MARTIN K. STARR

Professor
Graduate School of Business
Columbia University

IRVING STEIN

President
Cambridge Institute

D1541047

The Practice of
Management Science

PRENTICE-HALL, INC., *Englewood Cliffs, New Jersey*

Library of Congress Cataloging in Publication Data

Starr, Martin Kenneth,
    The practice of management science.

      1. Industrial management.   2. Decision making.
I. Stein, Irving, joint author.
II. Title
HD31.S687   658.4   75-23139
ISBN   0-13-693630-X

© 1976 by PRENTICE-HALL, INC.,
Englewood Cliffs, New Jersey

Printed in the United States of America

10 9 8 7 6 5 4 3 2 1

Prentice-Hall International, Inc., *London*
Prentice-Hall of Australia, Pty. Ltd., *Sydney*
Prentice-Hall of Canada, Ltd., *Toronto*
Prentice-Hall of India Private Limited, *New Delhi*
Prentice-Hall of Japan, Inc., *Tokyo*
Prentice-Hall of Southeast Asia (Pte.) Ltd., *Singapore*

Contents

Preface

Since World War II, there has been a rapid expansion in the mathematical and statistical techniques available to the managers in industry. The variety of applications is virtually unlimited; advances in computer technology have made almost all corporate problems subject to quantitative analysis. The potential benefits of application have been considerable.

Unfortunately, the very specialized (and sometimes complex) skills that are required by these techniques have led to a dichotomy of perspective among those who study and practice management. In the one camp are those who have become conversant with the required methodologies and enraptured with the elegance of quantitative analysis, at the expense of understanding the broader issues of management decision making. In the other camp are those who have little or no exposure to management science, who shy away from performing quantitative analysis, and who lack confidence in its results; this group tends to rely on more prosaic methods for its decision making.

It is our intent in this book to remove the barrier between these two groups. We have provided a basic, simple coverage of management science techniques to serve as introduction for those who are unknowledgeable in the field. We have provided materials that will allow those with primarily specialized interests in management science to become more aware of the qualitative issues that surround most decision problems.

The materials in this book were first developed to meet the needs of managers in industry who operated in both the camps described above. The managers who used these materials came from varying backgrounds—some had no college, some were college graduates with liberal arts degrees, and some had undergraduate or graduate degrees in business administration. We found the materials to be effective in conveying management science concepts, whether used in self-study or in the classroom. We later introduced the cases into the curriculum for students of management science at the graduate level and found them useful in providing simulations of real-world applications.

The Practice of Management Science can be used either as a supplement to basic textbooks in management science and management of operations or as an introductory text for those who want to acquire first-level familiarity with the practical application of management science techniques. The material is presented in workbook format and consists of eleven units, or modules. The units can be studied in sequence or in some other desired order. Since the book is not intended to be a comprehensive survey, the expository material has been made as simple as possible. Our aim is to present the basic concepts that underlie the more common management science methods rather than to explore any one technique in detail. We are trying to provide the student with a base for understanding the techniques within the practice of management. For example, in Unit 4, PERT is looked on less as a technique than an approach to planning and control and as an introduction to the many forms of network theory that exist.

The book is designed to give equal weight to quantitative and qualitative analysis. The text introduces the student to the management science concept and its mathematics; the case instructions guide the student to a rational and comprehensive consideration of the issues involved in a practical situation. The arithmetic has been simplified to enable the student to spend a minimal amount of time on number pushing.

The units consist of:

Technical Notes. These notes, which begin each unit, offer a concise discussion of the general concept of the unit. They are meant to provide the student with an efficient "bare-bones" explanation and hopefully with a point of view different from that of a full text; they are not meant to provided detailed coverage.

Short Questions and Answers. These exercises (found within the technical notes) are aimed at helping the student to verify his knowledge of the more mechanical points.

Problem-Solving Exercises. These problems (located after each case) are designed to consolidate the student's understanding of the methodology and to lighten the burden of arithmetic after the desired level of skill has been acquired. In one case, a simulation exercise has been provided.

Case instructions. We have found the average student to be scattered and abbreviated in his approach to case analysis. Our instructions (which precede each case) push toward good analysis by giving some hints and sample guides. It is our experience that the student begins to recognize the fundamentals of rational analysis after six or seven cases.

Cases. The cases are the heart of the book. They require the student to consider quantitative and qualitative issues from the standpoint of planning and control. While there is only one solution to each quantitative analysis, students may justifiably arrive at differing management decisions because of the qualitative issues.

The workbook format allows space for answering the questions and working out the exercise sets. The actual case analysis may be integrated into group discussions or may be used as a basis for written assignments.

We would like to offer our thanks to the many students who have used these materials and whose constructive criticisms have helped this book reach its final form. We also thank those who helped in the preparation of this book —Judith Dumas, Nancy Martland, and Lynn McWhood.

Use of the Case Method

The use of the case method in studying law, business, and economics is predicated on the belief that basic learning is hard work, not merely a matter of having an instructor pour out his ideas on a certain subject. Under the case method, the participant is expected to dig things out for himself, with the help of his fellow participants. He is expected to be active in this role, not passive. The worthwhileness of a case discussion thus depends primarily on each participant. The instructor does not tell him; he expects the participant to study the case and to tell his fellow participants what he has learned from it. The instructor is more a moderator than a lecturer. However, he does expect the participant to justify the position he takes; and he may from time to time indicate lines of direction for the group discussion.

A case is a statement of facts, opinions, and judgments more or less relevant to an actual situation in which a problem exists and a decision must be made. Frequently, a case contains one or more problems; that is, situations in which facts, opinions, and judgments are in conflict and some action must be taken by responsible executives.

A case is as accurate a description of a situation as it is possible to secure. Sometimes, the real identity of a company or individual is concealed, and numerical data may be altered enough to prevent revealing confidential information. Certain cases may only approximate actual situations, since it may be difficult to secure a completely accurate description of an event that has occurred or is occurring from people involved in it.

In working with cases, it is helpful to observe carefully all the available pertinent information and data. In certain cases, it may be found that insufficient information is provided. As mature people know only too well, this lack of information is quite common in actual situations. Additional knowledge, as well as foresight and perception of the immediate problem, must be supplied by the participant in the same manner that he would handle the problem in actual practice.

Next, the information and data are analyzed; that is, broken into components and carefully reviewed, in order to understand the significance of each component and the relationships, if any, between components. From the analysis, a search is made for possible decisions or actions to be taken. Usually, several alternative actions for dealing with the situation can be evolved.

Then the probable consequences from each alternate action are forecast. It is at this stage that actual experience is most helpful. The work of evaluating each alternate move leads to the selection of the recommended action—that is, the decision to be followed. The final step is to detail the specific action recommended, so that a clear, concise, and sound program is supplied.

It is important to remember that few cases have a *right* answer. Any solution or recommendation suggested for the problem should be supported by a logical structure of reasoning and argument. As informed managers know so well, there may be several plausible ways of proceeding. Thus, the specific solution suggested is less important than the reasoning with which it is supported. The participant may feel that this approach makes his objectives in handling a case somewhat indefinite. This is true, but it is equally true in real-life situations. As the participant gains experience in working with cases, he will come to realize that the requirements of this method give him considerable scope for his resourcefulness and ingenuity.

In summary, it is suggested that the participant use the following approach in preparing cases for group discussion:

1. Know the facts as given in the case.
2. From these facts, determine the main problem or issue to be settled.
3. Reach a decision through analysis of the material, considering all alternate possibilities.
4. State your recommended solution, indicating how and why you arrived at your particular decision.

Further observations concerning our use of the case method will be found in the concluding section of the text. It is entitled, "Feedback Cases: What Are They and Why Are They Used?"

Unit 1

Decision Theory

In this unit we shall present a mathematical model that applies to decision making under risk conditions. We shall explain decision theory and show how to construct a decision matrix. Then we shall demonstrate the use of this approach.

The major concept with which we are dealing is:

Formalization of the decision process can be accomplished without complex mathematics. Even simple decision models can provide the manager with significant ways to look at his problems.

A *decision matrix* is shown below. A matrix is an arrangement of data into rows and columns. Matrices are used to organize data and to facilitate mathematical operations on these data. The matrix illustrated represents a simple decision problem responding to the question, Which strategy should the manager use?

A Simple Decision Problem in Matrix Form

	Probability: States of Nature:	.1 Fog	.9 Clear
Strategy 1:	Plane	+$2,000	+$4,500
Strategy 2:	Train	+$3,000	+$3,000

Let us imagine that a salesman is faced with the question of whether to fly or take a train to an out-of-town customer's location. If the weather permits, he can fly in 2 hours portal to portal, whereas the train will take him 7 hours. If he takes the train, he will lose a day at his present location that he estimates could be used to generate $1,500 in sales. He has also estimated that the out-of-town customer will give him an order for $3,000 if he makes a personal call. Should he plan to go by plane but then be grounded by fog, he will be unable to visit in person and will be forced to use the telephone. This will reduce the size of the out-of-town order to $500, but he will still be able to get the $1,500 at the present location.

The data in the matrix shown above reflect these estimates for the different outcomes. In addition, some guesses are presented concerning the probabilities of fog (which will ground the flight but not affect the train) and clear weather. We see that an estimate of one in ten chances of fog occurring has been supplied. Further, the matrix shows that with Strategy 1 (taking the plane), if the weather is clear (.9 probability, or 9 chances in 10), the salesman estimates his sales will be $4,500 (referred to as an outcome). The other three outcomes can be explained in similar ways.

What should the salesman do in a case like this? What would you do? Later, after you are thoroughly versed in the decision-matrix method, come back to this problem and solve it. (After you have worked out your own solution, using the space on the next page for figuring, you might check it against the one given on page 6.

Let us now examine the structure of a decision matrix in more abstract form:

	States of the environment: various N's that are mutually exclusive (such as different weather conditions)		
	N_1	N_2 .... N_m	
The lower case p's represent the odds that each of the states of the environment will occur.	p_1	p_2 .... p_m	
Manager's first strategy:	O_{11}	O_{12} .... O_{1m}	
Manager's second strategy:	O_{21}	O_{22} .... O_{2m}	
.	.	.	.
.	.	.	.
.	.	.	.
Manager's nth strategy:	O_{n1}	O_{n2} .... O_{nm}	

The matrix of outcomes (for instance, O_{nm}) is read in the following way: If the manager uses his nth strategy and the state of the environment that occurs by chance is N_m, then the result will be O_{nm}. In reference to our previous example, if the salesman elects to fly (S_1) and the weather is clear (N_2), he can obtain total sales of $4,500 ($O_{12}$).

The outcomes are frequently called *payoffs,* and the matrix a *payoff matrix.* This usage arises from games of chance, but it is also applicable to profit and cost in business. We can construct cost, profit, brand-share, man-hour, productivity, and other matrices according to our objectives. The decision matrix is a model that can organize a lot of information about a problem in a very useful way.

First, each row represents a different strategy. The *strategy* must be composed only of *variables* that are *under the manager's control.* Whenever there are strategy alternatives, a decision problem exists.

Second, each column describes a different set of environmental conditions *(states of nature* or *environment).* These must be composed of all those variables that are *not under the manager's control.* Since they are not under the manager's control, he will attempt to *forecast* their probability of occurrence. That is what is meant by the odds (called p) that are shown in the matrix.

> *The probability of an event's occurring is stated as the ratio of the number of times that the event is likely to occur in 100 trials, divided by those 100 trials.*

Given a certain strategy and a specific state of the environment—in terms of our objectives—a particular *outcome* will result. If the outcome is not known for each possible strategy, it must be determined before a decision can be made. Determining outcomes is problem solving. This is what the salesman had to do to fill in his decision matrix. Some form of problem solving *always* precedes decision making.

For example, we can determine the corrosion resistance of plating with known thicknesses of nickel, copper, and chromium. This is a problem-solving question. There is no decision to be made. If, instead, we ask what the plating composition and thicknesses should be to meet specified salt-spray tests at minimum costs, where metal prices fluctuate, we would then be asking a decision question.

Price is an important variable for our objective but cannot be controlled. With the notion of varying price, we have added risk to the decision problem. *Risk* arises whenever *uncontrollable variation* can affect our results.

Some variables are under the manager's control. His alternative strategies include all feasible and reasonable arrangements of these controllable variables. But the manager must also recognize and enumerate all environmental conditions that can occur that could affect the results of his decision. The farmer will be concerned with rainfall; the financial manager will be involved with the ups and downs of the stock market; the inventory manager will list as paramount, in his states of nature, the demand for each item that he stocks. (His strategies will be the different stock levels and order quantities that he might use.) Forecasts (when they can be obtained) provide valuable information upon which to base action. For example, forecasts might indicate for the farmer that a dry season is twice as likely as a wet one; that is, that the probability of a wet season is 0.333, and that of a dry season 0.667.

> *We note that the probabilities sum to one. They must always do this.* Otherwise the decision matrix is incomplete, because certain states of the environment that could occur have been ignored.

Forecasts can be obtained in many ways. If there is recorded history, *and* the fundamental forces in the system have not changed over time, then we can base our estimates for the future on conditions that prevailed in the past. This is generally done by tabulating past occurrences and then counting the frequency of each type of event.

Assume that the farmer has records of weather for the past thirty years, and that 10 years were wet and 20 years were dry. These are the frequency counts that he converts to probabilities by recognizing that 10 out of 30 years ($10/30 = 0.333$) were wet seasons.

> In general, if we have n observations, and y of these are y-type events, z of these are z-type events, and so forth, then the probability of y is y/n, the probability of z is z/n, etc. Again, we note that $(y + z + ...) = n$, and $(y/n + z/n + ...) = 1$. *That is, the sum of the frequencies of the events must equal the total number of observations (n), and the sum of the probabilities must equal 1.*

The environmental states must be defined so that each is completely unique and separated from all others. In other words, each type of event must be a *complete* description of some possible state of the environment. For example, if both temperature and rainfall are relevant aspects of the environmental conditions, we would require complete descriptions of each possible combination:

N_1: dry, temperatures averaging 40-50 (not including 50)
N_2: wet, temperatures averaging 40-50 (not including 50)
N_3: dry, temperatures averaging 50-60 (including 50)
N_4: wet, temperatures averaging 50-60 (including 50)
etc.

What has happened in the past may, however, provide poor or misleading clues as to what will occur in the future. Perhaps new factors have entered the situation, or the environmental system may never have been sufficiently stable to count on it as an indication of future events. It is also possible that no history exists, perhaps because a really new product has been developed.

There may be other approaches to forecasting. The farmer turns to meteorology for a long-range forecast based on reports from the weather satellite. Alternatively, sometimes it becomes feasible to employ technology to gain control over the states of nature, rather than simply forecasting. The farmer could build a large greenhouse, but for any extensive farming, this strategy would price him out of the market. He might, therefore, turn to technology with a view to exploiting cloud-seeding methods. In many cases, the decision is deferred, and the problem is referred back to the drawing board or to R&D, for the development of new strategies.

AVERAGES

Here is an example which introduces the use of averages (also called means, or expected values):

The Babbitt Company is considering the expansion of its military-products division. Strategy A calls for building a new plant devoted solely to military products. Strategy B requires expanding the present capacity of this division. Strategy C is a do-nothing-now plan. The relevant environments are descriptions of states affecting government procurement policies. These might be: I—The present engagement of U.S. forces abroad is likely to stop within three years; II—The situation is likely to remain unchanged from present levels; and III—The commitment will increase substantially over the next three years. Management has estimated the three-year profits[*] associated with each plan and the relevant environmental conditions as follows:

Matrix of Payoffs (in $MM)

	I	II	III
Probability of environments:	p_I	p_{II}	p_{III}
Strategy A:	−20	−4	40
Strategy B:	−5	1	12
Strategy C:	0	0	0

This is a matrix of profits. Minus signs indicate losses. What would you do?

Clearly, if Environment III occurs, A is greatly to be preferred. But if A is used and I occurs, nobody around Babbitt is going to be very happy. The next step, then, is to gain consensus on the probabilities. These particular events are extremely difficult to forecast, but let us propose that agreement is reached where $p_I = 0.3$, $p_{II} = 0.5$, and $p_{III} = 0.2$.

The decision criterion always used under risk is to take an *average* for each strategy and then to choose the strategy that provides the most favorable average. To obtain the average value *(expected value)* for each strategy, multiply each probability by its respective outcome and sum these products together. The sense of the calculations is shown below.

$$\text{Average profit of strategy A} = p_I O_{AI} + p_{II} O_{AII} + p_{III} O_{AIII}$$

$$= p_I(-20) + p_{II}(-4) + p_{III}(40)$$

In this case, our averages will be:

$$\text{Average profit of strategy A} = 0.3(-20) + 0.5(-4) + 0.2(40) = 0$$
$$\text{Average profit of strategy B} = 0.3(-5) + 0.5(1) + 0.2(12) = 1.4$$
$$\text{Average profit of strategy C} = 0.3(0) + 0.5(0) + 0.2(0) = 0$$

Since maximum profit is the objective, strategy B would be chosen. If the probabilities had been 0.4, 0.5, and 0.1 for I, II, and III respectively, the average would be −6.0, −0.3, and 0. Then the third (do-nothing) strategy would be the indicated choice.

THE OUTCOME MATRIX

Simple variations in the design of the decision matrix permit us to model more complex situations. For example, we can treat the case in which probabilities of environmental states are affected by the choice of strategy. This kind of interaction is encountered quite frequently in the real world. For example, each different machine that performs a

---

[*]The choice of a three-year period was a management decision, properly related to the company's objectives.

particular job has its own characteristic distribution of product quality and conformance to tolerances. Also, industrial design, package, and advertising strategies are expected to alter the probabilities of demand levels for the product.

To deal with such situations, the average value of the outcome for each strategy is calculated using the probabilities that apply *to that strategy*. The averages are then compared, and the strategy with the most desirable average is chosen. Here is a brief example:

Two designs are being considered for a miniature vacuum tube. Their respective failure characteristics have been obtained by laboratory observations. The data shown below represent the *percentage of tubes remaining* after continuous use for T time units. (As will be noted, some vacuum tubes are faulty in manufacture and will fail at T = 0. That is why only 98 percent of the tubes of Design 1 remain at the beginning of the test.)

| | T (time units) | | | | | | | |
	0	1	2	3	4	5	6	7
Design 1	98	95	94	93	70	20	0	0
Design 2	97	92	92	92	91	60	15	0

These survival distributions are in cumulative form. We note, for example, that at the end of the fourth time unit, 91 percent of Design 2 tubes are surviving; 31 percent of these fail during the next time unit. We can obtain the percentage failing in each time class by subtraction and then convert it to probabilities by dividing by 100. Our calculations (below) compute the average value of tube life for Design 1 in time units:

$$
\begin{aligned}
(1.00 - .98 = .02) \times 0 &= .00 \\
(.98 - .95 = .03) \times 1 &= .03 \\
(.95 - .94 = .01) \times 2 &= .02 \\
(.94 - .93 = .01) \times 3 &= .03 \\
(.93 - .70 = .23) \times 4 &= .92 \\
(.70 - .20 = .50) \times 5 &= 2.50 \\
(.20 - .00 = .20) \times 6 &= 1.20 \\
(.00 - .00 = .00) \times 7 &= \underline{.00} \\
& 4.70
\end{aligned}
$$

The calculations for the second design are similar:

| | T (time units) | | | | | | | | |
	0	1	2	3	4	5	6	7	Average Time
Design 1	.02	.03	.01	.01	.23	.50	.20	0	4.70
Design 2	.03	.05	0	0	.01	.31	.45	.15	5.39

The decision matrix has been recast to make outcomes the states of the environment, and the entries in the matrix are the probabilities that each outcome state will occur. This is simply a transformation of the decision matrix into a new form that is more appropriate for this type of problem. It tells us that the average life of the second design exceeds that of the first design by 0.69 time units. A cost analysis is still required to determine whether this advantage is worth the price of achieving it.

Exercise

Which vacation, A or B, should I choose? A is a ski lodge, and B is a Caribbean island. I shall use a scale of preference where +10 is the most preferred and 0 is the least preferred. If the ski lodge has snow and I am there, I would rate it with the highest preference, +10; but if there is no snow, I have 0 preference for it. The Caribbean island always has sun, and I consider it to have a preference measure of +6. Based on past weather records, the probability of snow in the vicinity of the ski lodge in February (the month of my vacation) is 0.4.

What advice do you have for me after studying my problem in decision-matrix terms?

Your preference for the ski lodge is the same as mine, and you have told me that you can't make up your mind which vacation you would take. What preference rating does your statement imply for sun-drenched islands?

After you have tried your own hand at answering these questions, using the space below to work out your solution, you might like to make a comparison with our solution, given after the one to the preceding exercise.

Solution to Salesman Exercise

$$EV^* \text{ (plane)} = \$2{,}000 \text{ (.1)} + \$4{,}500 \text{ (.9)} = \$4{,}250$$
$$EV \text{ (train)} = \$3{,}000 \text{ (.1)} + \$3{,}000 \text{ (.9)} = \$3{,}000$$

Therefore, accept the risk of fog and take the plane.

Solution to Vacation Exercise

The matrix is simple to derive. It is:

				EV
	0.4	0.6		
Ski lodge strategy A	snow	no snow		
	+10	0		10(.4) + 0(.6) = 4
	0.0	1.0		
Caribbean strategy B	snow	no snow		
	—	+6		6(1) = 6

Your advice (based strictly on this matrix) would be to forget about skiing, since $EV_B = 6$ is better than $EV_A = 4$.

Since you are indifferent, it must be true that for you $EV_A = EV_B$. Then, let k = your preference rating for the island vacation.

$$\begin{array}{cc} \text{ski lodge} & \text{sunny isles} \\ 10(.4) + 0(.6) = & k(0) + k(1.0) \\ +4 = & k \end{array}$$

*EV = expected value (also called average or mean).

INSTRUCTIONS FOR PREPARING THE CASE

Verity Mining Corporation

Read the case carefully. Put yourself in the position of Dave Leone. You have been asked to recommend which site to acquire—Wild Oats or Never—and to report to Mr. Marden with a full justification of your position, listing alternative uses for each site.

Marden will expect you to present the criteria that you have used to justify the choice of one site over the other. As one criterion, bear in mind that Marden has told you that he wants the new site to achieve the greatest contribution over the next five years; he is also interested in contribution beyond five years. (But which is more important to him?) You will note that Marden is betting on Wild Oats as a place to hunt. (Is this as important to him as contribution?) You may find other criteria in the case; if so, spell them out.

Since this site acquisition is of tremendous significance to Verity, you should also make sure Marden is well aware of whatever assumptions underlie your recommendation. For example, the forecast of prices is only a guess on the part of the executive committee; for completeness, this is best stated as an assumption. If you accept the assumption in your analysis, state this, or if not, give reasons why you disagree. As another example, the probabilities for the grade of ore given in the table are assumptions—the truth will out only after considerable mining has been done. While you can't do much about the given data, if you questioned the sampling in real life, you could recommend that more test borings be made to give better information.

Verity has several alternatives to look at before making a decision:

Short Term:

1. Mine 30% more ore at New Mexico.
2. Mine 390,000 tons of ore at Never and ship to New Mexico.
3. Mine 390,000 tons of ore at Wild Oats and ship to New Mexico.

Long Term:

4. Build mill at Never; mine and mill there.
5. Build mill at Wild Oats; mine and mill there.
6. Mine at Never; mill at New Mexico.
7. Mine at Wild Oats; mill at New Mexico.

Since Marden is definitely interested in the short term, analyze the first three alternatives thoroughly. Add whatever insights you think feasible about the long-term alternatives.

You will find Problem-Solving Exercises at the end of the case. These are included to help you with some basic calculations.

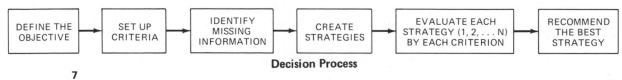

DEFINE THE OBJECTIVE → SET UP CRITERIA → IDENTIFY MISSING INFORMATION → CREATE STRATEGIES → EVALUATE EACH STRATEGY (1, 2, . . . N) BY EACH CRITERION → RECOMMEND THE BEST STRATEGY

Decision Process

CASE

Verity Mining Corporation

The mining properties and milling facility of this youthful but growing U.S. company are located in New Mexico. The company's present ore deposits are located 165 miles from the mill where uranium concentrate (yellowcake) is produced. The ore is trucked to the mill at a cost of $1.50 per ton. The mill has been operating at about 70% of full capacity. Its maximum milling tonnage is 1,300,000 tons of ore per year.

Verity has been engaged in mining uranium ore for approximately 15 years. During the greater part of that time, the Atomic Energy Commission has been the major consumer. With congressional backing, the AEC supported prices (currently at $8 per pound) to encourage uranium mining activities. At last, the developing requirements of atomic-power installations have begun to promise a commercial market for yellowcake, and this trend has prompted the AEC to announce that it would soon withdraw the support of prices.

Soon after the announcement by the AEC, the Verity executive committee met in a planning session. While the members agreed that the market for yellowcake would increase in the years ahead, they were far less certain as to what prices might be without support. On the basis of sales prospects, the committee decided to bring production at the mill to full capacity. They unanimously agreed to obtain mineral rights at a new location as quickly as possible, as an unusual amount of land speculation was taking place at all potential mining sites. When the president of Verity, Mr. Marden, asked for opinions about the future price of yellowcake, the consensus of the committee was that the price would probably drop and then rise as atomic installations became more prevalent. As a result of the various inputs, Marden stated an 80% probability that the price over the next 5 years would average $5 per pound, 10% that it would average $8 per pound, and 10% that the upturn would come sooner than expected, yielding an average of $10 per pound.

When Marden left the meeting, he called in Dave Leone, his manager of operations, and briefed him on some of what had transpired. He added, "The company plans to bring the mill up to full capacity as rapidly as possible. As you know, this mine in New Mexico has experienced a downgrading of ore quality, to the present 0.375%. We expect this figure to hold for another 5 years; then we anticipate that the vein will peter out. You know, also, that we have been prospecting for new sources and that we have narrowed our choices to the two best sites, Wild Oats, Wyoming, and Never, Nevada. We have to move fast on one of these locations. Let me have your recommendations as to which of these sites we should move on. Both sites have large deposits for the future. The question is which one will give us a greater contribution to expenses and profit. We are most interested in the next 5 years, but look beyond that as best you can. Ignore the costs of acquiring mining rights—I think we can make about the same deal at both locations. Incidentally, I don't want to bias your thinking, but I hope you find Wild Oats to be a better location—the hunting there is great, and there is a lot of game on the property."

Dave Leone quickly assembled the information that was available on both sites. He knew that both locations were thoroughly accessible. The preparation costs for exploitation at Wild Oats were considered to be 10% higher than at Never, but this was not an appreciable amount in view of the value of the ore to be withdrawn. He knew also that manpower was short at Wild Oats and that transport facilities for bringing ore to New Mexico would be more difficult to arrange from that site. Dave recalled from informal conversations that the man most likely to be chosen to supervise a new installation would resign rather than go to Never.

Dave Leone turned to the technical abstracts that had been compiled on both locations. He noted that mining studies had been translated into the table below:[*]

Grade (%)		Probabilities for the Grade of Ore at Each Location									
100 G =	0	0.10	0.20	0.30	0.40	0.50	0.60	0.70	0.80	0.90	1.00
Never	0	.05	.20	.20	.20	.15	.15	.05	0	0	0
Wild Oats	0	.10	.15	.15	.20	.30	.05	.05	0	0	0

Dave found in the technical memoranda the estimated costs of transporting ore from each location to the mill at New Mexico: $3.25 per ton for Wild Oats, and $4.10 per ton for Never.

APPENDIX
VERITY MINING CORPORATION

For convenience, we have listed a range of values of $\log_e x$:

$\log_e x$	x	$\log_e x$	x
0.100	1.105	0.385	1.470
0.200	1.221	0.400	1.492
0.300	1.350	0.500	1.649
0.375	1.455	0.600	1.822
0.380	1.462	0.700	2.014

Logarithms have interesting properties. Note, for example (using $\log_{10} x$), that $\log_{10} 10 = 1$, $\log_{10} 100 = 2$, and $\log_{10} 1,000 = 3$. Thus, here x grows by multiples of 10, but the log of x increases slowly, by the addition of 1. This diminishing-return attribute of the log of x depicts many real-life situations better than a constant return does. For an example, from this table, let $G = 0.0030$; then $100G = 0.300 = \log_e x$. Then $x = 10,000/C_1 = 1.350$, and, solving this equation, $C_1 = \$7407.40$.

[*]Dave was well aware that the cost of producing a ton of refined ore varies with the quality of the deposit. As a rough guide, managers used the following formula:

$$\log_e \frac{10,000}{C_1} = 100G$$

where $\log_e$ is the natural logarithm found tabled in most standard handbooks, and C_1 = cost per ton of refined ore, given that the deposit has a grade of G. (If G were 0.0010, for example, this would mean that the yield of refined ore is 0.10% of each extracted ton.)

PROBLEM-SOLVING EXERCISES

Verity Mining Corporation

To save you time on calculations, we have prepared a programmed series of problems for this unit that will help you to solve the case. There are three parts to the exercises—A, B, and C. If you solve Question 1 correctly in Parts A, B, and C, you may stop figuring and just look at the computations as done by us, since you have shown that you understand the method and the problem. If you can't do Question 1 correctly, look at the solution, try to find your mistake, and go on to Question 2 (or as directed in the instructions). Continue this process until you have solved at least one problem in all parts correctly. Do not look at the solutions except to check yourself.

PART A

Question 1.   What is the transportation cost per year for an increase in ore shipments equal to 30% of the milling-facility capacity if ore is mined in New Mexico and transported to the present milling facility?

You will find the solution to this problem on page 16.

Question 2.   What is the annual transportation cost for ore shipments equal to 30% of the milling-facility capacity if ore is mined at the Never site and transported to the present facility?

You will find the solution to this problem on page 16.

Question 3.   What is the annual transportation cost for ore shipments equal to 30% of the milling-facility capacity if ore is mined at the Wild Oats site and transported to the present facility?

You will find the solution to this problem on page 16.

PART B

Question 1.   What is the expected total annual milling cost for the 30% incremental production from the Never site when milled at the New Mexico facility?

You will find the solution to this problem on pages 16, 17.

Question 2.   What is the expected total annual milling cost for the 30% incremental production from the Wild Oats site when milled at the New Mexico facility?

You will find the solution to this problem on page 17.

Question 3.   What is the expected total annual milling cost for the 30% incremental production from the New Mexico site when milled at the New Mexico facility.

You will find the solution to this problem on page 17.

PART C

Question 1.   Compute the incremental revenue from yellowcake recovered from the Never site, at $8 per pound.

You will find the solution to this problem on page 18.

Question 2.   Compute the incremental revenue from yellowcake recovered from the Wild Oats site, at $8 per pound.

You will find the solution to this problem on page 18.

Question 3.   Compute the incremental revenue from yellowcake recovered from the New Mexico site, at $8 per pound.

You will find the solution to this problem on page 18.

Solution to Part A, Question 1:

Transportation costs to New Mexico milling facility, from New Mexico mine:

Amount of ore shipped: 30%(1,300,000) = 390,000 tons per year
Cost per ton: $1.50
Total: $1.50(390,000) = $585,000 per year

If you have completed the calculation correctly, you may go on to Part B, Question 1. If you have not completed it correctly, go on to Part A, Question 2.

Solution to Part A, Question 2:

Transportation costs to New Mexico facility, from Never site:

$$\$4.10(390,000) = \$1,599,000 \text{ per year}$$

If you have completed the calculation correctly, you may go on to Part B, Question 1. If you have not completed it correctly, go on to Part A, Question 3.

Solution to Part A, Question 3:

Transportation costs to New Mexico facility, from Wild Oats site:

$$\$3.25(390,000) = \$1,267,500 \text{ per year}$$

Now go on to Part B, Question 1.

Solution to Part B, Question 1:

Milling costs for 390,000 tons of raw ore from the Never site:

At Never there is a 5% probability that the grade is .10 = 100G. If the grade is .10 = 100G, then the cost per milled ton is $9,050. Also, the amount extracted would be 390,000 × .0010 = 390 tons.
Thus, there is a 5% chance that the annual output will be 390 tons and total annual milling cost will be ($9,050)(390) = $3,529,500.
Using this method, the table below presents the costs for each grade, and the expected annual output and expected annual cost.

P_i Probability	100G Grade	C_i Cost per ton[a]	O_i Annual Output (tons)	C_iO_i	$P_iO_iC_i$
.05	.10	$9,050	390	$ 3,529,500	$ 176,475
.20	.20	8,190	780	6,388,200	1,277,640
.20	.30	7,407	1,170	8,666,190	1,733,238
.20	.40	6,702	1,560	10,455,120	2,091,024
.15	.50	6,064	1,950	11,824,800	1,773,720
.15	.60	5,488	2,340	12,841,920	1,926,288
.05	.70	4,965	2,730	13,554,450	677,722

9,656,107

Expected annual output[b]: ΣP_iO_i = 1501.5 tons
Expected annual milling cost: $\Sigma P_iO_iC_i$ = $9,656,100 (rounded)

[a]As derived from the formula: $\log_e \dfrac{10,000}{C_i} = 100G$

[b]Σ is the Greek capital sigma, which stands for "sum of." The subscripts i denote that the values of P_iO_i should be summed for all values of i.

If you have completed the calculation correctly, you may go on to Part C, Question 1. If you have not completed it correctly, go on to Part B, Question 2.

Solution to Part B, Question 2:

For the Wild Oats site:

Using the method described in the solution to Part B, Question 1:

P_i	100G	C_i	O_i (tons)	C_iO_i	$P_iO_iC_i$
.10	.10	$9,050/T	390	$ 3,529,500	$ 352,950
.15	.20	8,190	780	6,388,200	958,230
.15	.30	7,407	1,170	8,666,190	1,299,928
.20	.40	6,702	1,560	10,455,120	2,091,024
.30	.50	6,064	1,950	11,824,800	3,547,440
.05	.60	5,488	2,340	12,841,920	642,096
.05	.70	4,965	2,730	13,554,450	677,722

Expected annual output: $\Sigma P_iO_i = 1,482$

Expected annual milling cost: $\Sigma P_iO_iC_i = \$9,569,390$

If you have completed the calculation correctly, you may go on to Part C, Question 1. If you have not completed it correctly, go on to Part B, Question 3.

Solution to Part B, Question 3:

The ore grade at the New Mexico mine is known, at .00375.

Output will be .00375 (390,000) = 1,462.5 tons per year.
Milling cost will be $6,873/ton (i.e., 1.455 = 10,000/C_i).
Thus, $6,873(1,462.5) = $10,051,763 is the expected annual cost.

Now go on to Part C, Question 1.

Solution to Part C, Question 1:

Expected annual output = 1,501.5 tons, or (1501.5)(2,000) pounds.
Thus, $8(2,000) (1,501.5) = $24,024,000 per year.

If you have completed the calculation correctly, you may stop. If you have not completed it correctly, go on to Part C, Question 2.

Solution to Part C, Question 2:

Expected annual output = 1,482 tons.
$8(2,000)(1,482) = $23,712,000 per year.

If you have completed the calculation correctly, you may stop. If you have not completed it correctly, go on to Part C, Question 3.

Solution to Part C, Question 3:

Annual output = 1,462.5 tons.
$8(2,000)(1,462.5) = $23,400,000

Unit 2

Decision Trees

Many decision problems involve a sequence of alternative choices, where each part of the action sequence is subject to risk. We call these multistage or sequential decision problems and to resolve such problems, we recommend the use of *decision trees*.

Let us take as an example a very simple game of chance, where one decision *must* be made and one chance event *must* occur.

Question: To play (Strategy A) or not to play (Strategy B)?
Specification of the Game: If you play, you must pay $50. If you win, you are paid $60. If you lose, you receive nothing. The odds of winning are 50/50.

We will draw a decision tree to represent the situation.

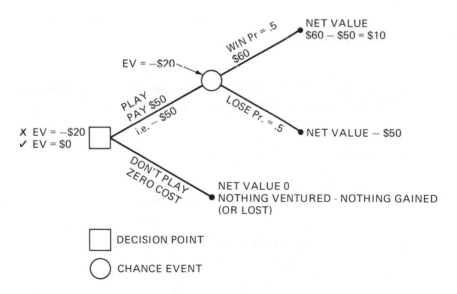

Note that the top branch of the decision tree represents playing, at a cost of $50, and the upper subbranch represents winning $60. The end node for this subbranch, therefore, is associated with a net value of $10. The lower subbranch of this alternative represents playing at a cost of $50 and losing all, so the end node shows a net value of −$50. The bottom end node of the tree has zero net value. The expected value of −$20 for the upper branch is obtained by adding the probable value of each branch extending from the chance node: 0.5 × $10 + 0.5 × (−$50) = −$20.

19

FIRST RULE FOR USING DECISION TREES

Draw the tree appropriate to your situation, starting with the various action alternatives that emanate from the first *decision point*. (There can be more than two lines fanning out from any decision-point box.)

Label the action alternatives with their costs. At the end point of each action alternative whose outcome will be affected by the particular state of nature that will occur, draw a *chance-event circle*. As many different events as can happen should fan out from the chance-event circle, and each event should be labeled with its appropriate probability, and the outcome value for that event.

Simply by tracing out the costs and profits encountered along any branch of the tree leading to a unique end point, the net value of that end point can be determined.

SECOND RULE FOR USING DECISION TREES

We start working backwards through the tree. Wherever two *or more* events (such as win, lose, or draw) merge at a chance-event circle, we obtain the expected value. In this case, the top and middle end points of the tree yield an expected value:

$$EV = .5(\$10) + .5(-\$50) = -\$20$$

The only chance-event node on the preceding tree is so labeled.

THIRD RULE FOR USING DECISION TREES

We continue working backwards through the tree. Whenever two *or more* action alternatives (such as play roulette, play craps, or don't play) merge at a decision-point box, we carry the largest net value to that box. For the preceding tree, the choice is between −$20 and $0. Since the latter is larger, we label the decision-point box with an expected value of zero.

FOURTH RULE FOR USING DECISION TREES

We follow that sequence of strategies that accounts for the expected value carried to the first decision-point box of the network. In the case of the preceding network, the strategy *don't play* is accepted.

DECISION MATRIX EQUIVALENT

Now that we have the basics, let us first see how the preceding tree would look in decision-matrix form.

Matrix of Net Payoff

	Pr.		EV
	.5 Win	.5 Lose	
S$_A$: Play	$10	−$50	−$20
S$_B$: Don't play	0	0	0

This matrix is much like those we have seen before. The reason is that the sequence included only one decision-point box.

DECISION SEQUENCES OF GREATER LENGTH

A more complicated game of chance is now proposed. Here are the specifications:

    1.   If you choose to play game A, and win, then you can go on to play game B, but you do not have to play game B.

    2.   To play each game costs $50.

    3.   If you win game A, you receive $50. Probability of winning game A is 0.8. If you win game B, you receive $200. The probability of winning game B is 0.6.

Following these game specifications, we construct the tree below:

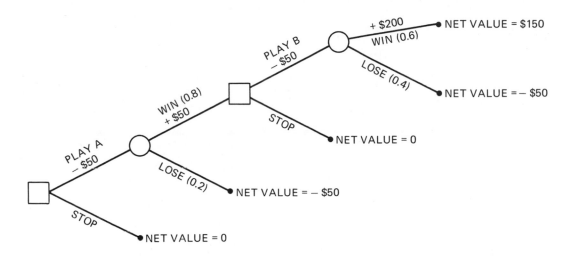

Following the first rule for using decision trees, we have completed labeling and determined net value for all unique end-point nodes. Next, we apply rules 2, 3, and 4 for using decision trees. The results are shown on the tree below.

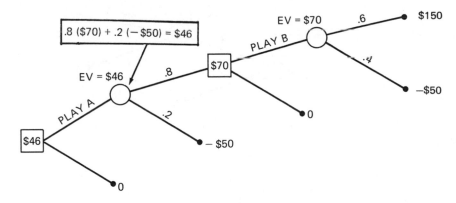

DECISION-MATRIX EQUIVALENT

When we convert this tree into its decision-matrix form, we begin to appreciate the economy of representation of the tree approach for large, multistage decision problems.

	Pr.			EV
	0.48	0.32	0.20	
	Win A	Win A	Lose A	
	Win B	Lose B	Stop	
S_A: Play A	0	0	−$50	−$10
S_{AB}: Play A and B	$150	−$50	−$50	$46
S_0: Don't play	0	0	0	0

The solution, to play both A and B, resulting in a maximum expected value of $46, is unchanged, of course. But the work required to obtain the solution is simply not as well organized by the matrix format as by that of the tree.

EXERCISE I

Change the multistage tree we have been using so that the cost of playing is only $5. What is the solution and its expected value?

After working it out, see the solution below. If you have the correct answer, proceed to the case. If not, go to Exercise II.

Solution to Exercise I

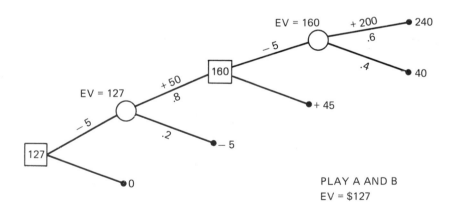

PLAY A AND B
EV = $127

EXERCISE II

Change the (original) multistage tree so that the cost of playing the first game, A, is $5, while the cost of playing the second game, B, remains $50. Also, let the probability of winning A remain unchanged, but lower the probability of winning B to 0.10.

Solution to Exercise II

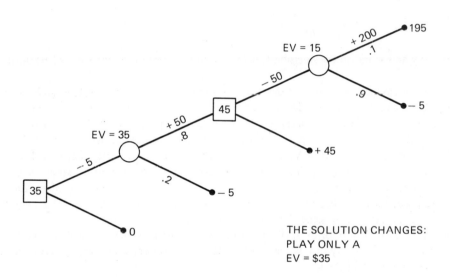

EV = 15

EV = 35

THE SOLUTION CHANGES:
PLAY ONLY A
EV = $35

INSTRUCTIONS FOR PREPARING THE CASE

Vulcan Specialty Rubber Company

Read the case carefully and work on the decision tree (Solution to Question 3, Parts A and B) until you understand it completely.

For the purpose of case analysis, assume that you are Fred Hooper. Your boss, George Vulcan, has told you that the buck stops with you; he expects a decision from you that is well thought out and documented. You have asked him the question, "Should Vulcan Specialty Rubber accept the proposition offered by the General Truck Company?" He has turned this decision question back to you and said you should answer it, with a full analysis.

You will find in the case that George Vulcan has laid out some goals (criteria) that you should consider in your analysis. Perhaps you can think of others, either personal or corporate. You will note also in the case that George has raised certain questions that are not answered by available information: Tom Carbon's probabilities might be too conservative; the purchasing agent's reaction to any request for a price change might be extremely negative. You might find that other information is missing, thereby constituting an obstacle to your analysis. Dispose of such obstacles by making a valid assumption, or by spelling out how you would get the information and how you would respond in the meanwhile. Finally, lay out all reasonable alternative strategies and select the one that best meets the goals (criteria) that you have established.

Decision Process

Vulcan Specialty Rubber Company

Jim Desmond bounced into the office of Fred Hooper, marketing vice-president of the Vulcan Specialty Rubber Company. "I've done it! After four years of calling on the General Truck Company in Detroit, I have finally sold them!"

Fred's enthusiasm took off at this news. "What's the order for? How big?"

"The deal shapes up like this, Fred. General Truck is having trouble with its present sources of supply in meeting specifications for parts for their new-model trucks to be introduced next year. I have talked them into letting us have a whack at their problems. Apparently the new model has some radical design changes to overcome severe criticism from their present customers. They want to see what we can do with three parts that are critical—one goes into the engine mount, one into the shock absorber assembly, and one into the bumper. The purchasing agent says his job is on the line, and he hopes we can produce. As long as our price is reasonable, he will go along with us, but he cannot make any compromises on meeting specifications. He says he is willing to give us a chance, but he wants us to show good faith by sharing his risk in switching to us as a new vendor."

Fred's soaring enthusiasm took a nosedive. "What do you mean, Jim?"

Jim was all salesman—his enthusiasm didn't waver. "General Truck will give us a chance to submit engine-mount parts from a sample mold. If these parts meet laboratory tests, he will give us an order for 100,000 parts and then give us a chance to submit samples for either the shock-absorber assembly or the bumper assembly—one or the other, but not both. If we succeed in passing the laboratory tests with the second set of samples, we can go on to qualify for the third or remaining part. The order quantities are 100,000 for all parts."

Fred feared the answer to his next question, but asked, "And what happens if we fail the tests? Do we get reimbursed?"

"No, the purchasing agent was clear on this point. This is our part of the 'sharing the risk.' If we don't meet specifications, we take the loss. But I think this is worth any gamble—you know what this account can mean to us. If we produce, we will be able to write our own ticket with this purchasing agent. He's in a bind. Obviously, the quantities are only enough to try us out."

"What's the timing on this, Jim?"

Jim replied, "We have a week to tell them if we are interested in the proposition. Then we have two months to deliver the first samples. I have a full set of drawings and specifications here."

Fred took the sheaf of papers from Jim and walked down the hall to the office of the plant manager, Tom Carbon, and explained the situation to him. Tom examined the specifications and frowned. "I can see why they are having trouble with these parts. These requirements are tough. I think the rubber compound formulations will be our biggest headache. The molds are intricate, but should present no problem that we can't lick. I want to go over this job with my department heads. I'll have an answer for you in three or four days."

Four days later, Tom met again with Fred. "As I suspected, this is one of the tougher jobs that we have been asked to do. I think our chances of success for the engine mount and bumper parts are about fifty-fifty. The shock-absorber part is a little easier."

"How much easier, Tom?"

Tom thought a moment. "Not that much easier—I'd say about sixty-forty."

Fred then asked, "Do you have any cost figures? How many dollars will we be gambling?"

Tom gave Fred some penciled numbers:

Direct costs for 100 samples, including laboratory formulations, molds, and labor:

Engine mounts—$8,000
Bumpers—$16,000
Shock absorbers—$10,000

At the following prices, we can meet our standard pricing policy of charging two times the direct costs—that is, 50% of the price will cover direct costs; 50% will cover overhead and profit.

Engine mounts—20¢ each
Bumpers—80¢ each
Shock absorbers—40¢ each

These prices are safe—*provided we can do the job at all.*

Fred took the figures and called the purchasing agent at General Truck to learn if the prices were acceptable if they decided to go ahead. Inwardly, he hoped that they would be far out of line, to save him from the difficult decision of whether to take the risks of proceeding with the job.

The purchasing agent said the prices were in line with those of his present suppliers.

Fred searched for a handle. He had never been confronted with a proposition such as this. He finally decided to take the path of many lesser men. He went into the office of his boss, the president of Vulcan, described the situation, and asked for a decision.

George Vulcan, president, had taken over the company just a few years ago, upon the death of his father. George was 28 years old, bright, and the holder of an M.B.A. from a leading university. While he had little knowledge of the technical intricacies of specialty-goods manufacture, he was aggressive and a good businessman. Under his stewardship, the company had grown in sales to its present $2 million annual level. His policy was to put profits back into the business in the form of new presses and other capital equipment; but while this posture enabled the company to take on new jobs at competitive prices, working capital was at a bare minimum to keep up with current operations. George was a firm believer in delegation; he was convinced that passing responsibility and accountability down the ladder was essential to corporate growth.

After hearing Fred's description of the General Truck Company proposition, he responded, "I would like you to make this decision. I think a decision-tree analysis could be revealing—you are familiar with this technique. I hope that your analysis shows that we should take this job—we want it. While there is no guarantee that these pilot runs will lead to additional major contracts, if we do well, the doors will be open. On the other hand, our cash position and projected flows will not permit us to lose any money on this work, no matter how slight. We should at least see a positive expected value fall out of your decision tree. We can take a gamble on our ability to produce—we gamble daily. Knowing Tom and his nature, I feel his odds on completing the work successfully are probably conservative. If you have to, you might consider the per-piece price of one or more of the parts, although there might be some problem in going back to the purchasing agent at General Truck with increased prices. Let me have your decision as soon as possible."

George went back to his desk and worked out a decision tree from the data that he had. Clearly, the expected value did not meet George's criteria. The question loomed—was there an alternative strategy that was viable?

PROBLEM-SOLVING EXERCISES

Vulcan Specialty Rubber Company

We have prepared a programmed series of problems for this unit that will help you to solve the case.

PART A

Question 1.   What does the engine-mount component of the decision tree look like with respect to both decision points and chance events? Label the branches with correct costs and revenues.

Construct your solution in the space below; then compare your answer with ours, found on page 32.

Question 2.   What does the decision tree look like when the engine-mount parts are followed by the bumper parts which are then followed by the shock-absorber parts—all with respect to both decision points and chance events? Label the branches with correct costs and revenues.

Construct your solution in the space below; then compare your answer with ours, found on pages 32, 33.

Question 3.   What does the decision tree look like when the engine-mount parts are followed by both sequences— i.e., bumper parts followed by shock-absorber parts, and shock-absorber parts followed by bumper parts—all with respect to both decision points and chance events? Label the branches with correct costs and revenues. *Note*: This is the final decision tree required for the case.

Construct your solution in the space below; then compare your answer with ours, found on page 33.

PART B

Question 1.   What is the decision and its expected value for the solution to Question 1 of Part A?

Work out your solution in the space below; then compare your answer with ours, found on pages 33, 34.

Question 2.   What is the decision and its expected value for the solution to Question 2 of Part A?

Work out your solution in the space below; then compare your answer with ours, found on page 34.

Question 3. What is the decision and its expected value for the solution to Question 3 of Part A? This answer represents a potential basis for solving the case.

Work out your solution in the space below; then compare your answer with ours, found on page 34.

Solution to Part A, Question 1:

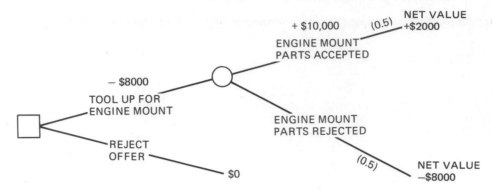

If you have completed the construction correctly, you may go on to Part A, Question 3. If you have not completed it correctly, go on to Part A, Question 2.

Solution to Part A, Question 2:

We assume that revenues are obtained for at least 100,000 units of all *accepted* parts. This is a best-case interpretation of the potential agreement. The worst case would be where *no revenues* are obtained until all three parts are accepted. Then:

$8,000 would be lost if Vulcan Rubber rejects the bumper-parts offer,
$24,000 would be lost if General Truck rejects the bumper parts.
$24,000 would be lost if Vulcan Rubber rejects the shock-absorber offer,
$34,000 would be lost if shock-absorber parts are rejected by General Truck.

If the agreement is not acceptable to the Vulcan Specialty Rubber Company under the best-case conditions, it surely would not be acceptable under worst-case conditions.

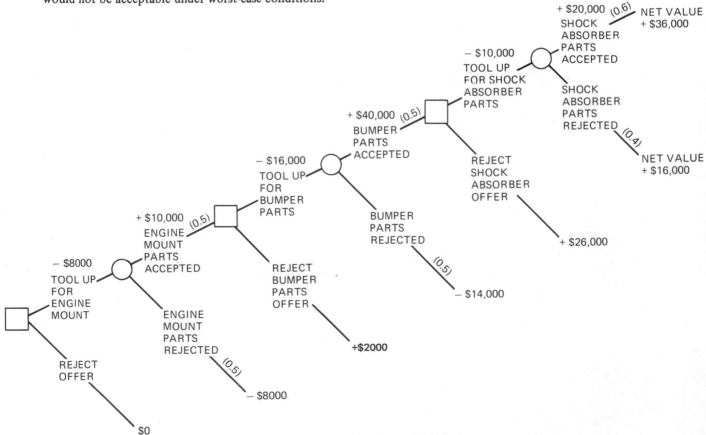

If you have completed the construction correctly, go on to the solution of Part A, Question 3. If not, first restudy our answers to Questions 1 and 2 of Part A and then go on to Part A, Question 3, and solve that problem.

Solution to Part A, Question 3:

We assume that revenues are obtained for at least 100,000 units of all accepted parts. See the discussion in the solution to Question 2, of Part A.

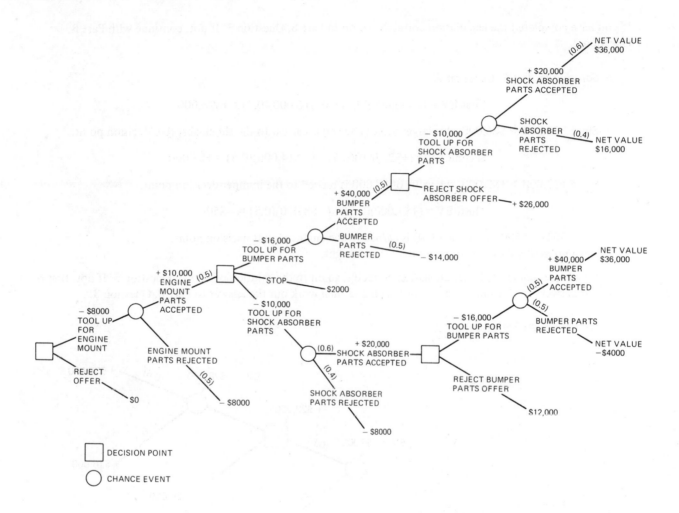

If you understand the tree constructions, go on to Question 1 of Part B.

Solution to Part B, Question 1:

$$EV = (+\$2,000)(0.5) + (-\$8,000)(0.5) = -\$3,000$$

The comparison is made:

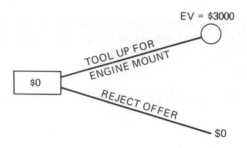

If you have completed the calculation correctly, go on to Part B, Question 3. If not, continue with Part B, Question 2.

Solution to Part B, Question 2:

$$\text{First EV} = (+\$36,000)(0.6) + (+\$16,000)(0.4) = +\$28,000$$

Since $28,000 > \$26,000$, this larger value (28,000) is carried to the shock-absorber decision point.

$$\text{Second EV} = (+\$28,000)(0.5) + (-\$14,000)(0.5) = +\$7,000$$

Since $+\$7,000 > +\$2,000$, the value of $7,000 is carried to the bumper decision point.

$$\text{Third EV} = (+\$7,000)(0.5) + (-\$8,000)(0.5) = -\$500$$

Since $\$0 > -\$500$, the value of $0 is carried to the engine-mount decision point.
The indicated solution is to reject the offer outright.

If you have completed the calculation correctly, go on to the solution of Part B, Question 3. If not, first restudy our answers to Questions 1 and 2 of Part B and then work out the answer to Part B, Question 3.

Solution to Part B, Question 3:

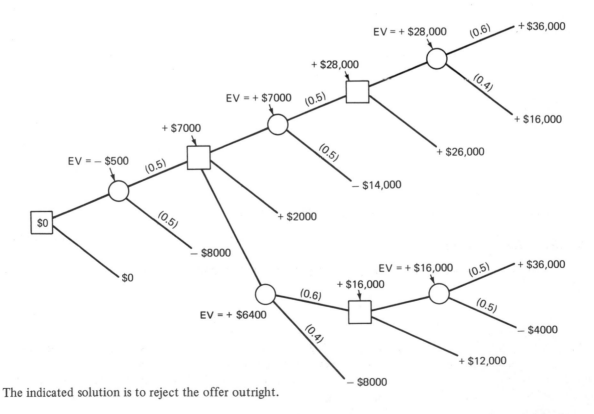

The indicated solution is to reject the offer outright.

Unit 3

Breakeven Analysis

Breakeven analysis is tried and true. It has found favor with many concerns. We shall begin this unit by developing the concepts and form of the breakeven chart. Then its strengths and weaknesses as an analytic tool will be discussed. At that point, not unexpectedly, our discussion will lead us to a decision-matrix representation of the breakeven chart.

Most rules of thumb are simple models that offer help but can severely distort reality when the extreme simplicity of their operating basis is not understood. Breakeven analysis, while a powerful planning tool for management, can fall into just this rule-of-thumb trap; it can mislead as well as guide. You should therefore use this technique at whatever level of complexity and sophistication you deem advisable and then apply your judgment and intuition.

A breakeven chart is shown below:

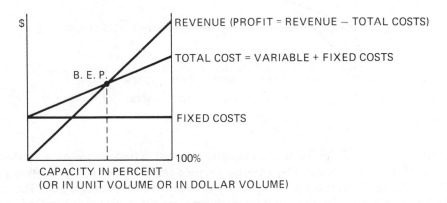

The construction of a breakeven chart involves two kinds of costs: *fixed* costs, which do not vary with output, and *variable* costs, which do change according to the output level. The fixed costs are a form of investment in equipment or facilities—say, a machine that costs $10,000. Whether you make ten pieces or a million on that machine, the $10,000 expenditure is fixed. Let's say that $0.30 of materials and $0.50 of labor go into making a part on the machine. Then the total variable (or operating) cost is $0.80 per part.

Assume that the capacity of our imaginary machine is 5,000 parts per year, and that we can sell each part for $2. Also, assume that our accounting practice is to depreciate machine investments evenly (called straight-line depreciation) over five years. Therefore, we can charge $2,000 per year ($10,000 ÷ 5 years) as fixed costs. Having invested in this machine, if we produce no parts, our fixed costs are still $2,000 for the year. The variable costs are $0, since no labor or materials are involved. Also, it follows that total cost is $2,000 and revenue is $0. This yields a net loss of $2,000.

Next, we shall assume production and sales of 500 units (or 10% utilization of capacity). What happens here? Fixed costs are $2,000; variable costs are $0.80 × 500 = $400; revenue is $1,000; total cost is $2,400. Consequently, our loss has been reduced to $1,400. Revenue minus total cost is profit. Negative profit is loss.

The chart below shows what would result in a number of different cases of production utilization as a percentage of total capacity (assuming everything we make is sold).

	0	10	20	33.3	50	80	100
				% of Capacity			
No. of parts	0	500	1,000	1,667	2,500	4,000	5,000
Fixed costs	$2,000	$2,000	$2,000	$2,000	$2,000	$2,000	$2,000
Variable costs	$0	$400	$800	$1,334	$2,000	$3,200	$4,000
Total costs	$2,000	$2,400	$2,800	$3,334	$4,000	$5,200	$6,000
Revenue	$0	$1,000	$2,000	$3,334	$5,000	$8,000	$10,000
Profit (or loss)	−$2,000	−$1,400	−$800	$0	+$1,000	+$2,800	+$4,000

The chart can also be shown as a graph:

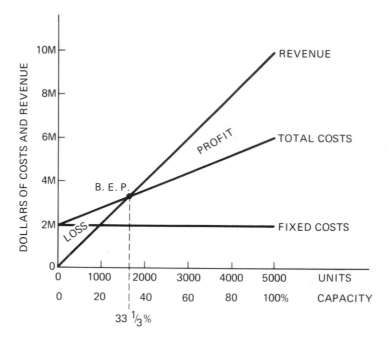

The breakeven chart is a great aid for planning. For example, it can tell us (roughly) at what breakeven load factor (breakeven point, or B.E.P.) a commercial airliner costing a certain amount (fixed costs) and having specified operating (variable) costs will begin to produce profit—given a known revenue per passenger mile. The same thinking can be applied to a factory or refinery. It is also useful for machinery, conveyors, materials-handling equipment, and so forth.

On the other hand, the breakeven model has weaknesses. Because of its simplicity, it could lull us into thinking that as a model, it is a perfect image of reality—whereas, in fact, it omits, oversimplifies, and incorporates estimates and accounting procedures that are crude and suspect. For example, breakeven analysis is not ideal for situations where many different products are made at the same facility. It is inappropriate if the system parameters are unstable over the planning period.

The straight lines that are used to represent variable costs and revenue are frequently close enough to the truth so that no problem exists with this simplification. However, when these economic and cost functions are not linear (that is, when a straight line does not properly represent the case), then it is feasible to work with graphs like the one below (and dangerous not to do so):

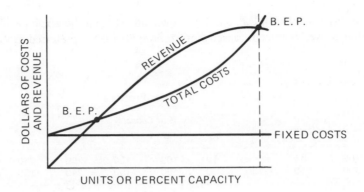

Another difficulty arises when we try to compare two plans, such as A and B in the graph below:

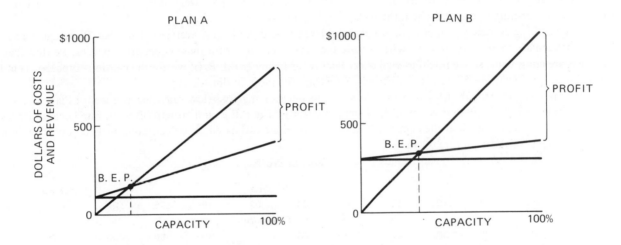

Comparing Two Plans with Different Costs and Revenues

Plan A has a superior (lower) B.E.P. to that of Plan B. However, note that after their respective B.E.P.'s are reached, Plan B has a better rate of profit growth. In fact, at 100% of capacity, B assures much greater profit than A. How does one decide which criterion to accept—the superior B.E.P., or the better profit rate?

We have stated that simple guides for managers, such as the B.E.P., are often weak taken by themselves. The more complex decision-matrix model can capture those essentials that interest the manager. Although in current B.E. practice this fact is frequently overlooked, there is growing awareness that the decision approach is required if most problems are to be properly analyzed.

Let us begin by recognizing that odds (probabilities) must be assigned to the likelihood of producing at the B.E.P. as well as over and under that threshold if our model is to be respected. Examination of the important characteristics of hypothetical Plans A and B will illustrate this.

	Plan A	Plan B
Fixed costs	$100	$300
Variable costs	$3 per unit	$1 per unit
100% capacity	100 units	100 units
Revenue	$8 per unit	$10 per unit
B.E.P. (% capacity)	20%	33 1/3%

We see that Plan A has a superior B.E.P. But if we now read off from the graph or calculate the profits at each capacity level, we see that above 50 percent capacity utilization, Plan B has preferred profits because of its greater profit growth rate.

Table of Profits

	0	10	20	30	40	50	60	70	80	90	100
					% of Capacity						
Plan A	−100	−50	0	50	100	150	200	250	300	350	400
Plan B	−300	−210	−120	−30	60	150	240	330	420	510	600

First, let's assume that we have no reason to believe that any operating percentage of capacity is more likely to occur than is another. This means we can set probabilities of 1/11 for each (capacity level) state of nature. In a horse race, this would mean that the odds are the same for every horse. If six horses were in the race, we would use 1:6 for each entry. If one horse were scratched, the odds would change to 1:5.

The resulting average profits for our 11 capacity levels would be: Plan A average = 150, Plan B average = 150. (You can calculate these for yourself.) When we use the decision matrix with these equal probabilities, we find that the plans are equivalent, so we might as well select Plan A for its lower B.E.P. (if we are the cautious type), or Plan B for its higher profits above 50 percent of capacity (if we are the more optimistic type).

If, however, the probabilities are those shown in the decision matrix below, then the average for Plan A is 222.0 and the average for Plan B is 279.6, so we would select B. The B.E.P. and growth of profit rate become far less influential in our thinking when the capacity-level probabilities are estimated. The decision model combines and integrates the effects of these factors for us.

Table of Profits

	.03	.07	.10	.15	.10	.03	.02	.10	.25	.15	*Average*
						Probabilities					
	10	20	30	40	50	60	70	80	90	100	
						% of Capacity					
Plan A	−50	0	50	100	150	200	250	300	350	400	222.0
Plan B	−210	−120	−30	60	150	240	330	420	510	600	279.6

The *ingredients* of the decision-matrix form of breakeven analysis are what count.

The decision model is a package demanding

> *complete cooperation among organizational divisions.*

The marketing department must supply sensible estimates for the probabilities of volume (or capacity utilization) at a given price and quality. (Quality is affected by both variable and fixed costs and by the ingenuity of the operations manager in terms of technology, methodology, and design.) Financial management exercises great influence, particularly in terms of the fixed-cost investments. Any breakeven analysis demands real synthesis of all functional area objectives—or the analysis becomes an academic exercise.

EXERCISE

You intend to rent a truck for the month of December to make Christmas deliveries. Two rental plans are available. Each has a monthly rental charge that is independent of how far you drive, and both have, in addition, a mileage charge that is fixed per mile. The following table presents these factors, which are relevant for comparing the plans.

	Plan A	Plan B
Monthly rental	$200.00	$150.00
Cost per mile driven	0.55	0.65

What is the breakeven point for the two plans? (We are using breakeven here to represent equality or indifference between these plans.)

If your estimate of delivery mileages has produced the following probability distribution, which plan would you use?

Delivery Miles per month	Probability
200	.25
300	.25
400	.25
500	.25

Use the space below for calculations to obtain your answer.

Solution to Exercise

The breakeven point occurs when the total cost of Plan A equals the total cost of Plan B. Let TC = total cost per month and M = miles driven per month.

$$TC_A = 200 + .55M$$
$$TC_B = 150 + .65M$$
$$200 + .55M = 150 + .65M$$

Solving, we find M = 500 miles. The appropriate decision matrix of total costs would be:

Probabilities	.25	.25	.25	.25
Miles per month	200	300	400	500
Plan A	$310	$365	$420	$475
Plan B	$280	$345	$410	$475

Clearly, Plan B is preferred. It has always lower or equal costs. There is no need to take the expected values to find that result. This is a case where the simple rule of thumb provided by breakeven analysis is sufficient without involving the decision-matrix approach. It is good to see an example where the old rule of thumb is perfectly suitable without complications.

INSTRUCTIONS FOR PREPARING THE CASE

Marquis Detection Company

Assume that you are the trusted right-hand assistant to Mr. Swinburne, director of the Newtown Public Libraries. He has asked you to analyze the situation described in the case and to tell him whether the Cole system should be installed.

Swinburne has told you that he knows you may want additional information that is not available in the time you have for your analysis. In such instances, he asks you either to (1) bank on careful assumption, explaining it in detail; or (2) let him know that you would have liked more information, specify it, tell him what you assume the results might be, and make your recommendations contingent upon the answer as provided by research.

Mr. Swinburne, being highly supportive, has "suggested" that you pay close attention to these points:

1. Does the nationwide survey showing 10% yearly growth in transactions apply to Newtown? to one or both libraries?
2. Is Cole's estimate of savings on theft reduction accurate?
3. How durable is the Cole system?
4. What is the cost of maintaining the system?
5. What will be its psychological effect on borrowers?
6. How effective will the system be (how easy will it be for a prospective thief to remove the tab or rip off the portion of the book containing the tab)?

Swinburne also says that your recommendation must accomplish certain things:

1. Any change must cost no more to the taxpayer than the present procedure does, starting with the first year.
2. If a change is recommended, it must make sense to the finance committee.
3. The present level of service to the community must not deteriorate in the slightest.

He also says he hopes that the recommended system will:

1. Not upset the library patrons appreciably.
2. Improve the level of service to the community.
3. Save money for the libraries.

Finally, Swinburne suggests that you analyze these alternatives:

1. Recommend installation in the main library only.
2. Recommend installation in the Avis branch only.
3. Recommend installation in both libraries.
4. Recommend that the Cole system be rejected for installation.

Decision Process

Marquis Detection Company

A recent news story:

> ### LIBRARY BOOK BUZZER BUGS STUDENT THEFTS
>
> *East Lansing, Mich. (AP)–Books that buzz are the latest gimmick to cut down on student thefts from the Michigan State University Library.*
>
> *All books on open shelves carry a magnetized metal plate. Unless the plate is de-energized at the check-out desk, it will lock the turnstile and sound a buzzer if a student attempts to smuggle the book out of the library.*
>
> *The new system is not perfect, an official said. Other metallic objects may also activate the buzzer, causing some temporary embarrassment.*

The Marquis Detection Company was found by Ransom Cole after his invention of a method for library protection had been patented. The Cole system is designed to help public libraries prevent thefts.

Under the Cole system, a small magnetic tab is permanently glued to the binding of every book (including reference works and bound magazines and periodicals). When a book is properly checked out, the tab is demagnetized, and the borrower passes through an exit turnstile without incident. However, a detection unit on the turnstile senses a tab that has not been demagnetized, and it locks the turnstile. When a borrowed book is returned, the tab is magnetized again.

Marquis Detection has set rental of the exit turnstile at $3,400 per year; there are no significant installation expenses. Cole says that the average cost of affixing the tab is $.05 per volume. This includes all material and labor costs.

Cole is currently negotiating with Mr. Swinburne, director of Newtown's two public libraries (main library and Avis branch). The director has agreed to install the Cole system if an analysis justifies it. Swinburne believes that he might be able to negotiate a lower rental rate if he starts by discussing only the main library, then later raises the possibility of an installation at the Avis Branch.

The main library has 160,000 volumes. Over the next several years, the director plans to buy about 15,000 new volumes per year (of which 5,000 are for Avis). The expected life of a book is 20 years. The main library has fixed costs of $200,000 per year. Both libraries assign a variable cost of $.25 for each book that is borrowed.

The frequency distribution shown below is based on a study of transaction records of the past 30 months at the main library. (Each borrowed book is a transaction; total transactions include many books borrowed more than once in a given year.) No trend exists in the number of transactions over the 30-month period. However, a nationwide survey of library activity showed that the number of transactions is growing at the rate of 10% per year. Cole contends that the trend confirms the economic feasibility of his system.

Table of Main-Library Transactions

Rate of Transactions	Frequency of Occurrence
100,000 per year	9 months
200,000 per year	12 months
300,000 per year	6 months
400,000 per year	3 months
	30

Cole states that book thefts will be reduced by approximately 1% of the total number of transactions. The library figures the average cost of a stolen book at $2.50, based on original cost and average age of the books. Average replacement cost is $6.00 per book.

The librarian of the Avis branch argues that the main-library calculations would not apply to his branch. He feels that Avis cannot grow beyond its present 100,000 volumes because of limited space; he does not expect transactions to increase above the level of last year, 120,000. Thus, there is a question of whether both libraries in the system would benefit equally. It is therefore necessary to identify the advantages and disadvantages of Cole's system at both the libraries.

Swinburne has turned to you, his assistant, for advice on whether the Cole system should be installed in one library or both, or in neither. He reminds you that funds for running the library come from an annual appropriation, and that any request for funds must first be approved by the Newtown Finance Committee, and later by the Town Council. He asks that if you recommend installation, your story be a convincing one, as taxes have soared over the past few years.

PROBLEM-SOLVING EXERCISES

Marquis Detection Company

To save you time on calculations, we have prepared a programmed series of problems for this unit that will help you to solve the case. If you solve Question 1 correctly in Parts A, B, C, and D, you may stop figuring and just look at the computations as done by us, since you have shown that you understand the method and the problem. If you can't do Question 1 correctly, look at the solution, try to find your mistake, and go on to Question 2. Continue this process until you have solved at least one problem in each of the four parts correctly. Do not look at the solutions except to check yourself.

PART A

Question 1. What is the breakeven point for installation of the alarm system in the main branch only, using the cash method of accounting? (Cash method means that all costs are written off in the year they occur, and savings are based on a replacement cost of $6 per book.)

Work out your solution in the space below; then compare your answer with ours, found on page 48.

Question 2.   What is the breakeven point for installation of the alarm system in the Avis branch only, using the cash method?

You will find the solution to this problem on page 49.

Question 3.   What is the breakeven point for installation of the alarm system at the main branch only, using the accrual method of accounting? (Accrual means that costs are written off over the period of estimated use—tabs on new books have an expected life of 20 years; those on old books average 20/2 = 10 years—and savings are based on a depreciated book value of $2.50.

You will find the solution to this problem on page 49.

Question 4.   What is the breakeven point for installation of the alarm system in the Avis branch only, using the accrual method?

You will find the solution to this problem on page 49.

PART B

Question 1.   For the total library system (both main and Avis branches), what is the net dollar change for the first year if the alarm system is installed in both branches? Use the cash method and assume no increase in transactions.

You will find the solution to this problem on pages 49, 50.

Question 2. For the total library system, what is the net dollar change for the second year if the alarm system is installed in both branches? Use the cash method and assume no increases in transactions.

You will find the solution to this problem on page 50.

PART C

Question 1. For the total library system, what is the net dollar gain for the first year if the alarm system is installed in both branches? Use the accrual method, assuming no increase in transactions.

You will find the solution to this problem on page 50.

Question 2.   For the total library system, what is the net dollar gain for the second year if the alarm system is installed in both branches? Use the accrual method, assuming no increase in transactions.

You will find the solution to this problem on pages 50, 51.

PART D

Question 1.   If transactions increase as predicted in the nationwide survey, what would be the net dollar change in year 1 of installation of the alarm system in both branches? Show both the cash method and the accrual method.

You will find the solution to this problem on page 51.

Question 2.   If transactions increase as predicted in the nationwide survey, what would be the net dollar change in year 2 of installation of the alarm system in both branches? Show both the cash method and the accrual method.

You will find the solution to this problem on page 51.

Solution to Part A, Question 1:

Breakeven:

$$\$3,400 + (\$.05)(160,000 \text{ volumes}) + (\$.05)(10,000 \text{ new volumes}) = (.01)\,(\text{Transactions})(\$6.00)$$
$$\$3,400 + \$8,500 = \$.06T$$
$$T = 198,333$$

The breakeven point for the main branch is 198,333 transactions yearly.

If you have completed the calculation correctly, you may go on to Part A, Question 3. If you have not completed it correctly, go on to Part A, Question 2.

Solution to Part A, Question 2:

Breakeven:

$$\$3{,}400 + (\$.05)(100{,}000\ \text{vol.}) + (\$.05)(5{,}000) = (.01)(T)(\$6.00)$$
$$\$3{,}400 + \$5{,}250 = \$.06T$$
$$T = 144{,}167$$

The breakeven point for the Avis branch is 144,167 transactions yearly. (We are given the yearly rate in the case, for the present year.)

Now go on to Part A, Question 3.

Solution to Part A, Question 3:

Breakeven:

$$\$3{,}400 + \frac{\$.05}{10\ \text{yrs.}}{}^{*}(160{,}000) + \frac{.05}{20}(10{,}000) = (.01)(T)(\$2.50)$$
$$T = 169{,}000$$

If you have completed the calculation correctly, go on to Part B, Question 1. If you have not completed it correctly, go on to Part A, Question 4.

Solution to Part A, Question 4:

Breakeven:

$$\$3{,}400 + \frac{\$.05}{10\ \text{yrs.}}(100{,}000) + \frac{\$.05}{20\ \text{yrs.}}(5{,}000) = (.01)(T)(\$2.50)$$
$$T = 156{,}500$$

Now go on to Part B, Question 1.

Solution to Part B, Question 1:

Breakeven:

$$\$6{,}800 + (\$.05)(260{,}000\ \text{volumes}) + (\$.05)(15{,}000\ \text{new volumes}) = (.01)(T)(\$6.00)$$
$$\$6{,}800 + \$13{,}000 + \$750 = .06T$$
$$T = 342{,}500$$

The present total transactions for both branches is 330,000.** Assuming that the thefts will indeed be reduced by 1% of transactions, we can say that the number of thefts will be reduced by 3,300 books yearly. At $6 per book, that is a savings of $19,800. This information may be arranged in table form as below:

Year	Rental	Tabs: Original Volumes	Tabs: New Volumes	Total Cost	Gross Savings	Net Gain
1	$6,800	$13,000	$750	$20,550	$19,800	–$750

*Expected life of a new book (and of its tab) = 20 years; average remaining life of a book in the present collection is 20/2 = 10 years.

**Estimated in the following way: Based on the last 30 months of data, present level = $\frac{100{,}000}{30}[(1 \times 9) + (2 \times 12) + (3 \times 6) + (4 \times 3)]$ = 210,000 main library transactions + 120,000 Avis transactions = 330,000 total transactions.

If you have completed the calculation correctly, go on to Part C, Question 1. If you have not completed it correctly, go on to Part B, Question 2.

Solution to Part B, Question 2:

Breakeven for year 2:

$$\$6,800 + (.05)(15,000) = (.01)(T)(\$6.00) \text{ No cost for tabbing volumes already tabbed.}$$
$$T = 125,833$$

If we arrange the second-year information in a table:

Year	Rental	Tabs: Original Volumes	Tabs: New Volumes	Total Cost	Gross Savings	Net Gain
2	$6,800	0	$750	$7,550	$19,800	$12,250

Now go on to Part C, Question 1.

Solution to Part C, Question 1:

Breakeven:

$$\$6,800 + \frac{\$.05}{10 \text{ yrs.}} (260,000 \text{ old vols.}) + \frac{\$.05}{20 \text{ yrs.}} (15,000) = (.01)(T)(\$2.50)$$
$$T = 325,500$$

The yearly rate of transactions remains the same at 330,000, and the reduction in thefts remains at 3,300. At a saving of $2.50 per book, gross savings for one year amount to $8,250.

Arranging this into a table:

Year	Rental	Tabs: Original Volumes	Tabs: New Volumes	Total Cost	Gross Savings	Net Gain
1	$6,800	$1,300	$37.50	$8,137.50	$8,250	$112.50

If you have completed the calculation correctly, go on to Part D, Question 1. If you have not completed it correctly, go on to Part C, Question 2.

Solution to Part C, Question 2:

Breakeven for year 2:

$$\$6,800 + \frac{\$.05}{10} (260,000) + \frac{\$.05}{20} (30,000) = .01(T)(\$2.50)$$
$$T = 136,255$$

Cost of tabbing new books doubles, due to yearly purchase of 15,000 additional books.

In the table:

Year	Rental	Tabs: Original Volumes	Tabs: New Volumes	Total Cost	Gross Savings	Net Gain
2	$6,800	$1,300	$75	$8,175	$8,250	$75

Now go on to Part D, Question 1.

Solution to Part D, Question 1:

Cash method. Assuming a 10% increase in T per year:

Year	Costs (from Part B)	Transactions	Gross Savings	Net Gain
1	$20,550	363,000	$21,780	$1,230

Accrual method. Assuming a 10% increase in T per year:

Year	Costs (from Part C)	Transactions	Gross Savings	Net Gain
1	$8,137.50	363,000	$9,075	$937.50

If you have completed the calculation correctly, you have reached the end of this exercise. If you have not completed it correctly, go on to Part D, Question 2.

Solution to Part D, Question 2:

Cash method. Assuming a 10% increase in T per year:

Year	Costs (Part B)	Transactions	Gross Savings	Net Gain
2	$7,550	399,300	$23,958	$16,408

Accrual method. Assuming a 10% increase in T per year:

Year	Costs (Part C)	Transactions	Gross Savings	Net Gain
2	$8,175	399,300	$9,982.50	$1,807.50

Unit **4**

PERT

PERT and other critical-path methods are powerful project planning and control aids. They are widely used and their acceptance is continuing to grow. These approaches require a network representation of the stages of a *project* from inception to completion. To create such a network requires an understanding of systems design, as well as the ability to estimate times, costs, and performances. The method is intended to *schedule* operations and to *allocate* resources in a near-optimal way.

> *Complex project planning can be assisted by a* <u>systematic</u> *and* <u>objective</u> *approach that allows the manager to assess how much he really* <u>knows</u> *and* <u>understands</u> *about his planning problems.* <u>Knowing what you know is essential</u> *when critical points could possibly be overlooked.*

The project network is like a chain that is only as strong as its weakest link. We shall therefore examine the various aspects of network methods.

A very simple PERT chart is drawn below.

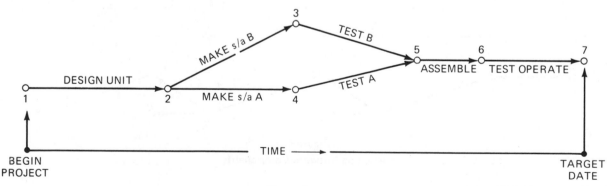

Figure 1

We see the network is composed of directed lines (or arrows) and nodes (or junctions, defined by two or more lines converging at or emerging from a single node). The network above should be viewed as a map of the activities that must be performed for the project to move from design of the item, through fabricating the subassemblies (s/a), ultimately to an operating assembly. Much of this particularly simple network follows a single path. But at the

53

second node (2) there is a junction where the two paths, A and B, can be treated separately. (Activities between nodes 2 and 5 parallel each other.)

Each step in the network is sequenced so that activities are shown in proper order. When two or more arrows emerge from a single node, work in both branches can occur simultaneously—for example, at node 2. At other times, two or more arrows may converge at a single node. This occurs in the diagram when test A and test B lead to the fifth node. An alternate form of drawing the network, shown below, emphasizes (by means of dotted lines) the fact that both test activities must be completed before the assembly step can be taken.

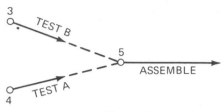

Figure 2

With only a few rules for establishing sequences of activities, we can begin to look at real project situations and construct useful PERT networks. First, however, it must be noted that the network is extensive. This means that it cannot loop back on itself, as in the following figure:

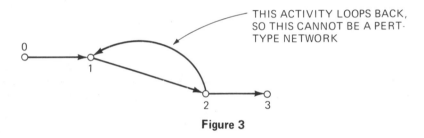

Figure 3

The figure above presents an impossible condition for an extensive network. Arrow 2-1 loops back; thus, activity 1-2 occurs again and again. Every activity in a proper critical-path network must be a unique activity that never repeats itself. All activities are sequentially ordered. This is so even when the same type of operation has to be repeated, as is shown below.

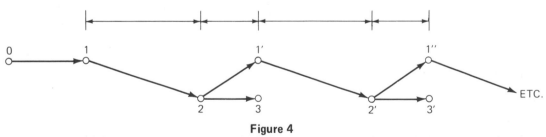

Figure 4
Repeating Network Components

DESIGN OF THE NETWORK

The network design must be technologically feasible and must adhere to good practice in the engineering and technological fields with which the project is involved. Questions of what constitutes good administration, successful leadership, acceptable coordination, and so on, are similarly determined by the network configuration. And not to be overlooked (as will be seen shortly) are cost, time, and quality considerations.

If the government takes bids, for example, on a proposed aircraft with specific performance characteristics and with a fixed target date, the competing firms are certain to come up with not only different designs but also with different project networks. Even when the product is totally specified, networks are likely to differ. One engineer may prefer to test individual components, while another tends to wait for assemblies. The design of an optimal program for testing "what and when" might be derived through a management-science study, but the present state of project planning usually leaves many degrees of freedom for the network's configuration. So, in general, we have no method that prescribes an ideal project sequence when a large number of feasible ones exist.

More specific to the network-construction problem, there is no way of saying how small or how large each activity link should be made. In other words, there is no way of specifying the number of arrows that should be used to represent the project. Make A, for example, could be broken into a large set of basic activities, such as blank and form in the press shop, drill two holes in the machine shop, trim, plate, and so forth. But it might instead consist of just two: machine and plate. Which should it be? The answer to the question is determined by the purpose to be served. The more detailed the network, the tighter the control that can be exercised and, at the same time, the more costly the PERT effort. This crucially important point concerning the cost of PERT must not be obscured by the seductive and compelling methodological advantages of network analysis. The estimation problem may shed some additional light on the degree of detail that should be used in constructing the network. The cost and benefits of controlling performance and schedule will also influence the configuration to be used.

ESTIMATING

Time and, if possible, cost estimates should be associated with each of the activity arrows in the network. Believable methods for estimating must be either available or developed if the advantages that can be derived from using these networks are to be realized. In some cases, especially when machines perform the activities, tight estimates can be obtained. As more human behaviors are involved in activities, greater variability enters the picture.

There is no simple answer to when it is appropriate to use complex statistical methods instead of some simpler approach. Management science is, however, beginning to learn how to ask the right questions about estimating procedures. We should use whichever method promises the required accuracy for an acceptable cost. The idea that a complex approach* will of necessity perform in a fashion superior to a simple off-the-cuff estimate is incorrect. Sometimes, on the other hand, complex procedures may be essential. If careful records are kept of what was estimated and what occurred, over time we can expect to improve our estimating performance. The empirical verification of estimating procedures is good management practice.

In summary, each of us is in a position to design his own set of methods for problems of estimation. This prerogative must be supported by consistency and logic. It should be accompanied by complete follow-up and checking.

> *Systematic data collection of what was guessed and what occurred is required if learning (and improvement) is to take place.* Without memory in the system, estimation procedures will remain an artist's game.

GANTT CHARTS

PERT networks and other critical-path variants (some of which we shall discuss shortly) are the formidable offspring of Gantt charts, an example of which is illustrated below. A moment spent with the history of the Gantt chart will enable us to understand the advances that PERT represents.

---

*In his article, "How to Plan and Control with PERT," *Harvard Business Review*, March-April 1962, Robert W. Miller describes one such approach: the Beta method. It is based on three estimates that are combined mathematically to yield the "best" single estimate.

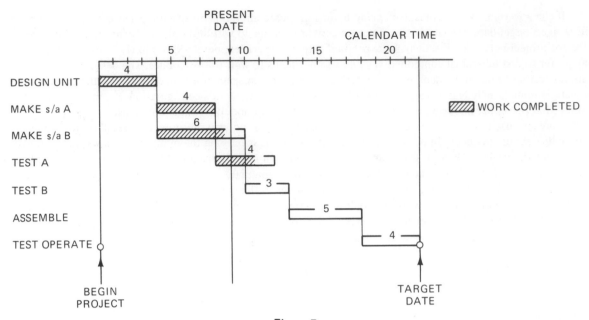

Figure 5

Henry L. Gantt (1861-1919) was the first to develop a systematized approach for setting down the design steps of the project as separate activities. The length of each bar in the Gantt chart reflects the allocation of resources to that activity. Some of these lengths are relatively fixed by the nature of the job. In other cases, a change in manpower allocation, different machines, or an alteration in the design specifications could alter the length of the bar. The sequence of steps is also indicated. For example, Test A doesn't begin until Make A is completed. Schedule control exists as well. We observe that at the "present date" in Figure 5, component A is ahead but component B is behind schedule. Frequently, the reasons for failure to meet schedule are noted on the chart.

Gantt charts helped organize and control projects. Relative to PERT, however, this is a comparatively weak method, in its ability to both allocate resources and follow up on the accomplishment of the activities. Nevertheless, neither Gantt nor PERT resolve the problem of how to design the network. Both methods involve time and cost estimates, but PERT/COST allows careful consideration of time and cost trade-offs that are not available through Gantt charts.

THE CRITICAL PATH

We repeat the network shown in Figure 1, but now it has the same time estimates that appeared in the Gantt chart, and these are associated with their respective branches or paths of the network.

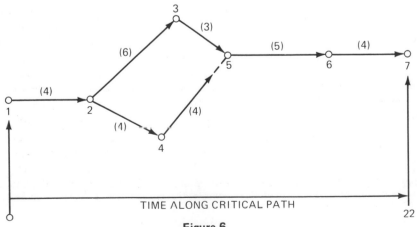

Figure 6

There are two distinct paths in the system. The first one (called A) consists of nodes 1, 2, 3, 5, 6, and 7; the second (called B) of 1, 2, 4, 5, 6, and 7. If we sum up the time estimates for each of these, we find that the path that includes making part A takes one day *longer* than the path involved with part B. Therefore, the A path is the critical path.

> *The longest path in the system is called the critical path.* The reason should be apparent; namely, if *any* slippage occurs in meeting schedule along the critical path, it will result in the project's not being completed in time. This longest time branch is *critical, since it* is the network route that *determines the total length of the project.*

In more complex networks, the same procedure prevails. For example, in the network below, we have five different paths.

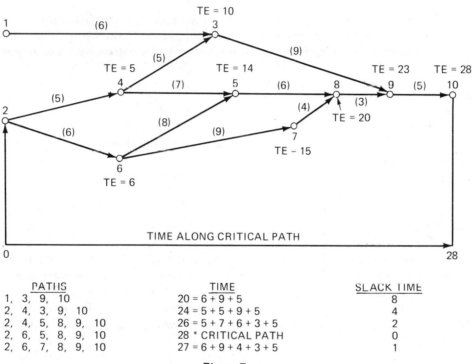

PATHS	TIME	SLACK TIME
1, 3, 9, 10	20 = 6 + 9 + 5	8
2, 4, 3, 9, 10	24 = 5 + 5 + 9 + 5	4
2, 4, 5, 8, 9, 10	26 = 5 + 7 + 6 + 3 + 5	2
2, 6, 5, 8, 9, 10	28 * CRITICAL PATH	0
2, 6, 7, 8, 9, 10	27 = 6 + 9 + 4 + 3 + 5	1

Figure 7

At each node, a *time estimate* is shown, which is called *TE*. TE represents the *greatest* cumulative total time of preceding activities that must be completed to get to that node. In other words, it is the actual clock time that is required to complete all prior activities. With the data of Figure 7, it is easy to compute TEs and then to determine which path is the critical one. It is the path (or paths) that determines all TE values. Thus, at node 5, path 2, 4, 5 has a total time of 12, whereas path 2, 6, 5 has a total time of 14. TE at node 5 is, therefore, set equal to 14. Path 2, 4, 5 cannot be on the critical path. Then, path 2, 6, 5, 8 dominates TE at node 8, and path 2, 6, 5, 8, 9 dominates TE at node 9. Accordingly, path 2, 6, 5, 8, 9, 10 is the critical path. Various search methods exist that are particularly adaptable to computer applications. They can provide systematic search through the network to determine the critical path. When a network is very complicated, with say, several hundred paths, it is easy to develop appreciation for a method that takes advantage of the computer's indefatigable abilities. One method first develops the TE measures and then goes backward through the network subtracting all activity times. Each node is labeled with the appropriate value, called TL. At a junction, where two or more activities converge, the smallest value equals TL. We note that TL − TE equals the slack time. Figure 8 on the following page.

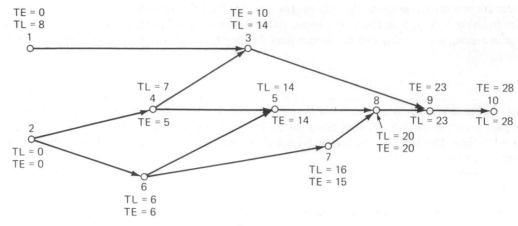

Figure 8
Along the Critical Path, TL — TE = 0

All paths that are less than critical have *slack time.* The critical path must then have zero slack. For our example, slippage of up to eight time units can be tolerated on the top path in Figure 7 without affecting the completion date of the project. Slippage of only one time unit is permissible on the bottom path. Let us recapitulate. Our steps are as follows:

1. Design the stages of the project.
2. Arrange them in proper sequence.
3. Provide best estimates of time.
4. Carry through the cumulative timing process to determine the critical path.
5. Compute slack time.
6. Analyze resource trade-off possibilities; i.e., balance resource allocations.

RESOURCE ALLOCATION TRADE-OFF

Our procedures do not necessarily end when we have found the critical path. The sixth step should be taken. It enables us to find out whether we can either bring new resources into the system to change some of the activity times, or transfer some of the resources from slack paths to the critical path. In this way we can utilize resource and manpower capacities more fully. If possible trade-offs between slack paths and the critical path can be accomplished, this produces the desirable result of decreasing the length of the critical path. Sometimes it may even switch the critical path to a new set of branches in the network. For example, assume that for the project in Figure 7, only one man works on each job, so that one man-day is equivalent to one calendar day. (This is an unrealistic assumption, but it will greatly simplify the example and the problem that follows.) If one man-day can be transferred from the branch 3, 9 to the branch 2, 6, the time along the top path increases by one day (to 21). The length of the critical path decreases by one day (to 27). There are now two critical paths of length 27. With two man-days transferred, we find three critical-path routes through the network. The length of these critical paths is 26. Knowledge of the technology and character of one's resources is essential to obtain the best possible trade-offs.[*]

Using PERT networks takes skill. (There is no question about the fact that practice improves performance.) A lot of accomplishments are required, and they are not simple ones. But the conceptual structure of the network approach is simple and simplifying. For this reason, many government organizations—the Navy, NASA, and so forth—require PERT or some other, similar network method for complex projects. The Navy was instrumental in developing PERT; it was first used to plan for the Polaris missile project.

---

[*]*Problem*: What occurs if one man-day can be transferred from the branch 3, 9 to the branch 5, 8? (Answer at end of technical note.)

SCHEDULE CONTROL

One of the by-products of the PERT network (especially when it is programmed for a computer system—and there are many such programs available, from all major computer manufacturers) is the ability to ask at any point in time, "At what stage is the *real* network as compared with the *planned* one?" The answer can be obtained immediately if the state of completion of all activities is regularly and frequently reported to the *information system* maintained by the computer. With even a very complex network, made up of many contractors and subcontractors, tight scheduling and efficient expediting are entirely feasible.

Within companies, trade-offs can be arranged. In one department, for example, the work may have proceeded faster than was expected. If that work is involved with the critical path, then the target date can be brought closer to the present. If it is along one of the slack branches, it means that additional slack has been generated that might be usable along the critical path. On the other hand, if it turns out that slippage has occurred along the critical path, this means an extension of project time and may lead to new resources' being brought into the system. Along the slack path, it means that less slack is now available than had previously been thought. Severe slippage might even turn a slack path into the critical path.

Schedule control also existed in the Gantt system. This was indicated in our Gantt diagram (Figure 5) by a vertical line that represented the present time. On the chart, each activity bar was shaded in to depict the degree of completion. Nevertheless, the Gantt system had less flexibility, no critical path, and, in general, a weaker story to tell. Trade-offs are also much harder to accomplish in the Gantt system. When elements are sequenced in the network fashion, the branching characteristics emerge, permitting even more powerful trade-off considerations when both time and cost are used.

PERT/COST

The major difficulty of PERT/COST is that the network method does not answer the question of cost and time trade-offs. However, if time vs. cost relationships can be estimated, such trade-off problems can be tackled effectively. Figure 9 shows such relationships.

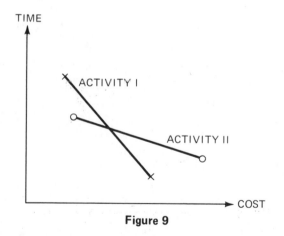

Figure 9

We see that Activity II does not lend itself to time cutting as well as Activity I does. A substantial increase in cost results in a minimal time saving as compared with the results of spending the same amount on Activity I. Naturally, that's not the whole story. We must know whether either activity is on the critical path, and if not, how much slack is associated with each of them. Costs might be reduced along slack paths to bring them more in line with the critical path as the branch activity times increase. (We have drawn linear relations between cost and time, which may not be an adequate representation.) The points at minimum times might be considered to be crash-program points. The other end of each line is the minimum-budget situation.

Some projects must be scheduled on a very tight time base. In these cases, cost is held to be of a secondary nature. The company is willing to assume large costs to achieve minimum project time. In other cases, cost is a major consideration and time becomes less important. It may be possible to let the project slip to a longer period, thereby decreasing its total cost. Most frequently, something in between these two extremes exists. The manager is charged with finding the best possible arrangement for the problem situation.

Solution to the Manpower Transfer Exercise

Two paths become critical; total slack decreases markedly.

Paths	Time	Slack Time
1, 3, 9, 10	21	6
2, 4, 3, 9, 10	25	2
2, 4, 5, 8, 9, 10	25	2
2, 6, 5, 8, 9, 10	27	0
2, 6, 7, 8, 9, 10	27	0

INSTRUCTIONS FOR PREPARING THE CASE

Teaneck Construction Company

After you have read the technical notes on PERT and studied the Teaneck case, make a PERT diagram for the project. Then go on to the Problem-Solving exercises that follow. When you have completed these exercises, analyze the management aspects of the case and make a decision regarding the following objective for analysis: *What exact bid for the Deerfield job should be recommended to the president of Teaneck?*

The case places you as project manager of Teaneck. Assume that the president has asked you to present a bid recommendation and to justify it with a full analysis. In a meeting with you, he has given you these instructions as to what he looks for in your recommendation:

He wants the bid to cover operating costs as a minimum.
He would like to gain as much contribution to overhead and profit as possible.
He will take a reasonable financial risk, recognizing that the possible strike would have impact on costs.
(He does not tell you what he means by "reasonable.")

The president tells you that if you think of other criteria that are important in weighing alternative strategies, you should add them to your report (with explanation). He also tells you that, as with most managerial decisions, you may stumble over the absence of information that you would like to have, and that if you do run up against such obstacles to analysis, you should list them and tell how you would dispose of them—that is, through assumption or research. Finally, he would like to be aware of all alternatives that you have considered, with the pros and cons given for each.

Decision Process

Teaneck Construction Company

The Teaneck Construction Company is a small organization operating in Northwestern Florida. Ninety percent of the company's dollar volume is obtained from contracts for municipal work.

Management has decided to submit a bid for the construction in April of a mile-long extension to the main sewer system in the nearby town of Deerfield. The extension is going into a residential area that until now has used septic tanks. The bidding is expected to be competitive, because whoever gets this contract will have some advantage in obtaining a contract that is to be awarded by the town later in the year, and that is worth approximately $1 million. In order to submit the most competitive bid possible, the project managers of Teaneck decided to evaluate the alternatives of using one, two, or three work shifts.

Table 1 shows time and cost estimates made by Teaneck's engineers. The trunk sewer extension is to be laid in a tunnel for one-third its length; the remaining two-thirds is to be constructed in trenches. To build the tunnel, a primary shaft must be excavated first. After this, the secondary shafts can be driven and the tunnel can be dug simultaneously. The trench is to be started at the same time as the primary shaft. Another crew of workers follows the trench workers, laying the pipes, pouring the concrete, and refilling the trenches as far as they have been excavated. The excavators lose no time as a result of this follow-up. A third group would be performing a similar function in the tunnel.

TABLE 1

		1 Shift		2 Shifts		3 Shifts	
	Activity	Time (days)	Cost ($)	Time (days)	Cost ($)	Time (days)	Cost ($)
A	Move in machinery & equipment	12	3,000	6	3,300	4	3,600
B	Excavate primary shaft	12	6,250	12	6,600	12	6,950
C	Excavate secondary shafts	60		24		12	
D	Excavate trenches	300	33,700	150	42,500	100	44,700
E	Excavate tunnel	305	36,150	155	39,100	105	40,000
F	Backfill (trenches only)	50	1,000	25	1,500	17	2,000
G	Pipelaying in trenches	50	8,500	25	8,200	17	8,900
H	Pipelaying in tunnel	46	5,500	25	5,700	16	6,000
J	Pour concrete in trenches	70	11,400	35	11,650	25	11,850
K	Pour concrete in tunnel	60	11,000	30	11,250	20	11,500
L	Landscape	10	2,000	8	2,900	6	3,000
M	Move out	6	500	3	750	2	1,000
	Total direct costs	$119,000		$133,450		$139,500	
	Total indirect costs	$140/day		$160/day		$180/day	

There is an additional complication that may have serious effects on the profitability of this job. There is a strong chance that the local Excavators Union will strike on the inception date of the project. At the last meeting of the project managers, there was consensus that the probability of such a strike fell somewhere close to 80 percent; at least, it was decided to use this figure for planning purposes. In case of a strike, the direct costs associated with the project would remain unchanged, since the issue involved was not one of wages; but indirect costs would accrue for the duration of the strike at the same daily rate as indicated in Table 1. Teaneck's direct labor is hired from union pools, the common practice of all construction companies in the area. General and administrative costs are put at 40% of the sum of direct and indirect costs. Normally, Teaneck aims at making a profit equal to 10% of total costs.

There was also a recognized need to develop some kind of estimate to describe the probability of the strike's duration. With a great deal of misgiving, the project managers came up with the following guesses:

TABLE 2

Length of strike in days	20	30	40
Probability of a strike of n days, on the condition that a strike occurs	.25	.25	.50

You are the project manager assigned to the Deerfield bid. The president of Teaneck and his two executive vice-presidents have asked you for a detailed recommendation, including the exact bid to be submitted.

PROBLEM-SOLVING EXERCISES

Teaneck Construction Company

To save you time on calculations, we have prepared a programmed series of problems for this unit, which will help you to solve the case. Part A involves the construction of a PERT diagram, for which there is more than one correct answer. The other Parts, B, C, and D, include questions that do have singular solutions. If you solve Question 1 correctly in Parts B, C, and D, you may stop figuring and just look at the computations as done by us, since you have shown that you understand the method and the problem. If you can't do Question 1 correctly, look at the solution, try to find your mistake, and go on to Question 2. Continue this process until you have solved at least one problem in each of the parts correctly. Do not look at the solutions except to check yourself.

PART A

Construct a PERT diagram for the Teaneck Company's sewer project. Disregard the possibility of a strike.
Here are some suggestions to make construction of the diagram easier:

1. Theoretically, laying the pipes, pouring the concrete, and refilling the trenches would have to begin some time after the excavation begins, and could not be completed until after the digging is finished. We suggest, however, that you regard these activities as if they were starting simultaneously; similarly, consider the pipelaying, concrete pouring, and refilling as being complete as soon as the digging is complete.

2. Do not begin your landscaping until both the tunnel and trench operations are completed.

3. Undoubtedly, a sophisticated operation could be designed if we choose to trade off resources and work on a multishift basis (one shift for some operations, two or three shifts for others). Designing this type of system, however, requires the use of a computer; implementing it would require strict control. For our purposes, we prefer that you determine which is best—a one-, two-, or three-shift operation; do not combine various numbers of shifts in your final plan.

4. Remember, too, that in PERT diagrams, nodes are usually drawn at the completion of an activity.

5. The indirect costs referred to in the case are comparable to manufacturing overhead.

Now go ahead with your diagram in the space on the following page. You will find one solution on page 70.

PART B

Question 1.   If only one shift were employed, what would be the largest cumulative time figures at each node for construction of the sewer extension? (Do not consider the strike in these calculations.)

You will find the solution to this problem on page 70.

Question 2.   If two shifts were employed, what would be the largest cumulative time figures at each node for construction of the sewer extension? (Disregard the strike.)

You will find the solution to this problem on page 71.

Question 3:   If three shifts were employed, what would be the largest cumulative time figures at each node for construction of the sewer extension? (Disregard the strike.)

You will find the solution to this problem on page 71.

PART C

Question 1.   Figure the bid analysis (costs, profit) if only one shift is employed, assuming that the strike does not occur.

You will find the solution to this problem on page 72.

Question 2.   Figure the bid analysis (costs, profit) if two shifts are employed, assuming that the strike does not occur.

You will find the solution to this problem on page 72

Question 3.   Figure the bid analysis (costs, profit) if three shifts are employed, assuming that the strike does not occur.

You will find the solution to this problem on page 72.

PART D

Question 1.   Figure the bid analysis (costs, profit) if only one shift is employed, assuming that the strike does occur.

You will find the solution to this problem on pages 72, 73.

Question 2. Figure the bid analysis (costs, profit) if two shifts are employed and the strike does occur. You will find the solution to this problem on page 73.

Question 3. Figure the bid analysis (costs, profit) if three shifts are employed and the strike does occur. You will find the solution to this problem on page 73.

Solution to Part A:

The diagram that appears below is *one* solution to the problem. There could be many others. However, the solutions to the remainder of the exercises are based on *our* PERT diagram. You must use *our* diagram to arrive at the solutions given. You may use our figures to solve the case if you choose to do so.

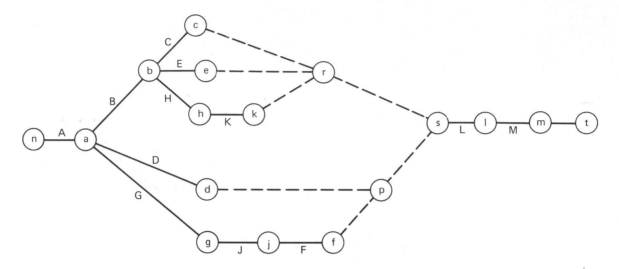

Now continue on with Part B, Question 1.

Solution to Part B, Question 1:

Largest cumulative total time, one shift:

Node	Time (days)
n	0
a	12
b	24
c	84
e	329
h	70
k	130
r	329
d	312
g	62
j	132
f	182
p	312
s	329
l	339
m	345
t	345

If you have completed the calculation correctly, go on to Part C, Question 1. If you have not completed it correctly, go on to Part B, Question 2.

Solution to Part B, Question 2:

Largest cumulative total time, two shifts:

Node	Time (days)
n	0
a	6
b	18
c	42
e	173
h	43
k	73
r	173
d	156
g	31
j	66
f	91
p	156
s	173
l	181
m	184
t	184

If you have completed the calculation correctly, go on to Part C, Question 1. If you have not completed it correctly, go on to Part B, Question 3.

Solution to Part B, Question 3:

Largest cumulative total time, three shifts:

Node	Time (days)
n	0
a	4
b	16
c	28
e	121
h	32
k	52
r	121
d	104
g	21
j	46
f	63
p	104
s	121
l	127
m	129
t	129

Now go on to Part C, Question 1.

Solution to Part C, Question 1:

Bid analysis (no strike) for one shift—345 days:

Total direct	$119,000
Total indirect	48,300
Operating cost	$167,300
40% G & A	66,920
	$234,220
10% profit	23,422
Bid	$257,642

If you have completed the calculation correctly, go on to Part D, Question 1. If you have not completed it correctly, go on to Part C, Question 2.

Solution to Part C, Question 2:

Bid analysis (no strike) for two shifts—184 days:

Total direct	$133,450
Total indirect	29,440
Operating cost	$162,890
40% G & A	65,156
	$228,046
10% profit	22,805
Bid	$250,851

If you have completed the calculation correctly, go on to Part D, Question 1. If you have not completed it correctly, go on to Part C, Question 3.

Solution to Part C, Question 3:

Bid analysis (no strike) for three shifts—129 days:

Total direct	$139,500
Total indirect	23,220
Operating cost	$162,720
40% G & A	65,088
	$227,808
10% profit	22,781
Bid	$250,589

Now go on to Part D, Question 1.

Solution to Part D, Question 1:

Bid analysis (with strike) for one shift—371 days:

The expected length of the strike will be:

$$.2[0 \text{ days}] + .8[(20 \times .25) + (30 \times .25) + (40 \times .5)] = 26 \text{ days}$$

With one shift, expected elapsed time = 371 days

Total direct	$119,000
Total indirect	51,940
Operating cost	$170,940
40% G & A	68,376
	$239,316
10% profit	23,932
Bid	$263,248

If you have completed the calculation correctly, you have reached the end of the exercises for this case. If you have not completed it correctly, go on to Part D, Question 2.

Solution to Part D, Question 2:

Bid analysis (with strike) for two shifts—210 days:

With two shifts, expected elapsed time = 210 days

Total direct	$133,450
Total indirect	33,600
Operating cost	$167,050
40% G & A	66,820
	$233,870
10% profit	23,387
Bid	$257,257

If you have completed the calculation correctly, you have reached the end of the exercises for this case. If you have not completed it correctly, go on to Part D, Question 3.

Solution to Part D, Question 3:

Bid analysis (with strike) for three shifts—155 days:

With three shifts, expected elapsed time = 155 days

Total direct	$139,500
Total indirect	27,900
Operating cost	$167,400
40% G & A	66,960
	$234,360
10% profit	23,436
Bid	$257,796

Unit 5

Decisions with Multiple Criteria

Multiple objectives are essential to many "real" systems. Frequently, these multiple objectives conflict with each other. (As one objective is improved, the others may deteriorate.) Dimensional analysis can help the manager make better decisions under such circumstances.

There are various dimensional approaches. We shall develop one of them that is particularly useful to cope with multiple objectives in a management planning situation. In addition, we shall attack the incorrect application of a method that is frequently used in the wrong way, leading to erroneous solutions. It will become clear that dimensionality is the key concept underlying acceptable evaluation procedures.

Let us consider some problems with important multiple outcomes. We choose our food for nutrition, taste, cost, and appearance; no one quality suffices to describe our objectives. The characteristics we look for in an executive are manifold: intelligence, energy, leadership, attitude, and so on. In a product design, we expect a variety of objectives to be fulfilled, such as safety, ease of using, ease of maintaining, low cost of producing, low cost of operating, marketability, and so forth. When we buy a new machine, we evaluate it in terms of its productivity, the cost of using it, the ease of maintaining it, its size, the date of delivery, the downtime on it, the setup costs, and many other crucial attributes.

SINGLE-SCALE SYSTEMS

It is vital to note: Multiple objectives are not a serious problem when they can all be evaluated on the same scale—for example, dollars. If we wish to evaluate our machines on one scale, we must try to convert all the factors of importance into dollar costs and dollar benefits. Then we can compare the machines in terms of the single scale of dollar profit. We know that dollars can be added and subtracted, and ultimately a single number can be derived for each machine. That is what we mean by a single scale. It is illustrated by the following diagram:

MACHINE B
$2400
⟶ DOLLARS OF ANNUAL COST OR PROFIT

0   MACHINE A
              $1000

We can sum a sequence of dollar objectives in terms of either cost or profit. If it is cost dollars in the diagram above, then we prefer Machine A; if it is profit dollars, we prefer Machine B. Furthermore, these final values are achieved after a process of adding and subtracting along that single scale of dollars.

We know it is often possible to evaluate all pertinent objectives on the single scale of dollars. However, it can get quite difficult, at other times, to do this. For example, try to evaluate the dollar value of the safety features of a product design; or the feeling of satisfaction that the manager might get by moving the plant to his home state of Wyoming; or the garment manufacturer's sense of pride at producing nothing less than a $20 dress. For such cases, we must abandon the dollar measure.

To retain a single scale, some kind of preference measure must be supposed. For example, if we're looking at an airplane and trying to evaluate its qualities in terms of several objectives—its ability to fly long distances, land on short runways, and be maneuverable; whether it has a good lift-to-drag ratio, substantial cargo and passenger capacity, and low operating costs—we can at least try to put down a preference measure for each design alternative with respect to every one of these objectives. Then, assuming you can assign a preference measure for each particular design across each one of the objectives, it would be possible to determine on a single scale, as shown below, a measure of the total preference for each design.

If this type of preference measure can really be achieved, the dimensionality problem is not serious. Frequently, however, people think that they can do this when, in fact, they cannot.

A hypothetical case is shown below in which each design is measured for preference independently for each objective.

TABLE OF PREFERENCES

Objective	Design A	Design B
1	3	9
2	7	1
3	4	2
4	2	5
5	5	3
Total preference (A is preferred to B.)	21	20

Large numbers indicate greater preferences than small numbers.

Sometimes, as a concession to the difficulty of achieving such a single scale of preference, the preference scores are weighted for each objective. This is illustrated below.

TABLE OF WEIGHTED PREFERENCES

Objective	Design A	Design B	Objective's Weight[*]
1	3 X 4 = 12	9 X 4 = 36	4
2	7 X 1 = 7	1 X 1 = 1	1
3	4 X 3 = 12	2 X 3 = 6	3
4	2 X 1 = 2	5 X 1 = 5	1
5	5 X 2 = 10	3 X 2 = 6	2
Total preference (B is now preferred to A.)	43	54	

[*]Larger numbers indicate greater importance.

We may note that the unweighted table is in fact weighted—but the weights are all one.

Again, if this type of preference measure (whether weighted or unweighted) can really be achieved, the dimensionality problem is not serious. The use of unequal weights merely testifies to the fact that simple transformations[*] of preference scale values exist, such as 12 inches = 1 foot, or 10 pennies = 1/10 of a dollar. The basic problem remains of whether such single-scale preferences can be given. Frequently, people (and managers, in particular) think they can assign such single-scale preferences when they cannot.[**]

INCORRECT (BUT VERY COMMON) USE OF THE SINGLE SCALE

Often a set of observations are made that are *treated* as though they were members of a single-scale system. For example, let us consider the comparison of two radios:

Objectives	Radio A[a]	Radio B[a]	Assigned Weights[b] Joe	Tom
Weight[c]	32	24	1	2
Size[d]	85	100	2	1
Tone[e]	2	4	2	3
Cost[f]	14	10	3	2

[a]Smaller numbers indicate greater preferences.
[b]Smaller numbers indicate greater importance.
[c]In ounces.
[d]In cubic inches.
[e]Scaled 1 - 10, 1 is best.
[f]In dollars.

We observe that Joe and Tom see things differently. Joe's evaluation:

$$\text{for RA} = (32 \times 1) + (85 \times 2) + (2 \times 2) + (14 \times 3) = 248$$
$$\text{for RB} = (24 \times 1) + (100 \times 2) + (4 \times 2) + (10 \times 3) = 262$$

Since the lowest weight, smallest size, rating of 1 for tone, and lowest cost are desired, Joe would choose Radio A, which has the smallest index number.

Tom's evaluation:

$$\text{for RA} = (32 \times 2) + (85 \times 1) + (2 \times 3) + (14 \times 2) = 183$$
$$\text{for RB} = (24 \times 2) + (100 \times 1) + (4 \times 3) + (10 \times 2) = 180$$

By the same reasoning, Tom prefers Radio B. We must specifically note how both Tom and Joe are acting as though the observed measures of ounces, cubic inches, tone-scaled values, and cost are (negative) preferences measured along a single scale.

The approach above is wrong! These observations are not all measured along the same single dimension (be it dollars of cost, dollars of profit, preference, or negative preference). The mistake that is being made here is the well-known one of "adding apples, bananas, and baseballs."

[*]See glossary definition.

[**]If unequal weights for the importance of objectives seem to apply, then it is quite likely that single-scale preferences are inappropriate. When the objectives have different dimensions, the same conclusion prevails.

Let us look at another example. Say that ABCO, Inc., a toy manufacturer, has as a policy a primary interest in the appearance of the product and the ease of manufacturing it. Clearly, appearance has to be evaluated on some kind of a scale that reflects the diverse opinions of the marketplace. Perhaps a market survey can produce a suitable index, but with toys, there is a short selling season and the market study is difficult to accomplish. "Expert" opinions will probably have to do. The "experts" may be buyers, production managers, industrial designers, marketing managers, and so on. Under these circumstances, what are the chances for total consensus? What should be done about real differences of opinion? The best answer is to talk it out; perhaps to spend some extra funds on studying issues of real disagreement that seem to affect the answer. Certainly, it would be foolish to incur data-collection and analysis costs on perfecting measures that will not change the problem's solution. Also, it should be observed, ABCO has at least got the benefit of putting the issues on the table where they can be studied by all and discussed. The second factor, relating to the ease of manufacturing, is somewhat easier (but not easy) to estimate for ABCO's engineers and production personnel.

These two measures come from different sources; they apply to different dimensions and probably produce unequal importance weights. Accordingly, a single scale for comparison is unacceptable.

After deriving numbers to describe the relevant outcome for each potential toy design, we must then obtain a set of weights to reflect the relative importance of appearance as compared to that of the ease of fabrication of the product. As we have seen (Joe and Tom), these weight assignments may differ between individuals. We might take an average of them, or we might just decide to use the president's estimates for a variety of organizational reasons that need little explanation. Assume that we have come up with the following numbers: W_1 for the weight of appearance, and W_2 for that of manufacturing ease. Then, according to present practice, we would multiply these weights by their respective measures. These products would then be added together to obtain a final, single, weighted index for each design. The various final weighted indices would then be compared and the best one chosen. But we have said this is wrong, so what *should* we do?

A CORRECT APPROACH TO MULTIPLE SCALES

It is necessary to <u>multiply</u> the outcome measures—not add them (when they are measured on different dimensions). [*] *Weighting factors become exponents where each is associated with its indicated objective.*

Let us return to ABCO for an example.

Objective	Toy A	Toy B	Importance Weight
Appearance (1)	A_1	B_1	W_1
Ease of manufacture (2)	A_2	B_2	W_2

We should obtain the comparison:

$$\frac{\text{Index of A}}{\text{Index of B}}$$

where: Index of A $= A_1^{W_1} A_2^{W_2}$

Index of B $= B_1^{W_1} B_2^{W_2}$

EXERCISE A

Here are some hypothetical numbers. What toy would you choose—assuming that you had "faith" in these numbers? (The method of using the numbers is at issue here.)

[*]See P.W. Bridgman, *Dimensional Analysis* (New Haven, Conn.: Yale University Press, 1922), pp. 21-22.

Objective	Toy A	Toy B	Weight
Appearance[a]	9	7	1
Ease of manufacture[b]	4	5	2

[a]Measured on a scale of 1 to 10, where 10 is best.
[b]Measured on a scale of 1 to 5, where 5 is best.

Use the space below for your calculations. The solution will be given on page 83.

Why is addition wrong and multiplication OK? Let us return to the radio example to demonstrate conclusively that addition is not allowable in these non-single-scale cases. We will use Joe's weights first, with the formula:

$$W_1 A_1 + W_2 A_2 = \text{Index of A}$$
$$W_1 B_1 + W_2 B_2 = \text{Index of B}$$

It will be remembered that, using addition, Joe found:

$$\text{Index for Radio A} = 248$$
$$\text{Index for Radio B} = 262$$

Now let's assume that Joe measured radio weight in pounds rather than ounces. This change of scale should *in no way* affect the answer, if the addition method is to pass our test. Then:

$$\text{Index for Radio A} = \ (2 \times 1) + \ (85 \times 2) + (2 \times 2) + (14 \times 3) = 218$$
$$\text{Index for Radio B} = (1.5 \times 1) + (100 \times 2) + (4 \times 2) + (10 \times 3) = 239.5$$

It looks OK. Joe still chooses Radio A. Now, let us consider Tom's weights. Previously (before the change from ounces to pounds), Tom's indices were:

$$\text{Index for Radio A} = 183$$
$$\text{Index for Radio B} = 180$$

Using pounds, they are:

$$\text{Index for Radio A} = \ (2 \times 2) + \ (85 \times 1) + (2 \times 3) + (14 \times 2) = 123$$
$$\text{Index for Radio B} = (1.5 \times 2) + (100 \times 1) + (4 \times 3) + (10 \times 2) = 135$$

Tom's previous preference for Radio B has now shifted to Radio A, and this *cannot be tolerated,* since the only change that was made was a legitimate transformation of scale. There was nothing sacrosanct about ounces. *An acceptable system of comparison must be* invariant *to the unit of measure.* Whether pounds, tons, kilograms, grams, or grains (all simple transformations of weight) are used, the solution must remain the same. Similarly, whether feet or inches, dollars or cents, pints or gallons are the scale of measure, we rely on the method of comparison to be insensitive to such scaling transformations.

The ratios of these indices obtained by multiplication *are not sensitive* to the unit of measure. For Joe's weights:

(in ounces)

$$\frac{\text{Index of Radio A}}{\text{Index of Radio B}} = \frac{(32)^1(85)^2(2)^2(14)^3}{(24)^1(100)^2(4)^2(10)^3} = 0.661$$

(in pounds)

$$\frac{\text{Index of Radio A}}{\text{Index of Radio B}} = \frac{(2)^1(85)^2(2)^2(14)^3}{(1.5)^1(100)^2(4)^2(10)^3} = 0.661$$

Joe prefers Radio A, as before, no matter how weight of the radio is measured. And for Tom:

(in ounces)

$$\frac{\text{Index of Radio A}}{\text{Index of Radio B}} = \frac{(32)^2(85)^1(2)^3(14)^2}{(24)^2(100)^1(4)^3(10)^2} = 0.370$$

(in pounds)

$$\frac{\text{Index of Radio A}}{\text{Index of Radio B}} = \frac{(2)^2(85)^1(2)^3(14)^2}{(1.5)^2(100)^1(4)^3(10)^2} = 0.370$$

Again, whether the problem is formulated in ounces or pounds, the multiplication method produces consistent results. And, as it turns out, Joe and Tom are on the same side of the fence. It so happens that when the correct evaluation method is used, they agree; both prefer Radio A.

PURE NUMBERS

When the ratio of two index numbers is taken, we require that a pure (dimensionless) number result. It tells us by how many times one thing is better than another. Because the ratio number is pure, we know that both things are being compared on the same basis. If we don't have a pure number, then our comparison of the two index numbers does not tell us the *relative measure of goodness between the choices compared.*

The addition method does not produce a pure number in ratio, except for single-scaled objectives. For example:

$$\frac{\$ + \text{inches} + \text{pounds}}{\$ + \text{inches} + \text{pounds}} = \frac{\$}{\$ + \text{inches} + \text{pounds}} + \frac{\text{inches}}{\$ + \text{inches} + \text{pounds}} + \frac{\text{pounds}}{\$ + \text{inches} + \text{pounds}}$$

whereas by multiplication, we obtain a pure number:

$$\frac{(\$)(\text{inches})(\text{pounds})}{(\$)(\text{inches})(\text{pounds})} = \text{a dimensionless number}$$

This further explains the rationale behind the multiplication method. After all, our whole purpose is to make a valid comparison.

USE OF LOGS TO SIMPLIFY CALCULATIONS

Using exponents and powers can lead to difficult computations. On the other hand, by employing logs we obtain additive quantities. Using Tom's weightings, we can compute as follows:

$$\log (\text{Index}^* \text{ of Radio A}) = 2 \log 32 + \log 85 + 3 \log 2 + 2 \log 14$$
$$= 2(1.50515) + 1.92942 + 3(0.30103) + 2(1.14613)$$
$$= 8.13507$$

$$\log (\text{Index}^* \text{ of Radio B}) = 2 \log 24 + \log 100 + 3 \log 4 + 2 \log 10$$
$$= 2(1.38021) + 2 + 3(0.60206) + 2$$
$$= 8.56660$$

Then, by subtraction:

$$18.13507 - 10$$
$$- \ 8.56660$$

The antilog of:

$$9.56847 - 10 \text{ is } 0.370$$

The log form is interesting for another reason. A set of evaluations that are transformed into log terms could be written:

$$\log \text{Index A} = W_1 \log A_1 + W_2 \log A_2 + \ldots + W_N \log A_N$$
$$\log \text{Index B} = W_1 \log B_1 + W_2 \log B_2 + \ldots + W_N \log B_N$$

$$\vdots$$

$$\log \text{Index Q} = W_1 \log Q_1 + W_2 \log Q_2 + \ldots + W_N \log Q_N$$

Then, we can write this in decision-matrix form:

	W_1	W_2 ————————	W_N	Expected Value
Strategy A:	$\log A_1$	$\log A_2$ ——————————	$\log A_N$	$\log$ Index A
Strategy B:	$\log B_1$	$\log B_2$ ——————————	$\log B_N$	$\log$ Index B
	.	.	.	.
	.	.	.	.
	.	.	.	.
Strategy Q:	$\log Q_1$	$\log Q_2$ ——————————	$\log Q_N$	$\log$ Index Q

If the weights (Ws) are replaced by probabilities, p_j's, then this is a typical decision matrix—but one where *all* outcomes have been *transformed into logs of outcomes.* The log of outcomes is frequently used as a type of utility transformation. *So we observe that the use of the multiplication method of evaluation is really equivalent to the additional method where logs of outcomes are added. This is a correct method for proceeding with an evaluation where no single scale can be found.*

THE USE OF A STANDARD FOR COMPARISON

It is sometimes beneficial to propose a standard, S, against which all contenders can be compared. That is:

*In ounces.

$$\frac{\text{Index A}}{\text{Index S}} = ?$$

$$\frac{\text{Index B}}{\text{Index S}} = ?$$

$$\frac{\text{Index S}}{\text{Index S}} = 1$$

The design of the standard is at the discretion of the decision maker. One possibility is to use the best outcomes that appear in any alternative for each objective. For example, here is a possible standard for comparing Radios A and B:

Objectives	Radio A	Radio B	Radio (Standard) (best value in each row)	(Joe's) Weights
Weight	32	24	24	1
Size	85	100	85	2
Tone	2	4	2	2
Cost	14	10	10	3

The standard provides a fixed point from which the other alternatives can be measured. It also can show the relative goodness of each alternative in terms of the standard. If we know how good the standard is, the comparisons can provide useful information. To illustrate, assume that:

$$\frac{\text{Index A}}{\text{Index B}} = \frac{2}{1}$$

We don't know how far the value of 2 is from the value of 1. It might be:

```
      STD.           B            A

      |--------------|------------|

       1            10           20
```

or it might be:

```
      STD.           B            A

      |--------------|------------|

       1           1,500        3,000
```

Without the standard, these two cases would appear to be alike. In fact, they are very different. So the standard helps to introduce a sense of distance—measured solely, of course, in terms of the standard.

Important: If all the terms in the evaluation are taken so that small values are desired (for example, with respect to cost), then the index associated with the smallest number will be chosen. If all terms are taken so that large values are desired (for example, with respect to profits), then the index of the largest value will be chosen. If, however, a mixture of these two types of values is present, this matter is simply handled by using the inverse of those observations that run counter to the sense of the problem. Thus, if the objective is the smallest index, then all profit-type outcomes should be entered as 1/Profit. Similarly, if the objective is the largest index, then cost-type outcomes should be recorded as 1/Cost.

Assume that in the radio example, the tone scale was reversed, and 10 became the best result. We shall assume that Radio A has a value of 2, which is not as good as Radio B's value of 4. The problem would be formulated as follows:

Objectives	Radio A	Radio B	Radio (Standard)	(Joe's) Weights
Weight	32	24	24	1
Size	85	100	85	2
Tone	1/2	1/4	1/4	2
Cost	14	10	10	3

The objective is identified by the smallest index. Now, 1/4 is less than 1/2, so Radio B has a superior tonal contribution—which was assumed above.

Solution to Exercise A

If we use the *incorrect* approach, we obtain:

$$\text{Quality of Toy A} = 1(9) + 2(4) = 17$$
$$\text{Quality of Toy B} = 1(7) + 2(5) = 17$$

$$\frac{\text{Index A}}{\text{Index B}} = \frac{17}{17} = 1.00$$

indicating no preference for either toy.

Turning to the correct method for this example:

$$\text{Quality of Toy A} = (9)^1 (4)^2 = 9 \times 16 = 144$$
$$\text{Quality of Toy B} = (7)^1 (5)^2 = 7 \times 25 = 175$$

$$\frac{\text{Index A}}{\text{Index B}} = \frac{144}{175} = 0.82$$

Since large numbers are desirable—or, equivalently, since a ratio greater than 1 would indicate that the numerator option should be chosen—ABCO would choose Toy B.

INSTRUCTIONS FOR PREPARING THE CASE

Lafayette Furniture Company

The case, Lafayette Furniture Company, is more than just an exercise in quantitative analysis. You will note that you have been asked to make a recommendation using "unbiased rationality." To do so, you must integrate the information derived from quantitative tools with other considerations that are equally important, but that may not be subject to precise definition.

Your assignment is to determine: Which plant site would you recommend?

In asking you for your analysis, Mr. Davidson, your boss, cautions you not to forget the human stresses that accompany decisions of possible plant relocation.

In your approach to this assignment, we suggest that you read the case carefully, then list just what goals (criteria) you intend to achieve in your recommendation. While many of the considerations of site location are identified in the case, you might identify other criteria that you feel must be achieved or would be nice to achieve, such as contentment in one or all of the executives; validity of the decision over the long-range time span, etc.

As you read about the problems of the Lafayette Furniture Company, you may think of strategies that go beyond the choice of a plant location. You might see location of warehouses, having more than one manufacturing plant, relocation of sales offices, etc. Bear in mind that since all the information you will have to make your recommendation is provided in the case, you should not be overambitious. Stay within the scope of your assignment. On the other hand, should you feel handicapped in carrying out your assignment by the lack of information, identify this lack and make a feasible assumption to dispose of it.

As you lay out possible alternatives for solution, you will be confronted with the question of how to handle the weightings of the different decision makers. You could take an average of all four; Abbott alone; or the average of the other three executives. When you get to this part of the analysis, we suggest that you refer to the problem-solving exercise as an example of methodology.

Decision Process

CASE

Lafayette Furniture Company

The Lafayette Furniture Company has been engaged for many years in the production and distribution of a line of inexpensive furniture sold exclusively under the brand name "Lafayette." The line consists primarily of low-priced bedroom, dining-room, kitchen, and living-room furniture. Gross revenues in the latest fiscal year were $3,248,000.

All manufacturing and assembly operations of the company are consolidated in an old plant in South Philadelphia. The factory is a rented one-story building with 120,000 square feet. The lease expires at the end of the next fiscal year. The property, while not ideal, has been relatively satisfactory—at least, up to this time. The total operation was originally located in Baltimore, Maryland. Now executive and sales offices are located in New York City, and regional sales offices are maintained in Chicago and Los Angeles.

The company was founded by the Abbott family in 1912. Started as a small family concern, Lafayette is now owned by four people: Mr. Abbott, the grandson of the founder, has a controlling financial interest, is president of the company, and is head of the New York office; Mr. Wiltsee is manager of the Philadelphia plant; Mr. Dumas heads up the Chicago office; and Mr. Jones is in charge of the Los Angeles office.

Recently, Lafayette submitted a great number of bids to furnish various military installations and officers' quarters. In each case, the contract was awarded to one of Lafayette's competitors. This was very disturbing. Mr. Wiltsee investigated each case and found that under no circumstances could Lafayette have done any better. The company had submitted the lowest possible quotations *consistent with its costs,* he contended. And the other three partners had no doubt that this was a correct evaluation.

The loss of the contracts was not unexpected, although a zero batting average was pretty hard to take. Nevertheless, all agreed that it was symptomatic of what was happening to Lafayette in its other markets, where it had been gradually losing ground to all its competitors in the last few years. In fact, the profit margin on consumer goods was also dropping. There was no doubt that competition was beginning to jeopardize the long-established market for Lafayette furniture.

The management-consulting firm of Davidson & Dubarry was hired to conduct an investigation of the problems that the company faced and to recommend a solution. The essence of the first report by D&D was as follows:

> Lafayette's labor costs are higher than those of its larger competitors; its productivity is lower. Most of these firms have at least some of their plants located in the Carolinas, Georgia, Tennessee, and Alabama. Lafayette's major problem is geographic. A superior location must be found if Lafayette is to regain its competitive position.

It was not surprising to any of the partners that the southern factories were able to operate at lower wage scales than the northern plants. In the first place, many of the southern plants were not organized by labor unions. Furthermore, abundant local labor supplies permitted lower wages. At its present location, Lafayette was definitely confronted with a diminishing labor supply. Even where the unions had succeeded in organizing southern workers, there still appeared to be advantageous wage differentials as compared with the North.

Lafayette has been unionized for many years, and the local union has caused many difficulties for the management. A continuous stream of grievances exists, and the union has been insistent in its demands for higher wages and lower productivity standards.

Of equal importance is the differential in productivity between southern and northern plants. This conclusion was less apparent to the partners, but they have come to accept it. The productivity of the more modern southern factories, they learned, is greater on the average than that of northern plants. Only part of this greater productivity can be traced to more modern plants and equipment, and there are many convincing indications that a large part of the differential can be attributed to the motivation and attitudes of the workers. To quote from the report, Davidson & Dubarry stated that "Lafayette's productivity has declined with the growth of restrictive practices as negotiated by collective bargaining. The problem seems to lie with the history of negotiations in this plant and can be traced as far back as the 1930s." At the same time, little differential in material costs appears between the two regions. Although some materials, such as wood, are cheaper in the South, others, like upholstery and steel frames, are cheaper in the North.

The analysis of sales on a regional basis indicated that a considerable shift has taken place in the last twenty years. In the 1940s, Lafayette marketed the greatest share of its output in the East, Northeast, and Midwest. Since 1947, a growing demand has appeared on the West Coast. Lafayette has always sold its merchandise f.o.b. factory. This practice, all agreed, should now be examined, since transportation to the Pacific Coast is such an important factor for Lafayette. Currently, *40 percent* of production goes to *the New York area, 50 percent to Chicago* and environs, and *10 percent to Los Angeles* and surrounding areas. Shipments to L.A. were found to be growing at about 3% per year. The New York market has remained substantially unchanged, and the Chicago market has been decreasing at about 1% per year.

In line with the conclusions of D&D, Lafayette began to investigate moving the factory from Philadelphia to a new location that would improve its competitive position. After considerable analysis, two locations, which we shall designate as cities A and B, were selected as the most attractive choices to the partners.

City A has a population of approximately 18,000. It is located in northeastern Mississippi, which is an area served by the TVA. This city, in contrast to the other, has been actively engaged in a program of attracting industry. It has indicated that it is prepared to offer a number of concessions. An extensive program of street paving, sewer construction, and school building has been under way. However, only the earliest stages have been completed. The area surrounding the city is primarily agricultural. There appears to be substantial migration from the rural areas to City A.

City B is in Georgia, located about fifteen miles from Atlanta. The population, which is approximately 24,000, is increasing. Evidence of increasing union activity in City B exists; in particular, a number of firms in Atlanta as well as City B have been organized in the last three years.

At President Abbott's request, Davidson & Dubarry have prepared a table of information that, according to standard practice, is relevant to a plant-location decision. (See Table 1.)

TABLE 1

Item	Present Location	City A	City B	Hypothetical Weights			
				Wiltsee	Abbott	Dumas	Jones
Estimated manufacturing costs at present volume	$1,900,000	$1,500,000	$1,600,000	10	10	10	10
Freight costs based on last year's shipments				7	6	8	3
Community attitude toward industry	fair	excellent	good	1	6	3	2
Water availability	good	fair	good	2	1	3	2
Availability of suitable manpower	poor	good	excellent	1	2	4	5
Probability of a union within the next 10 years	1.00	.10	.90	2	8	6	4

Cultural attributes	good	poor	good	3	1	3	1
Schools (average pupil-teacher ratio)	25	35	30	5	1	1	1
Airline service	excellent	poor	good	4	1	3	4

Note: Don't forget that the lowest outcome is the best. Assign your own quantitative scale for qualitative factors.

The average railroad freight rates to selected cities from the proposed locations were also obtained by Davidson & Dubarry (Table 2). Prices were quoted per square feet of load (the company shipped approximately one million square feet in the previous year).

TABLE 2

Railroad Freight Rates (per square feet)

	From		
	Present Location	City A	City B
TO			
New York	$ .39	$1.14	$ .86
Chicago	1.24	.99	1.24
Los Angeles	1.72	1.49	1.52

A meeting of the four partners was called by Davidson & Dubarry in order to discuss the proposed sites. During that meeting, Mr. Davidson attempted to ascertain the opinions of the executives concerning the relative weights of importance they felt should be assigned to each (location) variable in Table 1. He then modified the executive opinions into ratings scaled from 1 to 10, where 10 represented the most important. Dubarry suggested that the set of executive weights (which were obtained independently) be correlated to determine how much consensus existed in the group. The correlation was weak, and during subsequent discussion it became evident to both Davidson and Dubarry that each of the executives had a particular bias. Wiltsee wanted to remain as close to Philadelphia as possible; Abbott seemed to favor the plant in Mississippi, at least in part for social reasons; Dumas seemed convinced that to minimize the cost of freight was the crucial factor; Jones had an apparent preference for Atlanta, his birthplace.

All this information has been communicated to you by Mr. Davidson. He has suggested that you use some type of dimensional analysis to determine which site the company should choose. He states, "Our only hope is to bring an unbiased rationality to bear."

PROBLEM-SOLVING EXERCISES

Lafayette Furniture Company

To save you time on calculations, we have prepared a programmed series of problems for this unit, which will help you to solve the case. There are two parts to the exercises. If you solve Question 1 correctly in Parts A and B, you may stop figuring and just look at the computations as done by us, since you have shown that you understand the method and the problem. If you can't do Question 1 correctly, look at the solution, try to find your mistake, and go on to Question 2. Continue this process until you have solved at least one problem in each part correctly. Do not look at the solutions except to check yourself.

PART A

Question 1.   What are the freight costs of last year's shipments from the present location, based on the freight rates quoted in the case?

You will find the solution to this problem on page 91.

Question 2.   What is the estimated freight cost from City A, based on last year's shipments and the rates quoted in the case?

You will find the solution to this problem on pages 91, 92.

Question 3.   What is the estimated freight cost from City B, based on last year's shipments and the rates quoted in the case?

You will find the solution to this problem on page 92.

PART B

Question 1.   Compute the index number for the present location, based upon the information given in the case, using the average weight of the four executives.

You will find the solution to this problem on page 92.

Question 2.   Compute the index number for the City A location, based upon the information given in the case.

You will find the solution to this problem on page 92.

Question 3.   Compute the index number for the City B location, based upon the information given in the case. You will find the solution to this problem on pages 92, 93.

Solution to Part A, Question 1:

Freight rates, per square foot of load:

	Division of Year's Total	
To	Shipments	From Present Location
N.Y.	0.4	X ($ .39) = $.156
Chicago	0.5	X ($1.24) = $.620
L.A.	0.1	X ($1.72) = $.172
		$.948

($.948)(1,000,000 sq. ft. shipped) = $948,000

If you have completed the calculation correctly, go on to Part B, Question 1. If you have not completed it correctly, go on to Part A, Question 2.

Solution to Part A, Question 2:

Freight rates, per square foot of load:

	Division of Year's Total	
To	Shipments	From City A
N.Y.	0.4	X ($1.14) = $ .456
Chicago	0.5	X ($ .99) = $ .495
L.A.	0.1	X ($1.49) = $ .149
		$1.100

($1.10)(1,000,000 sq. ft. shipped) = $1,100,000

If you have completed the calculation correctly, you may go on to Part B, Question 1. If you have not completed it correctly, go on to Part A, Question 3.

Solution to Part A, Question 3:

Freight rates, per square foot of load:

To	Division of Year's Total Shipments	From City B	
N.Y.	0.4	$\times$ ($ .86) =	$ .344
Chicago	0.5	$\times$ ($1.24) =	$ .620
L.A.	0.1	$\times$ ($1.52) =	$ .152
			$1.116

($1.116)(1,000,000 sq. ft. shipped) = $1,116,000

Now go on to Part B, Question 1.

Solution to Part B, Question 1:

Index for present location = $(1,900,000)^{10}(948,000)^{6}(3)^{3}(2)^{2}(4)^{3}(1.00)^{5}(2)^{2}(25)^{2}(1)^{3}$

Log of index for present location = 10 log 1,900,000 + 6 log 948,000 + 3 log 3 + 2 log 2 + 3 log 4 + 5 log 1 + 2 log 2 + 2 log 25 + 3 log 1

equals:

10(6.2787) + 6(5.9768) + 3(0.4771) + 2(0.3010) + 3(0.6021) + 5(0.0000) + 2(0.3010) + 2(1.3979) + 3(0.0000) = 105.8852

Antilog 105.8852 = 7.677×10^{105}

If you have completed the calculation correctly, you may stop calculating. If you have not completed it correctly, go on to Part B, Question 2.

Solution to Part B, Question 2:

Index for City A = $(1,500,000)^{10}(1,100,000)^{6}(1)^{3}(3)^{2}(2)^{3}(0.10)^{5}(4)^{2}(35)^{2}(4)^{3}$

Log of index for City A = 10 log 1,500,000 + 6 log 1,100,000 + 3 log 1 + 2 log 3 + 5 log .10 + 2 log 4 + 2 log 35 + 3 log 4

equals:

10(6.1761) + 6(6.0414) + 3(0.0000) + 2(0.4771) + 3(0.3010) + 5(0.0000−1) + 2(0.6021) + 2(1,5441) + 3(0.6021) = 100.9653

Antilog 100.9653 = 9.232×10^{100}

If you have completed the calculation correctly, you may stop. If you have not completed it correctly, go on to Question 3.

Solution to Part B, Question 3:

Index for City B = $(1,600,000)^{10}(1,116,000)^{6}(2)^{3}(2)^{2}(1)^{3}(.90)^{5}(2)^{2}(30)^{2}(2)^{3}$

Log of index for City B = 10 log 1,600,000 + 6 log 1,116,000 + 3 log 2 + 2 log 2 + 3 log 1 + 5 log .90 + 2 log 2 + 2 log 30 + 3 log 2

equals:

10(6.2041) + 6(6.0477) + 3(0.3010) + 2(0.3010) + 3(0.0000) + 5(0.9542−1) + 2(0.3010) + 2(1.4771) + 3(.3010) = 104.0624

Antilog 104.0624 = 1,155 × 10^{104}

Unit 6

Systems: Storage of Resources

> What is an inventory problem? In generalized terms, it is a situation in which we need to find out how to order and stock some particular resource to meet a demand.

We shall differentiate between orders placed with a vendor (usually delivered at one time) and orders sent to one's own production department. We shall note that inventory problems involving more than one item can create special circumstances with respect to order frequency and order quantity.

The resources we are talking about do not have to be physical materials that are stored in bins or on a warehouse shelf. They can be an inventory of executive talents required to manage a company; of energy, stored in batteries or available upon demand from a head of water; or of cash needed to keep an organization sufficiently liquid. These are all inventory problems, but some of them—such as talent and liquidity—are particularly hard to handle. This is not because of the mathematical requirements of the inventory models, but because it is difficult to obtain "realistic" measures of costs and benefits that can be used with these models.

Under certain circumstances, competent managers can intuitively achieve results quite similar to those obtained from mathematical models. But many exceptions exist, particularly where the complexity of the situation is great. This may be so because very many items must be handled, or the demand is statistically distributed, or perhaps the delivery period is variable. Given such complex cases, mathematical models may be the only sensible route to follow. Even if they can do no better than intuition, they can do it faster and more reliably.

Most "real" systems are disturbed by chance events over time. Frequently, the manager's intuitive approach is not given the chance to arrive at the best possible solution. But mathematical models can be designed specifically for such disturbances; they may be updated continually to provide pertinent decisions under changing systems conditions.

In this unit, we shall design a *major operating control system*. It will reflect fundamental managerial *policies* with respect to the storage of resources. The foundation must first be built in terms of existing logical approaches for dealing with these situations. We shall resort to only simple mathematical models. We shall observe that models are pointless until we know how to estimate the kind of values (called systems parameters) these models require if they are to have *any* operational significance.

In the material that follows, we shall explore two variants of the type of inventory situation where the demand can be estimated with a fair degree of certainty and where it is regular and remains relatively constant *over time*. We shall classify this situation as an inventory problem of the dynamic variety.

The first variant will apply to inventories purchased from vendors.
The second variant will treat inventories that are manufactured by a serial-type production line.

THE DYNAMIC INVENTORY MODEL

Let us consider a *dynamic* inventory situation, one where *the same resource continues to be stocked over time*—as with soap flakes, paper clips, or chocolate pudding mix. In such cases, we are not faced with the possibility of having a certain amount of material that is overstocked at the end of the selling season and that must then be dumped.* Rather, we are concerned with carrying neither too much nor too little stock. The definition of what is "just right" involves balancing the costs associated with different ordering policies and inventory levels.

Why is it that a company does not order every day? In that way, it could keep a very small amount of stock on hand. Why is it, on the other hand, that a company doesn't order just once a year and save itself the bother and expense of preparing orders every day?

Some housewives never buy more than one unit of anything at a time. Others are known to buy dozens of similar items at one time—e.g., tubes of toothpaste, bars of soap, and provisions for the freezer—to save themselves the trouble of continually running to the store. Frequently, the latter kind of buyer doesn't even get a discount for such large purchases, and her husband may not believe that she has found a realistic inventory policy. But what makes him so sure? Can he tell her what amount of goods should be stocked in the medicine cabinet and food closet of the household? On what basis? We shall now look for answers to these types of questions, whether they apply to a company's inventory policy or to that of the household.

ORDER FREQUENCY VERSUS THE AVERAGE STOCK ON HAND

We know that if a company orders daily, it can maintain very small stocks of goods on hand. If it orders infrequently, it will have to buy and carry much larger inventories. Let us look at this relationship between order frequency and stock on hand (SOH) in diagrammatic form.

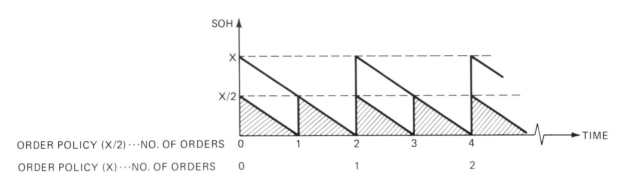

Two different patterns of sawtooth waves appear in our diagram. An order quantity of x (where SOH diminishes regularly) will result in half as many orders as an order quantity of x/2. It is a simple matter to show that the policy of ordering x units entails twice the average inventory of ordering policy x/2.

Note: The average inventory = $\frac{a+b}{2}$, where a is the starting stock, and b is the final stock. So the average inventory for ordering policy x is $\frac{x+0}{2}$, which equals twice that for ordering policy $\frac{x}{2}$, which is $\frac{\frac{x}{2}+0}{2} = \frac{x}{4}$. If we used an ordering policy x/4, once again we would double the order frequency and cut the average inventory in half. This relationship is quite regular; we shall be able to find a mathematical expression for it.

---

*There are inventory problems in which the materials can be stocked for only one period, and just one decision can be made concerning how much to order. This would describe the problem of a Christmas-tree retailer. He has to decide how many trees he should have on hand before his season. He has no chance to correct this decision because the selling season is too short. The same applies to the newspaper boy, the buyer of Christmas toys, or the Easter-bonnet buyer. This kind of problem, called a *static* situation, is also discussed in this text.

LEAD TIME

To this point, we have been assuming that as soon as the stock on hand is used up, an order can be placed and immediately filled. If this is not the case (and it seldom is), then we can move closer to reality by assuming that some lead time (LT) exists.

> *The lead time is defined as the elapsed interval between the placing of an order and its delivery.*

More precisely, it is the interval that includes delays in placing the order, delivery time, and delays in putting the delivered stock in the physical inventory. The situation is shown in the diagram below.

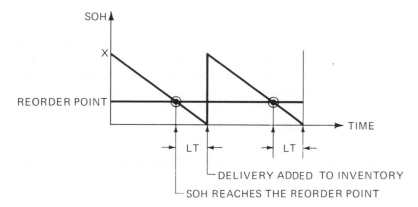

Please note that we assume that no variability exists with respect to the lead time; the lead time is treated as constant. This requires positive knowledge that the stock on hand has dropped to that level of SOH called the *reorder point*. The order is placed within a fixed period. The delivery is made in some constant number of days or weeks, or whatever time unit is involved. The order is received, inspected, and placed in stock with no variability. When LT variability is more than can be overlooked, special inventory models are required that we shall not consider here. For a great number of cases, the assumption that LT is constant is acceptable.

SELF-SUPPLY: BATCH-TYPE

We have treated the situation in which the replenishment quantity arrives at a single moment in time. This is exemplified by ordering from an outside vendor. But it is also characteristic of batch production methods in our factory. In other words, we process a number of items through several different stages, and all units must be completed at each one of the stages before they can move on. Therefore, all the units are considered completed at the same point in time. This is a batch process, represented in the diagram below.

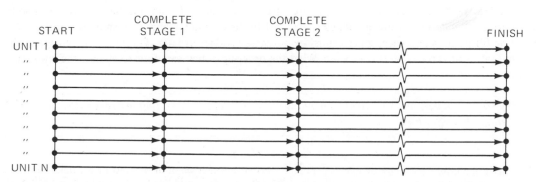

SELF-SUPPLY: SERIAL-TYPE

The first model we shall develop applies to production of the batch type within our plant as well as to ordering from outside vendors. But let us contrast this with a serial type of production line, as shown in the diagram below. In this case, items are completed in sequence—one after the other.

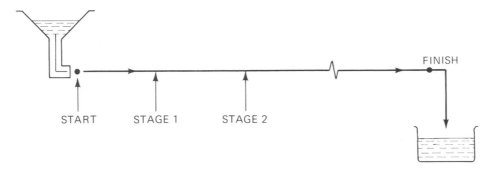

The serial system requires a model that is somewhat more complicated than the batch-type or vendor model, which we shall develop shortly. This model will tell us how to determine the best possible production run. But for the moment, let us return to the vendor model, which is frequently called the economic order quantity model.

ECONOMIC ORDER QUANTITY MODEL (EOQ)

In this (vendor's) type of system, two major kinds of costs are usually considered. We have illustrated them below.

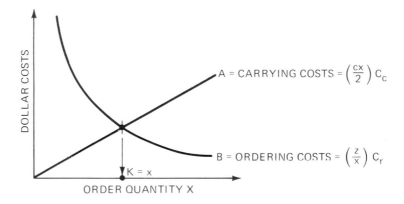

The first cost, labeled A, is a straight line (linear), which increases with x. This represents the way in which *carrying charges* increase when the order quantity, x, is increased. The total carrying cost is the average number of units carried, x/2, multiplied by the per-unit cost (c) of the item—i.e., cx/2. Then this is multiplied by the carrying-cost* rate, C_c, which yields $(cx/2)C_c$.

We note that with a dynamic situation, there is no point in comparing the cost of goods that are ordered under alternative policies. We assume here that quantity discounts do not apply. Therefore, the total cost of goods does not vary with ordering policies. Over time, all policies must satisfy the demand z, and we assume the dollar volume cz will be the same for all policies. These z parts must be purchased sooner or later. Therefore, no change in the inventory policy can save us from having this expense. What the ordering policy can do is to change the amount of cash tied up in inventory.

> *The only costs it makes sense to include in an inventory model are those that are responsive and variable to the policy that we adopt.*

---

*A percentage applicable to the cost of an item per unit of time. It is composed of the interest (% per time) lost on money that is tied up in inventory. But it must also include other temporal expenses, such as those of storage, insurance, and taxes.

By adding the two types of variable costs, A and B, we obtain the total variable cost curve. Its equation is simply the addition of the A and B costs, as shown below.

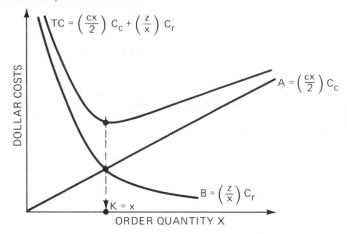

Fixed costs have no relation to the control we exercise and no relation to the strategic decisions we can make.

The second kind of cost is labeled B. As the order quantity x increases, the B-type cost decreases continuously but at a decreasing rate. The B cost is the ordering cost. It is associated with the number of orders that must be placed when an item is ordered in different quantities, x. Let us assume that the annual demand, z, is known with certainty. Now, if our order size is x units, then z divided by x gives us the number of orders that must be placed within the year. Dimensionally: z(units per year)/x(units per order) = n(orders per year).

Say that z equals 10,000 units per year. Then if we order one unit at a time, we shall have 10,000 separate orders. On the other hand, if we order 10,000 units at one time, we shall have only one order per year. The curve marked B represents a given value of z, divided by all values of x, multiplied by the cost of an order (C_r) (or the set-up charges for batch-type production).* We should note why this curve drops off as it does. When we divide 10,000 by 1, we get 10,000; when we divide 10,000 by 2, we have cut it in half; dividing 10,000 by 3, we obtain 3,333; dividing by 4, we get 2,500. It is clear that as x increases, z/x decreases at a decelerating rate. For some, these verbal descriptions are far more easily grasped by studying the diagram of cost functions.

In these diagrams, we have written in the mathematical expressions for each one of the lines. Line A is associated with a cost $(cx/2)C_c$. Let us review how this expression is derived. x/2 is the average number of units of inventory that we have on hand. We take this average number of units and multiply it by the cost per unit. This gives us an average cost over time. But, as we said before, we require the carrying charge, not the direct cost, and so we multiply cx/2 by the carrying-cost rate, C_c.

Line B is associated with a cost $(z/x)C_r$. Here, z/x is equal to n (the number of orders per year), and C_r equals either the cost per order or setup costs for batch production.

When we add these A and B costs together, we get the equation:

$$TC = \text{total variable costs} = \left(\frac{cx}{2}\right) C_c + \left(\frac{z}{x}\right) C_r$$

THE OPTIMAL ORDER QUANTITY ASSURES MINIMUM VARIABLE COSTS

Referring to the diagram of the total variable costs (TC), we see that a minimum value occurs for one particular order policy (i.e., a specific value of x). We can always find this minimum value by trial and error. It's acceptable to do this, but rather wasteful of our time, since we have much faster ways of getting the exact and precise value of x that will minimize the total cost.

When we want the minimum (or maximum) of a mathematical function, we can use calculus. (You will remember that the minimum [or maximum] is obtained by setting the derivative of that function equal to zero.) Those who have studied calculus will be able to apply the derivate. But note that an alternative method exists. For this particular case, the minimum total cost occurs at that point where the two types of cost are equal to each other. Let's say that x = K at this point; i.e., K = optimum order quantity. Then the minimum total cost would be:

*See definitions in Glossary.

$$\text{MIN TC} = \left(\frac{cK}{2}\right) C_c + \left(\frac{z}{K}\right) C_r$$

K can be derived as follows:

Set:

$$\frac{cKC_c}{2} = \left(\frac{z}{K}\right) C_r$$

Clearing denominators:

$$K^2 = \frac{2zC_r}{cC_c}$$

Taking square root:

$$K = \sqrt{\frac{2zC_r}{cC_c}}$$

It is easily proved that an order policy of (K + 1) or (K − 1) will produce a larger total cost than K. Let us show this, using the numbers of a specific example.

EXERCISE

Assume that John consumes 20 tubes of toothpaste per year. He pays $1.00 per tube. (We won't get involved with quantity discounts—they require more complex models, which are readily available.) Assume that John's carrying-cost rate for money is the same as the interest rate he gets from the savings bank—say, 5%. Businessmen will generally have much higher rates. We shall discuss the nature of these cost factors shortly. The cost of placing an order is still needed. Perhaps John would be willing to pay, say, 50 cents in order to avoid running out to get a tube of toothpaste.

Realistically, John buys a number of items each time he goes to the store. Here too, then, we are making another concession—a compromise so that we can use our model. We have various elegant ways of handling such multiple-item order cost problems, but the mathematics are unnecessarily complex for our purposes.

Let us agree not to get involved in deep complications, for the following reasons: First, many situations do not allow multiple-item orders. Second, it is perfectly reasonable to try to estimate the proper *share* of the order cost for toothpaste—given multiple-item orders. Third, we are only trying to develop guidelines for John's toothpaste-inventory policy.

Managers make this kind of concession frequently. Correctly, they expect to interpret mathematical results—taking into account all the relevant factors that have been left out. Talking aloud at this point has helped us to show that in *any* model-building situation, it gets costly to be perfectly realistic. Every pragmatic soul makes simplifying assumptions. And that's quite all right if we know what we are doing. *The manager must take into account what has been included and what has not been included when he comes to interpreting the answer derived from the formal model.*

Now let us determine John's minimum optimum (minimum cost) order for tubes of toothpaste.

$$K = \sqrt{\frac{2(20)\,(0.50)}{(1.00)\,(0.05)}} = \sqrt{400} = 20 \text{ tubes}$$

In other words, John *should* buy a year's supply of toothpaste at one time—if we assume that the costs in the model (the systems parameters) are correct. How does the total cost of 20 tubes compare with the costs if 21 or 19 tubes are bought?

$$\text{TC per year (20 tubes)} = (1.00) \frac{20}{2} (.05) + \frac{20}{20} (0.50) = 0.500 + 0.500 = 1.000$$

$$\text{TC per year (21 tubes)} = (1.00) \frac{21}{2} (.05) + \frac{20}{21} (0.50) = 0.525 + 0.476 = 1.001$$

$$\text{TC per year (19 tubes)} = (1.00) \frac{19}{2} (.05) + \frac{20}{19} (0.50) = 0.475 + 0.526 = 1.001$$

First, we observe that both the A and B costs are equal to 0.5 when K = 20. From our prior discussion, we expected these costs to be equal when TC is a minimum. Second, by adding or subtracting one unit from the order quantity, K, the total costs increase—certainly only slightly, but enough to show us the effect that we were looking for.

Nevertheless, John may say to us, "This is a ridiculous result." Perhaps it is, but only because the costs John gave us are ridiculous. Our model is not ridiculous. It may not be perfect, but it is a reasonable description of what is happening in this system.

If John states that his order cost is only 12½ cents (not 50 cents), then the optimal order quantity, K, would be:

$$K = \sqrt{\frac{2(20)\,(.125)}{(1.00)\,(0.05)}} = \sqrt{100} = 10 \text{ tubes}$$

Is that better, John?

Let's work backwards and assume that John insists that two tubes of toothpaste is the most he will tolerate purchasing at one time. Then, we can write:

$$2 = \sqrt{\frac{2(20)C_r}{(1.00)\,(0.05)}}$$

Squaring both sides:

$$4 = \frac{2(20)C_r}{(1.00)\,(0.05)}$$

and C_r = $0.005, or 1/2 cent.

So that is what John thinks his time is worth! Invoking the concept of multiple-item orders will at least improve the result; i.e., if (say) on the average 10 items make up one multiple-item order, then the order cost might be estimated to be 10 C_r = 5 cents.

EXERCISE A

Now, try an example for yourself. Use whatever numbers seem appropriate for your own situation. The question: What order cost does your automobile's gas-tank capacity imply? Assume that it is of optimal size. Use the economic order quantity model. A typical answer is given at the end of this note.

THE ECONOMIC LOT SIZE MODEL (ELS)

The inventory vendor model can be modified to cover the self-supplier, serial-production case. The shape of the sawtooth stock-on-hand diagram would be altered as shown below:

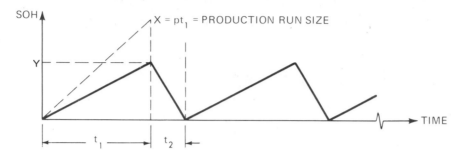

During the period t_1, the production facility is being utilized. Items are entering inventory at a daily rate $(p - d)$, where p is the production rate per day, and d is the stock withdrawal rate per day. At the end of t_1, the production run of x units is completed. The facilities are turned over to some other job. In the off-line period, t_2, *production makes no additions to stock, and the demand depletes the stock on hand at the rate of d units per day.* Reference to the diagram above will show that the *maximum actual* stock on hand, y, will be:

$$(1) \qquad y = (p - d)t_1 = dt_2$$

The total variable cost model can be formulated for the two kinds of costs, carrying (C_c) and setup (C_s).[*] It would be:

$$(2) \qquad \text{TC per year} = \left(\frac{cy}{2}\right) C_c + \left(\frac{z}{x}\right) C_s$$

Noting that $t_1 = x/p$ (since $x = pt_1$), and substituting for t_1 in equation (1), it is apparent that:

$$(3) \qquad y = (p - d)\frac{x}{p}$$

Now, substituting for y in equation (2), we obtain:

$$(4) \qquad \text{TC per year} = \left(\frac{cx}{2}\right)\left(\frac{p - d}{p}\right) C_c + \left(\frac{z}{x}\right) C_s$$

The derivative from calculus would be the fastest way to obtain the value of x that minimizes the total cost. Cut-and-try methods can also be used. But once again, we can set the two costs equal to each other in order to find the optimal value of x (which we have been calling K). Then:

$$\left(\frac{cK}{2}\right)\left(\frac{p - d}{p}\right) C_c = \left(\frac{z}{K}\right) C_s$$

$$K = \sqrt{\left(\frac{2zC_s}{cC_c}\right)\left(\frac{p}{p - d}\right)}$$

Also, the values of t_1, t_2, and y for optimal cost would be found by substituting K for x in the appropriate formulas. Thus:

$$t_1 = \frac{K}{p}; \quad t_2 = \left(\frac{p - d}{pd}\right) K; \text{ and } y = \left(\frac{p - d}{p}\right) K$$

Look, for a moment, at the square-root formula for K. Let's suppose that p = 1,000 units per day, and d = 2

[*]See Glossary for definitions.

units per day. In effect, $\left(\dfrac{p}{p-d}\right)$ approximates 1, and the formula becomes almost identical with the economic order quantity model for vendors or batch production. That's just what we would expect when the production rate is *very* much greater than the demand withdrawal rate. So that result squares with our intuition. How about when $p = d$? Then $(p - d) = 0$, and $p/(p - d) = \infty$, which means continuous running of the line or, euphemistically, mass production. That too jibes with our intuition.

EXERCISE B

Try another example for yourself. Let z (demand) = 2,000 units per year; C_s (setup cost) = $100; c (unit cost) = $5 per part; C_c (carrying cost) = 10% per year; p (production rate) = 10 units per day, with 250 working days per year. What is the optimal run size, and what are the optimal on-line and off-line times? What is the proper amount of storage space required for these optimal conditions? There is space for your calculations. The solution will be found at the end of the note.

THE DERIVATION OF COSTS

In all model building, finding the right numbers to describe the "real world" is one of the most difficult parts of the problem-solving, decision-making process. Here, this applies to the numbers to be used in describing the costs.

Let us consider the *carrying costs.* As a general rule, manufacturers prefer to have minimum inventory quantities. They don't like to keep a lot of money tied up in their inventories because there are other things they could do with this money. We have already used an example in which we chose the carrying-cost rate based on the potential earnings from the savings bank. Many organizations have substantial growth requirements. They can use their money to produce far greater returns than 5 percent. A great number of these larger companies consider their carrying-cost rate for money to be in the neighborhood of 10, 15, or even 20 percent. After all, by accumulating a wise portfolio, an individual can frequently obtain a *return on investment* of 10 percent or better. In setting the rate, allowance is made for the degree of risk in the investment.

In addition to investment considerations, the inventory carrying costs should also include *storage costs,* as well as *insurance* and *taxes* on stored inventory. Further, we must take into account *obsolescence, spoilage,* and *pilferage* charges. When we finish adding up all these contributions, we have estimated the percentage to be used for our carrying cost rates.

As a rule of thumb, small companies have carrying-cost rates in the neighborhood of 10 to 12 percent; medium-sized firms might have 15 to 18 percent; and large companies generally use a rate in excess of 20 percent, with a few rising as high as 30 percent. Any error in estimating the carrying-cost rate will obviously affect the solution we obtain from our inventory model. How then does one know what the correct carrying-cost rate is? Can our accountants give us this figure? It is true that in recent years, accountants have become far more interested in developing such important figures; nevertheless, not all of them are currently in a position to cope with such questions. Financial managers have helped most large companies to determine an appropriate carrying-cost rate. (In Lucky Bell's case, you should certainly question whether or not the given carrying-cost rate seems realistic. You might also wish to find out what happens when some divergence is allowed from the controller's figure.)

Now, let us treat the *ordering cost*. Every time a purchase requisition is drawn up, a number of fixed and variable costs are involved. The fixed costs occur because certain people who work in the ordering department would be paid their salaries even if it were not drawn up. On the other hand, if we overtax the ordering department's capacity, more people may have to be added. This reasoning indicates that certain ordering costs are variable with the number of orders.

Variable costs are incurred with respect to *salaries,* whereas *equipment and overhead charges* generally contribute to fixed ordering costs (unless they are chargeable according to the load on the ordering department). Some variable costs are straightforward to identify—such as the *purchase requisition form* and the charge for sending (or phoning) the purchase requisition to the vendor. *Inspection* costs and *receiving* costs may also vary as a result of the number of orders placed rather than on the basis of the individual units handled. *Delivery* costs are frequently dependent in part upon the number of deliveries made. For each cost element, the appropriate portion should be entered into the variable ordering cost. While it is not an easy task to obtain a good estimate for the ordering cost, nevertheless, some guidelines are available; for instance, many companies have found that their ordering costs are in the neighborhood of from $4 to $6 per order. This figure can differ radically depending on the nature of the business and the way the purchase requisition must be drawn. If, each time an order is placed, a *bidding* process must be used, this will normally entail large ordering expenses. If *engineering specifications* have to be checked and changed with each purchase requisition, this too will have the effect of raising the ordering cost greatly.

Setup costs, which are characteristic of the batch-type production system, will generally be much higher than vendor ordering costs. These costs could be anywhere from a few dollars up to many thousands, since the utilization of tools and dies, fixtures and jigs, and so on, involves technical skills and, furthermore, generally causes a period of downtime on the equipment. (In determining whether the setup cost for the case in this unit is proper, you will have to consider its specific circumstances.)

Can an accountant give us a good figure for an ordering cost or for a setup cost? In general, he cannot. A systems study is required, wherein all variable and fixed costs are traced to their true sources and a proper determination of what constitutes an operationally efficient ordering system is available. The production manager is generally in a better position than the accountant to estimate the setup costs.

> Which takes us to a most important point: *It is unwise to develop costs based on an inefficient system.* If we develop an ordering cost for a poorly run ordering department, then we are carrying the inefficiency penalty into our inventory policy. It is, therefore, necessary and advisable first to have a systems study to determine the best procedures and then to determine the costs. Further, we should not ignore the cost implications of the design of the product, which have impact on spoilage, obsolescence, and even pilferage.

In most inventory systems, there are many other costs to be taken into account. With more complicated models, we have to take into consideration the costs of being *out of stock* and the way in which such costs arise. This usually entails evaluating *goodwill costs,* which are about the most intractable of the lot. There are also *systemic costs*—that is, the costs of processing the data that underlie the inventory system's controls. There are costs of *unrealized discounts,* costs of *production interruptions, salvage costs,* and *expediting costs,* to name just a few more. In realistic circumstances where additional study expenses seem to be warranted, more of these costs will be brought into the inventory model.

Solution to Exercise A

A typical answer might be as follows:

Let's assume you drive 10,000 miles per year and you get 20 miles per gallon of gas. This means your yearly demand for gas is $10,000/20 = 500$ gallons $= z$. Let the gas tank hold $x = K = 20$ gallons. You pay 70 cents per gallon. We will use $C_c = 5\%$ per year. So:

$$20 = \sqrt{\frac{2(500)C_r}{(.70)(0.05)}}$$

$$400 = \frac{2(500)C_r}{(.70)(0.05)}$$

$$C_r = \$.014$$

This is certainly a very low figure. Most of us would be happy to pay far more than that to be able to avoid going into the gas station to fill up the tank. But the problem here is that an obvious interaction exists because of the technological space constraints in the design of a car. The present gas tank is about as big as it can go.

Solution to Exercise B

$$d = \frac{z}{250 \text{ days per year}} = \frac{2,000 \text{ units per year}}{250 \text{ days per year}} = 8 \text{ units per day}$$

Then, the optimal run size is:

$$K = \sqrt{\left(\frac{2(2,000)(100)}{5(0.10)}\right)\left(\frac{10}{10-8}\right)} = 2,000 \text{ units}$$

Optimal on-line time is:

$$t_1 = \frac{K}{p} = \frac{2,000}{10} = 200 \text{ days}$$

which is 4/5 of the working time per year.

Optimal off-line time is:

$$t_2 = \left(\frac{p-d}{pd}\right) K = \left(\frac{10-8}{80}\right) 2,000 = 50 \text{ days}$$

and this just happens to be the remaining 20% of the working time per year. *Note:* $t_1 + t_2$ do *not* have to sum to one year.

The proper amount of storage space is equal to the optimal value of y, since this is the maximum amount of stock on hand that will occur under optimal conditions. This is:

$$y = \left(\frac{p-d}{p}\right) K = \left(\frac{10-8}{10}\right) 2,000 = 400 \text{ units}$$

INSTRUCTIONS FOR PREPARING THE CASE

Lucky Bell Company

First, read the case. Then reinforce your grasp of the concepts you will use by completing the Problem-Solving exercises that follow. The numbers you generate for the Problem-Solving Exercises may be useful in your analysis of the case.

Assume that you are head of production planning, and Mr. Smith has asked you to work out a schedule to serve as a commitment to General Appliances. As Mr. Smith gives you this important assignment, he tells you he would like Lucky Bell to go on-stream at the earliest possible date to obtain revenues; in the same breath, he cautions you that schedules must be met at minimum cost. Mr. Smith also says he recognizes the differences of opinion regarding carrying and setup costs, and he would like you to minimize any risks in making the wrong assumptions. He says that because he realizes Lucky Bell's lack of computer facilities forces you to cut and try numbers in setting up a production schedule, you should not spend more than two hours on this part of the task. He says his primary interests are a policy for deviation from optimum run size and an analytical approach, which includes handling of missing information (assumptions), criteria used in setting the recommendation, and alternative approaches.

| DEFINE THE OBJECTIVE | → | SET UP CRITERIA | → | IDENTIFY MISSING INFORMATION | → | CREATE STRATEGIES | → | EVALUATE EACH STRATEGY (1, 2, . . . N) BY EACH CRITERION | → | RECOMMEND THE BEST STRATEGY |

Decision Process

Lucky Bell Company

In 1930, after his graduation from college with a mechanical engineering degree, D.K. Bell founded the Lucky Bell Company. The company's first and primary product was a mechanical alarm clock (with the "lucky bell"). Later, the company began to manufacture an expanding line of clocks, including some electrical models. The company was located in a small New England town that had a population of 14,000 people, assuring a reasonable supply of technically able workers.

At first the company was highly profitable, but during the late 1930s, it ran into serious financial difficulties. Unable to solve his problems, Mr. Bell accepted the opportunity of a merger when it was offered to him. This came about when a large national corporation, General Appliances, offered to purchase Lucky Bell with the intention of maintaining it as an autonomous division. Mr. Bell was retained as division manager, with a favorable salary plus stock options and profit sharing.

During World War II, General Appliances altered its product line in order to obtain government contracts. At that time, it was decided that Lucky Bell would no longer produce clocks and should instead manufacture precision components to be assembled into products made for the armed services by the parent company. The division marketing staff was disbanded, and Lucky Bell became basically a captive manufacturing unit of G.A. The war ended, but the same arrangement was maintained. The Lucky Bell division was profitable, but was still tied to government contracts, which continued to increase. By 1960, Lucky Bell's sales volume had stabilized at close to $6 million.

Mr. Bell ultimately retired and bought a ranch in Arizona. G.A. replaced him with R.A. Smith, one of its most successful young executives. Smith had a reputation for never sitting still; since he had joined G.A., every division he was ever with had grown faster than other parts of the enterprise. There was consensus among the executives of Lucky Bell that Smith would soon make changes to bring growth to the division.

This prediction turned out to be quite accurate. Smith revealed his plans at an executive board meeting of Lucky Bell, telling of two actions he had taken with the parent company: He had secured substantial additional financing from G.A.; and G.A. had agreed to let Lucky Bell take over a number of items that were currently subcontracted with outside companies. These items were parts for refrigerators and washing machines, and precision items for aerospace contracts. At this meeting, Mr. Smith made it clear that he wanted to get this production onstream as quickly as possible, in order to realize increased revenues and profits; he also stressed that heads would roll if all commitments to G.A. were not met—profitably.

Smith outlined the conditions he expected to prevail. General Appliances expected to phase out the subcontractors as Lucky Bell was able to fill the demand. Once Lucky Bell had begun to supply G.A., it was unequivocally understood that it would continue to do so, regularly and reliably—meeting not only schedule commitments but product quality specifications as well. *Daily* shipments of each item would be made to G.A. For each item, these were to begin on a different preplanned day. G.A. had given Mr. Smith absolute freedom with respect to the scheduling of production runs, but asked for a schedule specifying when deliveries of each item would start.

General Appliances specified the requirements for the next year:

G.A.'s Estimated Requirements for the Next Year

Component	Annual Quantity	Demand Rate/Day
x101	10,000	40
x102	2,000	8
x103	5,000	20
x104	7,500	30
x105	250	1

All necessary blueprints and complete specifications for each component were transferred to Lucky Bell's engineering staff. They studied the requirements and indicated the minimum times needed to get these items into production. The dates were as follows:

Item	First Possible Date for Production
x101	January 15
x102	January 1
x103	March 1
x104	April 1
x105	January 15

The engineering department planned for a *single* production and assembly line, through which all the items would be processed in a mass-production, serial fashion. It was a system requiring careful planning—but, given such planning, it had great operating advantages. The entire system would be set up and ready to go by January 1. However, the tools and fixtures needed for each item would take different lengths of time, as shown in the table detailing "First Possible Date for Production."

After studying the specifications and blueprints, Lucky Bell's engineers developed the following cost estimates:

Estimated Cost and Selling Prices

Component	Production (units per day)	Setup cost	Cost per Part
x101	100.0	$3,000	$ 120
x102	50.0	1,500	60
x103	250.0	2,300	45
x104	187.5	1,700	50
x105	5.0	750	2,400

The carrying-cost rate per year had been estimated by the company controller at 10%. Mr. Smith thought this to be very low; he believed it to be about 15%. The other executives of Lucky Bell were of the opinion that the controller was right—as of then—and that if Smith's reputation held, he would be right—in the near future. On another point, Smith believed that the setup-cost estimates were accurate, but doubted that they were based on efficient work procedures. He felt that with some methods study, setup costs could and should be reduced, and that a target of 30% reduction was possible.

At the time, Lucky Bell scheduled on the basis of 250 working days per year. Smith had already indicated that he was dead against planned overtime or an increased number of working days per year. He had also intimated that by means of methods and value analysis, he intended to reduce the cost of manufacturing the parts.

Prepare the production schedule for items x101 through x105. Remember that you must indicate the initial shipment date for each item. Bear in mind that Mr. Smith will want to know *how* you have chosen this schedule, and *why*. The schedule is needed immediately.

Lucky Bell Company

To save you time on calculations, we have prepared a programmed series of problems for this unit, which will help you to solve the case. There are two parts to the exercises, A and B. If you solve Question 1, a and b, correctly in Parts A and B, you may stop figuring and just look at the computations as done by us, since you have shown that you understand the method and the problem. If you can't do Question 1 in Part A correctly, look at the solution, try to find your mistake, and go on to Question 2 of Part A. Continue this process until you have solved at least one problem in both parts correctly. Do not look at the solutions except to check yourself.

PART A

Question 1a.   For component x101, what is the economic lot size, based on the controller's figures (C_s = $3,000; C_c rate = 10%)?

Question 1b.   For component x101, what is the economic lot size, based on Smith's figures (C_s = $2,100; C_c rate = 15%)?

You will find the solution to these problems on page 115.

Question 2a.   For component x102, what is the economic lot size, based on the controller's figures (C_s = $1,500; C_c rate = 10%)?

Question 2b.   For component x102, what is the economic lot size, based on Smith's figures (C_s = $1,050; C_c rate = 15%)?

You will find the solution to this problem on page 115.

Question 3a.   For component x103, what is the economic lot size, based on the controller's figures (C_s = $2,300; C_c rate = 10%)?

Question 3b.   For component x103, what is the economic lot size, based on Smith's figures (C_s = $1,610; C_c rate = 15%)?

You will find the solution to this problem on page 115.

Question 4a.   For component x104, what is the economic lot size, based on the controller's figures (C_s = $1,700; C_c rate = 10%)?

Question 4b.   For component x104, what is the economic lot size, based on Smith's figures (C_s = $1,190; C_c rate = 15%)?

You will find the solution to this problem on pages 115, 116.

Question 5a.   For component x105, what is the economic lot size, based on the controller's figures (C_s = $750; C_c rate = 10%)?

Question 5b.   For component x105, what is the economic lot size, based on Smith's figures (C_s = $525; C_c rate = 15%)?

You will find the solution to this problem on page 116.

PART B

Question 1a: For component x101, what are the values for t_1, t_2, and t, based on the controller's figures?*

Question 1b: For component x101, what are the values for t_1, t_2, and t, based on Smith's figures?*

You will find the solution to this problem on page 116.

*Round your answer to the nearest whole number.

Question 2a: For component x102, what are the values for t_1, t_2, and t, based on the controller's figures?

Question 2b: For component x102, what are the values for t_1, t_2, and t, based on Smith's figures?

You will find the solution to this problem on page 116.

Question 3a: For component x103, what are the values for t_1, t_2, and t, based on the controller's figures?

Question 3b: For component x103, what are the values for t_1, t_2, and t, based on Smith's figures?

You will find the solution to the problem on page 117.

Question 4a: For component x104, what are the values for t_1, t_2, and t, based on the controller's figures?

Question 4b: For component x104, what are the values for t_1, t_2, and t, based on Smith's figures?

You will find the solution to this problem on page 117.

Question 5a: For component x105, what are the values for t_1, t_2, and t, based on the controller's figures?

Question 5b: For component x105, what are the values for t_1, t_2, and t, based on Smith's figures?

You will find the solution to this problem on page 117.

Solution to Part A, Question 1a:

Economic lot size = 2,886 = K
$p = 100; d = 40; z = 10,000; C_s = \$3,000; c = \$120; C_c = .10$
Used in the formula:

$$K = \sqrt{\left(\frac{2zC_s}{cC_c}\right)\left(\frac{p}{p-d}\right)}$$

Solution to Part A, Question 1b:

Economic lot size = 1,972 = K
$p = 100; d = 40; z = 10,000; C_s = \$2,100; c = \$120; C_c = .15$

Using the same formula as that used in the solution of Question 1a, above.

If you have completed the calculations correctly, you may go on to Part B, Question 1. If you have not completed them correctly, go on to Part A, Question 2.

Solution to Part A, Question 2a:

Economic lot size = 1,091 = K
$p = 50; d = 8; z = 2,000; C_s = \$1,500; c = \$60; C_c = .10$

Using the same formula as that used in the solution of Question 1a.

Solution to Part A, Question 2b:

Economic lot size = 745 = K
$p = 50; d = 8; z = 2,000; C_s = \$1,050; c = \$60; C_c = .15$

Using the same formula as that used in the solution of Question 1a.

If you have completed the calculations correctly, you may go on to Part B, Question 1. If you have not completed them correctly, go on to Part A, Question 3.

Solution to Part A, Question 3a:

Economic lot size = 2,358 = K
$p = 250; d = 20; z = 5,000; C_s = \$2,300; c = \$45; C_c = .10$

Using the same formula as that used in the solution of Question 1a.

Solution to Part A, Question 3b:

Economic lot size = 1,610 = K
$p = 250; d = 20; z = 5,000; C_s = \$1,610; c = \$45; C_c = .15$

Using the same formula as that used in the solution of Question 1a.

If you have completed the calculations correctly, you may go on to Part B, Question 1. If you have not completed them correctly, go on to Part A, Question 4.

Solution to Part A, Question 4a:

Economic lot size = 2,464 = K
$p = 187.5; d = 30; z = 7,500; C_s = \$1,700; c = \$50; C_c = .10$

Using the same formula as that used in the solution of Question 1a.

Solution to Part A, Question 4b:

Economic lot size = 1,680 = K
$p = 187.5; d = 30; z = 7,500; C_s = \$1,190; c = \$50; C_c = .15$

Using the same formula as that used in the solution of Question 1a.

If you have completed the calculations correctly, you may go on to Part B, Question 1. If you have not completed them correctly, go on to Part A, Question 5.

Solution to Part A, Question 5a:

Economic lot size = 44 = K
$p = 5; d = 1; z = 250; C_s = \$750; c = \$2,400; C_c = .10$

Using the same formula as that used in the solution of Question 1a.

Solution to Part A, Question 5b:

Economic lot size = 30 = K
$p = 5; d = 1; z = 250; C_s = \$525; c = \$2,400; C_c = .15$

Using the same formula as that used in the solution of Question 1a.

Now go on to Part B, Question 1.

Solution to Part B, Question 1a:

$$t_1 = 29; t_2 = 43; t = 72$$

Using the formulas:

$$t_1 = \frac{K}{p}$$

$$t_2 = \left(\frac{p - d}{pd}\right) K$$

$$t = t_1 + t_2$$

Solution to Part B, Question 1b:

$$t_1 = 20; t_2 = 30; t = 50$$

Using the same formulas as those used in the solution of Question 1a.

If you have completed the calculations correctly, you may stop. If you have not completed them correctly, go on to Part B, Question 2.

Solution to Part B, Question 2a:

$$t_1 = 22; t_2 = 115; t = 137$$

Using the formulas given in the solution to Question 1a.

Solution to Part B, Question 2b:

$$t_1 = 15; t_2 = 78; t = 93$$

Using the formulas given in solution to Question 1a.

If you have completed the calculations correctly, you may stop. If you have not completed them correctly, go on to Part B, Question 3.

Solution to Part B, Question 3a:

$$t_1 = 10; t_2 = 108; t = 118$$

Using the formulas given in solution to Question 1a.

Solution to Part B, Question 3b:

$$t_1 = 6; t_2 = 74; t = 80$$

Using the formulas given in solution to Question 1a.

 If you have completed the calculations correctly, you may stop. If you have not completed them correctly, go on to Part B, Question 4.

Solution to Part B, Question 4a:

$$t_1 = 13; t_2 = 69; t = 82$$

Using the formulas given in solution to Question 1a.

Solution to Part B, Question 4b:

$$t_1 = 9; t_2 = 47; t = 56$$

Using the formulas given in solution to Question 1a.

 If you have completed the calculations correctly, you may stop. If you have not completed them correctly, go on to Part B, Question 5.

Solution to Part B, Question 5a:

$$t_1 = 9; t_2 = 35; t = 44$$

Using the formulas given in solution to Question 1a.

Solution to Part B, Question 5b:

$$t_1 = 6; t_2 = 24; t = 30$$

Using the formulas given in solution to Question 1a.

Unit 7

Linear Programming

Product-line changes can have significant impact on the *composition* as well as the quantity of production output. Products for which the company is best known can be phased out; the company may find itself doing new kinds of business, needing altered corporate images, resorting to different methods of distribution, and so on. More frequently, however, product-line changes adjust the output quantities of the various items that are regularly made. One key to the management of such changes is in the class of methods known as *programming models*. The specific type of programming model to be used here is *linear programming* (LP).

As will be seen, programming methods deal with multiple objectives in a system by selecting one objective as the kingpin and letting the others serve as constraints on the system. Linear programming, for example, can be used to minimize the cost of feed for cattle while assuring that they receive in their diet at least their minimum nutritional requirements. LP can also be used to maximize the profit for a plant of specified capacity, with other limited resources.

> *When viewed in proper perspective, linear programming requires the participation of production, marketing, and financial executives. Without this crossing of traditional department lines, only attenuated solutions can be obtained.*

The reliance to be placed on an LP solution will vary for many reasons. In some instances (such as oil refinery blending), the solution will be used *unchanged*, just as it comes from the computer. At other times, the results will be modified as necessary to account for factors that have not been programmed and included in the model. Frequently, the results can be construed as only a rough guide.

> *Beware the illusions that come with elaborate computer printouts.*

LP programs of all sizes and refinements are available as computer software. They are impressive—in both what they demand as input and what they produce as output. The fact that the computer never hesitates as it proceeds in lightning fashion to "solve" gigantic LP problems (a one-man-week computational problem can be solved by a large computer in a couple of minutes) does not reflect the quality of the input data, the completeness of the model (that is, the number of *relevant* variables used), and the appropriateness of the LP model to capture the reality of the situation. In other words, once the problem is formulated as a linear programming model, the solution is automatically computed. If the model truly represents the problem, then the solution is directly applicable. But the solution is never better than the representation.

A familiar form of the decision problem occurs when the manager (knowing that he can't have his cake and eat it too) accepts the idea of maximizing his attainment of only *one major* objective. He treats all other objectives as restrictions on what he can do. We call this approach to a decision problem *single goal programming*.

Frequently, the constraints are imposed by limited resources—for instance, plant capacity, executive time, materials, or capital. Requirements that must be met—minimum daily vitamin intake, power required to drive a generator, production to supply a market, or capital to undertake a project—are another form of constraint. Constraints of both types are variants of objectives that lend themselves to the programming format.

The manager is often faced with a wide range of constraints that define the decision conditions. As a result, he must choose from among a large number of interrelated alternatives—and the best choice may be far from obvious. An intuitive solution may never uncover the best approach. A rational approach to such problems requires a systematic way to represent the key objective, to describe the constraints under which the system must operate, and to arrive at the one best policy out of the many possibilities. Linear programming provides a rational approach.

In this unit's case, the Chocoban Company has a problem well suited to the programming format. For Chocoban, all objectives *except the main one* (as chosen by the manager) will be relegated to the role of constraints. The manager desires to maximize his profits with a given configuration of facilities and a limited amount of manpower and materials.

It is in the nature of constraints to require that either some minimum amount must be achieved, some maximum amount must not be exceeded, or both—this last being specified as a *range* of acceptable values. We indicate these conditions (using mathematical symbols for inequalities) as follows:

Language equivalent	Inequations
x_1 must be equal to or less than b;	$x_1 \leqslant b$
x_1 must be less than b;	$x_1 < b$
x_2 must be equal to or greater than b;	$x_2 \geqslant b$
x_2 must be greater than b;	$x_2 > b$
x_1 must be equal to or less than b and equal to or greater than a; the *range* of acceptance values includes both a and b;	$a \leqslant x_1 \leqslant b$
x_1 must be less than b and greater than a; the *range* of acceptance values does not include either a or b.	$a < x_1 < b$

Other possible range statements might be $a < x_1 \leqslant b$ or $a \leqslant x_1 < b$, which can be interpreted with no difficulty now that the symbols are understood.

THE POWER OF INEQUATIONS

The use of inequations is a very important addition to the methodology of applied mathematics. Problems expressed in this way, rather than as equations, have many more degrees of freedom for solution, and consequently better solutions that are consistent with managerial objectives can be found. This is a most critical point, so let us also put it in another way.

If the manager states that he requires equalities (such as $x_1 = b$, $x_2 = a$) when, in fact, a range will do, he is wasting his decision opportunities. If he requests an equality when (at most) some specific threshold conditions must be met (such as no more than b, $x_1 \leqslant b$, or no less than b, $x_1 \geqslant b$) he has overspecified and overconstrained his problem. He has cut down on the latitude of tolerable conditions under which his problem can be solved. Most of the time, severe penalties must be paid for such unnecessary restriction.

First, note the meaning of the constraints $x_1 \geqslant 0$, $x_2 \geqslant 0$ in the diagram following.

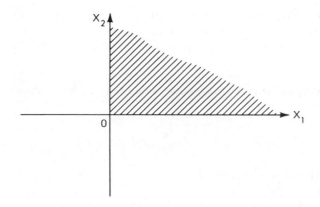

The only solution space is the upper right-hand quadrant (called the first quadrant).* Any set of values for x_1 and x_2 that does not lie in the solution space violates the constraints and must be rejected. (Thus, negative production amounts are prohibited.)

EXERCISE A

To examine your understanding of inequalities, draw the solution space for $x_1 \geqslant a$, $x_2 \geqslant b$, where both a and b are positive numbers. The solution is at the end of this note.

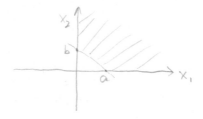

Now, let us compare the solution space for the two problem formulations (A and B) given below.

	Equalities		Inequalities
A.	$2x_1 + x_2 = 10$	B.	$2x_1 + x_2 \leqslant 10$
	$x_1 + 2x_2 = 8$		$x_1 + 2x_2 \leqslant 8$

The solution of the two equations in A is a *single point*. It is $x_1 = 4$, $x_2 = 2$. It is obtained directly by algebra. There are two equations and two unknowns. Thus:

*Including all points on the axes that have positive values.

$$\text{(Minus)} \quad \begin{array}{r} 2x_1 + x_2 = 10 \\ 2x_1 + 4x_2 = 16 \\ \hline 3x_2 = 6 \\ x_2 = 2 \end{array}$$

Substituting the value of 2 for x_2 in the first equation, we obtain:

$$\begin{array}{rl} 2x_1 + 2 = 10 \\ 2x_1 \;\;\;\;\; = 8 \\ x_1 \;\;\;\;\; = 4 \end{array}$$

A graphic solution can also be used, as here:

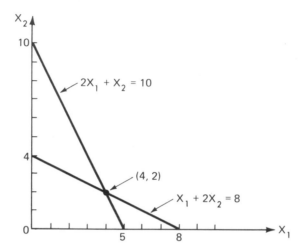

The important fact to realize is that, because equalities are required in A, *nothing* but a single point will satisfy both equations. That's what this problem formulation (the A model) states. Suppose that we get $3 of profit for each x_1 unit we make, and $7 for each unit of x_2. (In the equality case, the profits per unit have no relation to the values we select for x_1 and x_2.) Then our total profit, P, will be: $P = \$3x_1 + \$7x_2$.

For situation A, the single-point solution produces a profit of:

$$P = \$3(4) + \$7(2) = \$26$$

And it is now time to turn to formulation B, which is identical to A except that it is given in terms of *inequations* rather than equations. Here again is B:

$$\text{B.} \quad \begin{array}{ll} 2x_1 + x_2 \leqslant 10\text{:} & \text{first resource constraint} \\ x_1 + 2x_2 \leqslant 8\text{:} & \text{second resource constraint} \end{array}$$

The reason for each inequation might be that we have limited resources—say, only 10 pounds of the first resource and 8 gallons of the second.* Interpreting these inequations, we use 2 pounds of the first resource for each unit of x_1 that we make (that is, $2x_1$). We require only one pound of the first resource for each unit of x_2 (that is, x_2).

When equalities were used (in formulation A), it meant that we *had to use up (entirely)* all 10 pounds and all 8 gallons. With inequalities (as in formulation B), we are stating only that we can't exceed what we have on hand. And this seems eminently reasonable. Certainly, it includes the possibility of entirely using up both kinds of resources. If that solution is the best one, then formulation B will find it too. The equality is, after all, only a special case of the inequations as in formulation B. But if some other set of values for x_1 and x_2 will maximize the profit, P, then formulation A *cannot* find it. It should be evident, therefore, that the inequations allow flexibility, whereas the equations offer none. And usually, inequations come far closer to expressing what the manager *really means* to say. His objective is to maximize the profit, P. If he can do so without using up all his resources, so much the better. This is a vital conceptual point.

*Note that the dimensions of the constraints do not have to be the same.

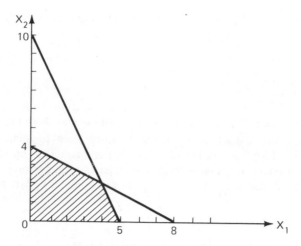

The diagram above shows the solution space (shaded) for the inequations. (Should you need to be convinced, this statement can be tested by selecting various point values of x_1 and x_2—some from the shaded and some from the unshaded portions of the diagram—and trying them in the inequations.) We have added the two additional constraints, $x_1 \geqslant 0$, $x_2 \geqslant 0$ (for our example they make evident sense). They both state that we can't produce negative quantities of either x_1 or x_2. Alternatively, we must plan to have zero or more units for both x_1 and x_2. Correspondingly, no negative values are shown for x_1 or x_2 in the diagram. We see that any one of the points in the shaded area might be our answer. Consequently, an infinite number of new possibilities exist for combinations of x_1 and x_2. Which of these values for x_1 and x_2 will maximize the profit, P? That is what we must determine. On the face of it, it would seem that we have really complicated our problem.

However, the analytical strength of linear programming lies precisely in its ability to substantially cut down on the amount of search necessary to find our answer. *Our theory tells us that one of the vertex points of the (shaded) polygon must produce the maximum profit, and this is proved quite simply by the mathematician.* We will bypass the mathematics and test the profit at each vertex point. (Here there are only four.)

Possible Solutions	Profit
(0,0)	$3(0) + $7(0) = $00
(0,4)	$3(0) + $7(4) = $28
(5,0)	$3(5) + $7(0) = $15
(4,2)	$3(4) + $7(2) = $26

We see that the profit derived in formulation A can be improved from $26 to $28 by using the (inequation) formulation of B. Assuming that the inequations express the manager's real intent, then it is clear that these extra degrees of freedom have been rewarding. But why is it that a solution that fully utilizes all resources might produce a smaller profit than one that leaves some resources unused? Note that with the solution (0,4), we have 6 units of the first resource left over. First resource: $2(0) + (4) = 4$, which is less than 10 by 6. Second resource: $(0) + 2(4) = 8$, which is fully utilized. Although 6 units of the first resource are left over, the profit is greater than if both resources had been fully utilized.

The key to understanding this result is to know that linear programming focuses on maximizing profits (or minimizing costs) rather than on using up resources. Input resources can be combined in various ways to produce different outputs. Each combination of inputs has a different cost, and each output has a different profit margin. The object of the linear program is to find a product mix that maximizes production of products with high profit margins while minimizing the use of inputs with high costs—with due consideration for constraints on available resources. *There is no reason to suppose that a combination that fully utilizes the input resources will produce the greatest profit. Full utilization of inputs may emphasize low-profit-margin activities, as in the situation we have just seen.*

To satisfy *equations* we often have to produce more of some product than is most profitable. Requiring equality can force us to engage in less-profitable ventures (in this case, to produce x_1); it may lead us to produce greater-than-optimal quantities of items with low profit margins or high-cost inputs. We would be better off if we used inequations and underutilized the first resource.

Maximum profit is not necessarily associated with full resource and total capacity utilization.

Let us look at another example:

Assume that the manager of the local brewery has come to you with the following problem. He has 100 gallons of light brew ingredient and 80 gallons of dark brew ingredient. Assume that these two basic ingredients can be combined in various ways to produce different products, but four brews are most popular. The brewmaster wants to know how much of each brew to make from the ingredients he has on hand. His objective is to maximize his daily profits. The table below presents the information necessary to understand and resolve this problem. The total daily number of bottles that will be produced is $x_1 + x_2 + x_3 + x_4$. For example, if $x_1 = 0$, then no True Dark Brew will be made.

Table of Brew Information

	Number of Bottles Produced Daily				Ingredient Quantities Available
	x_1 (True Dark)	x_2 (Dark Brew)	x_3 (Half and Half)	x_4 (Light Brew)	
Dark ingredient (gallons per bottle)	1/16	1/20	1/32	0	80 gal.
Light ingredient (gallons per bottle)	0	1/80	1/32	1/16	100 gal.
Profit per bottle	8¢	10¢	10¢	7¢	

What advice can you give the brewery manager to help him maximize his total profit for this period? What does your intuition tell you? It will be worthwhile if you try to answer that question before we begin to examine the combinations in a trial-and-error fashion.

THE CRUDE BUT RATIONAL APPROACH

First, consider the following production schedule: $x_1 = 1,280$ bottles, which uses up all 80 gallons of the dark ingredient, since $1,280/16 = 80$; and $x_4 = 1,600$ bottles, which consumes all of the light ingredient, since $1,600/16 = 100$. Then, $x_2 = 0$ and $x_3 = 0$, meaning that neither Dark Brew nor Half and Half will be made or sold. The day's profit that this production schedule yields is:

$$(\$.08)\, x_1 \quad + \quad (\$.07)x_4 \quad = \text{Profit}$$
$$(1,280 \times \$.08) + (1,600 \times \$.07) = \$214.40$$

Are you satisfied with this result—or can we do any better?

Let's try the marketing strategy of emphasizing dark brew. If $x_2 = 1,600$ bottles, we shall have used up all 80 gallons of the dark ingredient, since $1,600/20 = 80$, and 20 gallons of the light ingredient—$1,600/80 = 20$. This leaves an excess of 80 gallons of the light ingredient, which can only be used for the light brew.* Therefore, $x_4 = 1,280$ bottles of light brew ($1,280/16 = 80$). This product mix yields a one day's profit of:

$$(\$0.10)x_2 \quad + \quad (\$0.07)x_4 \quad = \text{Profit}$$
$$(1,600 \times \$.10) + (1,280 \times \$.07) = \$249.60$$

There has been an improvement in the profit—but again we ask, is there yet a better result available? The answer happens to be yes! The best combination is this one: $x_1 = 0$, $x_2 = 0$, $x_3 = 2,560$, $x_4 = 320$. This yields a one

*Since there is no excess of the dark ingredient.

day's profit of $278.40 and happens to use up entirely both types of ingredients. How do we know that this is the very best solution? We have used the mathematical approach of linear programming to obtain it. How long might *you* have continued to search for this optimal solution? Perhaps for quite a while, small as the problem is. Far more significant, how could you have known when to stop searching because you had found the best possible solution? Our purpose in using this example was to demonstrate that even a small problem begins to exceed the capabilities of cut-and-try methods.

> *The method of linear programming is powerful. Once this technique has been learned, large problems can be tackled with ease. You need not know all the mathematical theory underlying the formulation of the model. After you learn the concepts of LP, you will be able to use the method, by employing the appropriate computer program.* *

Let us now look at the basic concepts of linear programming.

SYSTEMATIC TESTING OF VERTICES

Assume, in our brewing problem, that the brewer tells you to consider only the Dark Brew and Half and Half. Linear programming can be used to find the solution. Our problem format follows:

	Number of Bottles Produced Daily		Ingredient Quantities Available
	x_2	x_3	
Dark ingredient (gallons per bottle)	1/20	1/32	80 gal.
Light ingredient (gallons per bottle)	1/80	1/32	100 gal.
Profit per bottle	10¢	10¢	

We can write the following inequations to express our constraints on the availability of the ingredients where $x_2 \geqslant 0$, $x_3 \geqslant 0$.

$$\text{(Dark)} \quad 1/20\ x_2 + 1/32\ x_3 \leqslant 80$$
$$\text{(Light)} \quad 1/80\ x_2 + 1/32\ x_3 \leqslant 100$$

And our objective function is:

$$\text{Maximize } (\$.10\ x_2 + \$.10\ x_3)$$

We have already seen how to represent the constraints geometrically. They are diagrammed below, for the particular values. Clearly, the constraint of the dark ingredient dominates that of the light ingredient. We can say that the light ingredient constraint is superfluous. The two vertices to be tested are $x_2 = 0$, $x_3 = 2,560$ and $x_2 = 1,600$, $x_3 = 0$.

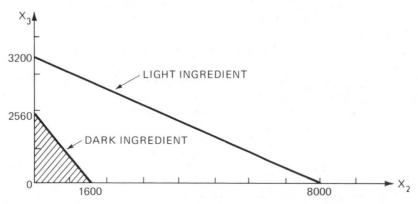

*Use of the computer, in this regard, can be learned in under an hour. Thus, the LP model is already programmed for the computer. The user must know only how to feed it relevant information and how to read the solution.

Whence: Profit $(0,2560) = \$0.10(0) + \$0.10(2,560) = \$256.00$
Profit $(1600,0) = \$0.10(1,600) + \$0.10(0) = \$160.00$

The first solution is the best one in this case.[*]

All we need to do is determine the values of our x's *for all vertices and test the profit at each one.*

Sometimes when two adjacent vertices yield the same profit, all combinations of the x's that lie on the line connecting these two vertices will also yield the same profit. For example, let the profit per bottle for x_2 be 16 cents (instead of 10) and the x_3 profit remain 10 cents. Then:

Profit $(0,2560) = \$0.16(0) + \$0.10(2,560) = \$256.00$
Profit $(1600,0) = \$0.16(1,600) + \$0.10(0) = \$256.00$

Take any point on the (dark ingredient) line; say, $x_2 = 400$, $x_3 = 1,920$.

Profit $(400,1920) = \$0.16(400) + \$0.10(1,920) = \$256.00$

which proves our point by example. The case of equal profits along the connecting line is not important with respect to techniques and method. It is conceptually significant with respect to implementation, because it means that *when two vertices have almost the same optimal profit, the manager has flexibility in his decision.*

BELIEVABILITY AND SENSITIVITY

We must bear in mind that many of the numbers used in LP formulations either are estimates, or vary with time. Such ranges of potential inaccuracy and variability should be recognized. *The validity of LP solutions is no better than the underlying assumptions and data used.* If the possible range of variability is great, there may be no "real" basis for preferring one solution to another. If the manager has some idea of the chance of error in estimating the values used in the LP formulation, he can decide pretty quickly how much belief to place in his results. Assume that he knows there are estimates that could be as much as 100 percent off. This fact alone means nothing. What counts is how *sensitive* the solution is to such potential errors.

For example, assume the profit per bottle for x_3 has been overestimated by 50 percent. This is a large error; yet the solution does not change as a result of this error, so we can say the system is insensitive to this overestimate. We observe:

Profit $(0,2560) = \$0.10(0) + \$0.15(2,560) = \$384.00$
Profit $(1600,0) = \$0.10(1,600) + \$0.15(0) = \$160.00$

so we continue to make no Dark Brew and 2,560 bottles of Half and Half. It is true we will experience a profit different from what we had expected, but our indicated actions remain unchanged. Proceeding with the same kind of reasoning, we note that a 40 percent error of underestimation for x_3's profit per bottle will change the indicated solution.

Profit $(0,2560) = \$0.10(0) + \$0.06(2,560) = \$153.60$
Profit $(1600,0) = \$0.10(1,600) + \$0.06(0) = \$160.00$

We would switch to 1,600 bottles of Dark Brew and make no Half and Half. The system is sensitive to a substantial underestimate of x_3's profit rate.

Our examples have been not only simple but gross. In this way we could quickly home in on crucial concepts, and that is our purpose here. Sensitivity analysis can be used for all estimates in the LP formulation, and the sensitivity levels to be tested are usually much finer than we have experienced here.

For sensitive parameters, it is worthwhile to spend time and money to get better information. For insensitive ones, it is wasteful.

---

[*]We don't even bother to test the vertex point (0,0). Quite obviously, it has zero profit. We can hardly maximize our profit by going out of business.

All members of the firm are likely to be party to the LP input information, and if they aren't, they should be. Take the brewer's situation, for example. His production personnel must be able to tell him how much of each resource must be used up to create one unit of finished product (that is, a bottle of each of the x's). The resources involved may be labor, materials, machine time, and so on. Product and process design affect these measures directly. A change in design could alter the solution. Thus, production design and process technology can influence marketing and financial activities.

Financial management is crucial in determining the investment in plant, materials, and other resources; with a different investment configuration, many of the resource-utilization measures would be changed. Also, the constraints on available resources would be influenced by financial considerations and materials-management policies.

Marketing management decisions are also crucial. In determining profit, a price must be set for each type of item in the product line. Further, marketing management plays a large part in specifying the nature of the product (for instance, the ingredients, the shapes, the advertising images). From all of the factors above, it should be evident that estimates required for LP must frequently cross traditional departmental lines, and decisions cannot be arrived at without interdepartmental consultation.

THE COST FORMULATION

Many times it is reasonable to minimize costs rather than to maximize profit. The same method is used. The only difference is that the solution space lies in the opposite direction. The vertices of cost space are tested. That vertex associated with the minimum cost is the solution.[*]

EXERCISE B

Let us try a cost example, to which the answer will be found at the end of this note. Assume that each of two ingredients I_j (used in a cattle-feed mix) has a given amount of vitamins A and C per pound; also, that to sell our product we must have minimum quantities of these vitamins present. We shall let these equations stand for the situation:

$$I_1 \geqslant 0, I_2 \geqslant 0$$

(Vitamin A)	$.01\,I_1 + .03I_2 \geqslant 1.8$	I_j = ingredient j
(Vitamin C)	$.04\,I_1 + .02I_2 \geqslant 2.0$	(j = 1,2)
(Cost)	Minimize $[\$.20\,I_1 + \$.30\,I_2]$	

Interpreting these equations: First, we cannot have negative amounts of the ingredients. Second, there is .01 unit of vitamin A in a pound of ingredient 1, and .03 units of vitamin A in a pound of ingredient 2. Third, there are .04 units of vitamin C in a pound of ingredient 1, and .02 units in a pound of ingredient 2. Fourth, the cost per pound of ingredient 1 is 20 cents; of ingredient 2, it is 30 cents. Fifth, we want to have *at least* 1.8 units of vitamin A and 2.0 units of vitamin C in our final mix. Sixth, we want to minimize the total cost. Do this as an exercise, making certain that you correctly identify the solution space.

---

[*]As with profit, an entire line of equivalent cost solutions might be found.

LIMITATIONS OF LP

The material on linear programming contained here is introductory in nature. From this exposure you should have enough conceptual understanding to know when and where to use LP, relying on technicians for implementation. To round out this managerial perspective, you should be aware of a few important assumptions and limitations underlying LP:

The constraints and profit (or cost) coefficients are assumed to be linear over the range of possible solutions. If, beyond a certain number of units, the profit (or cost) per unit changes, then special steps must be taken. When the profit *rate* decreases with an increasing number of units, or when the cost *rate* increases with an increasing number of units, straightforward transformations can be used and the problem will remain suitable for LP—otherwise, nonlinear programming methods must be applied.

The limitation of only two factors (x's, I's, and so on) with any given number of constraints has been used here only because we wanted to employ geometric representation to determine the composition of all vertices of the solution space. Three dimensional models can also be built, using three x's, I's, or other variables. For more than three factors, the analyst must go to algebraic forms of representation.

Solution to Exercise A

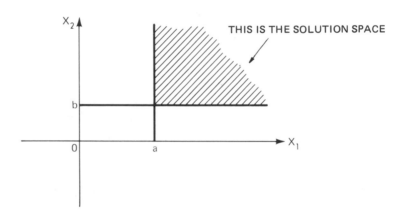

Solution to Exercise B

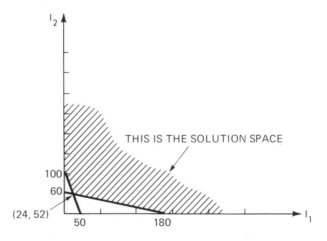

Testing each vertex of the solution space, we have:

$$\text{Total Cost } (0, 100) = \$.20(0) + \$.30(100) = \$30.00$$
$$\text{Total Cost } (24,52) = \$.20(24) + \$.30(52) = \$20.40$$
$$\text{Total Cost } (180,0) = \$.20(180) + \$.30(0) = \$36.00$$

So we will buy 24 pounds of ingredient 1 for each 52 pounds of ingredient 2.

INSTRUCTIONS FOR PREPARING THE CASE

Chocoban, Ltd.

Read the case carefully. Without reference to the exercises found after the case, use the principles of linear programming to derive the optimal mix of Chocodant and Chocomer with a daily constraint of 1,200 pounds of cocoa beans, and with a goal of maximum contribution. Should you find this calculation too difficult, or should you want to check your answers, refer to the exercise.

To benefit fully from this case, look at the situation with total perspective; place yourself in the position of Henry Sampson. You will soon have to meet with your partner to decide whether Chocoban will introduce a lower-priced line of chocolates. Explore the goals of Chocoban (Sampson and Jonas). Analyze the possible alternatives in the light of these goals. Identify the uncertainties that surround your analysis, brought about by information that is either unavailable or subject to variability—for instance, cost of cocoa beans; dispose of these uncertainties through assumption or sensitivity analysis. Bear in mind that this is more than just an exercise in linear programming—your analysis should encompass all parts of the total corporate activity.

Decision Process

CASE

Chocoban, Ltd.

Chocoban, Ltd., was a well-established producer and marketer of the finest boxed chocolates. The company had been started ten years previously by two partners, Henry Sampson and John Jonas. Prior to their going into business together, Sampson had been marketing vice-president in a candy company with national distribution; Jonas had served as comptroller in the same company. The two men agreed at the outset that Sampson would devote his attentions to distribution and marketing, while Jonas would be "Mr. Inside," concentrating on production, accounting, and the finances of the company; overall planning and major decisions would be agreed upon by both.

The two partners had decided to position the company product in the medium-high price range. They were successful in developing and selling a quality chocolate and enjoyed an edge over competition. The single manufacturing plant, located in Newark, New Jersey, served a densely populated market in the surrounding area. With increased customer acceptance, twenty retail outlets were opened. Until recently, growth seemed limited only by financial resources.

Within the past several months, each partner unearthed information that proved disturbing to both. In a review of cost data, Jonas discovered that production costs per pound of candy were rising with each new retail outlet opened. In retrospect, he recognized that the company had outgrown the production expertise of the present management staff.

Sampson's revelation was even more disturbing. He noted that sales had begun to drop off in several of the stores. On investigation, he found that in each instance, an aggressive competitor with a lower-priced line had moved into the market territory. In a meeting with Jonas, he observed, "People can't taste quality any more. I feel strongly that we should develop a cheaper line as quickly as possible, to sell for around half our present price. We should cut our production of the premium line to half its present rate and use the extra cocoa beans for our new line." As a result of this meeting, Jonas agreed to look into recipes, costs, and schedules.

A week later, Jonas met with Sampson again, this time to report his findings. "Our kitchen has developed two recipes that we can make at a lower price. We think each recipe will satisfy the public, but neither comes near our premium line in quality. We have names to suggest for each formulation: Chocodant and Chocomer. The only new equipment we will need is a mixer and a molder, and I have located both, available on a lease arrangement with immediate delivery. I have put some costs together that include the leasing arrangement, new boxes, and all other expected production expenses. I have put this information, schedules, etc., on this memo, which you can look over, then we can decide. However, I think it fair to tell you that I have done some pencil pushing, and I don't think this lower-priced line makes for good business. You will see that every 100 pounds of the premium line now yields $86 in contribution, while Chocodant will yield only $63 and Chocomer $54. We are strapped financially, and our cocoa-bean suppliers will not increase their shipments to us by more than 10%, because of greater demands and level supply. Finally, I question whether we should go to an inferior candy that might destroy our quality image. Are you sure we can sell candy to our customers at these prices?"

Sampson looked over the memo and then replied, "I would like to study this information for the next few days. The prices that you have here aren't geared to marketing and will have to be adjusted up or down by a few pennies, but I will accept them as they are for my thinking. In reply to your last question, let me say that we not only can sell all the candy we can make at these prices, but we are in for trouble if these new lines don't make financial sense."

The two partners agreed to meet again in a few days to make a decision.

Memo to Mr. Sampson
From Mr. Jonas
Re: New Product Considerations

I. New Equipment

There is no restriction on how the mixer and molder can be used, except that only one or the other product can be on the mixer at one time, and the same applies to the molder. Thus, Chocodant can be on mixing while Chocomer is molding. The reverse is also true. Both products require these same two manufacturing stages and they must share time on the equipment.

The mixing machine can process 500 lbs. of Chocodant daily or 300 lbs. of Chocomer. The molding machine can process 271 lbs. of Chocodant daily or 633 lbs. of Chocomer.

II. Costs and Pricing

Production costs (exclusive of cost of cocoa beans):

Premium line: $50 per 100 lbs.
Chocodant: $12 per 100 lbs.
Chocomer: $11 per 100 lbs.

The cost of cocoa beans as presently carried on the books is $19 per 100 lbs. In the past, the cost has ranged from $15 to $25 per 100 lbs.

Cocoa bean requirements:
Premium line: 1 lb. of candy, 6 lbs. beans (present daily allocation, 2,400 lbs. of beans)
Chocodant: 1 lb. of candy, 4 lbs. beans
Chocomer: 1 lb. of candy, 3 lbs. beans

Projected selling prices:
Premium: $2.50/per lb. (present price)
Chocodant: $1.51/lb.
Chocomer: $1.22/lb.

PROBLEM-SOLVING EXERCISES

Chocoban, Ltd.

To save you time on calculations, we have prepared a programmed series of problems for this unit, which will help you to solve the case. There are four parts to the exercises. If you solve Question 1 correctly in Parts A, B, C, and D, you may stop figuring and just look at the computations as done by us (you will need to look at the solutions in each part before you go on to the next part), since you have shown that you understand the method and the problem. If you can't do Question 1 correctly, look at the solution, try to find your mistake, and go on to Question 2. Continue this process until you have solved at least one problem in all parts correctly. Do not look at the solutions except to check yourself.

PART A

Question 1.   Set up the appropriate inequation for producing Chocodant and Chocomer, using the daily capacity of the mixing machine as a constraint. Work in units of 100 lbs. of candy.

You will find the solution to this problem on page 137.

Question 2.   Set up the appropriate inequation for producing Chocodant and Chocomer, using the daily capacity of the molding machine as a constraint. Work in units of 100 lbs. of candy.

You will find the solution to this problem on page 137.

Question 3.   Set up the appropriate inequation for producing Chocodant and Chocomer, using the daily supply of cocoa beans as a constraint. Work in units of 100 lbs. of candy.

You will find the solution to this problem on page 138.

PART B

Question 1a.   Graph the preceding inequations and identify the solution space.

You will find the solution to this problem on page 138.

Question 1b.   Locate (give coordinates of) vertices a and b.

You will find the solution to this problem on pages 138, 139.

Question 2.   Locate vertices c and d.

You will find the solution to this problem on page 139.

PART C

Question 1.   Compute the contribution for 100 lbs. of Chocodant.

You will find the solution to this problem on page 139.

Question 2.   Compute the contribution for 100 lbs. of Chocomer.

You will find the solution to this problem on page 139.

PART D

Question 1.   Test vertices a and b for maximum contribution.

You will find the solution to this problem on page 139.

Question 2.   Test vertices c and d for maximum contribution.

You will find the solution to this problem on page 139.

Solution to Part A, Question 1:

The mixing machine can process either 500 lbs. of Chocodant daily or 300 lbs. of Chocomer. Therefore, to make x_1 units of Chocodant will take $\frac{1}{5}x_1$ days. Extending this reasoning, and with a constraint of one day's machine time:

$$\frac{1}{5}x_1 + \frac{1}{3}x_2 \leqslant 1 \quad \text{or} \quad 3x_1 + 5x_2 \leqslant 15$$

If you have completed the calculation correctly, you may read the solutions to the other questions in Part A and go on to Part B, Question 1. If you have not completed them correctly, go on to Part A, Question 2.

Solution to Part A, Question 2:

The molding machine can process 271 lbs. of Chocodant or 633 lbs. of Chocomer daily. With a constraint of one molder, the inequation for one day's production is:

$$\frac{1}{2.71}x_1 + \frac{1}{6.33}x_2 \leqslant 1 \quad \text{or} \quad 6.33x_1 + 2.71x_2 \leqslant 17.15 \quad \text{or} \quad 7x_1 + 3x_2 \leqslant 19$$

If you have completed the calculation correctly, you may read the solution to the other question in Part A and go on to Part B, Question 1. If you have not completed them correctly, go on to Part A, Question 3.

Solution to Part A, Question 3:

The available quantity of cocoa beans is 1,200 lbs. per day. Chocodant uses 400 lbs. of cocoa beans and Chocomer uses 300 lbs. for each 100 lbs. of candy. Usage of cocoa beans will then be $4x_1$ for Chocodant and $3x_2$ for Chocomer. The inequation is:

$$4x_1 + 3x_2 \leqslant 12$$

Now go on to Part B, Question 1.

Solution to Part B, Question 1a:

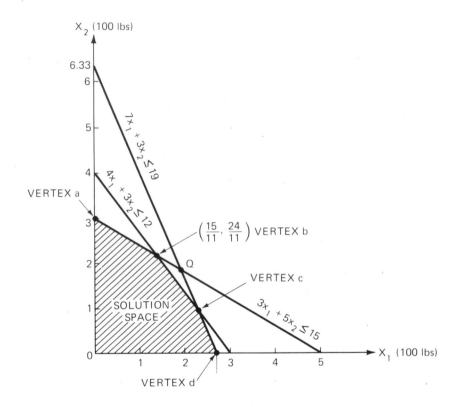

Solution to Part B, Question 1b:

Vertex a:

$$3x_1 + 5x_2 \leqslant 15$$
$$x_1 = 0, \text{ then,}$$
$$5x_2 = 15$$
$$\text{and } x_2 = 3$$

This vertex is located at 0,3.

Vertex b:

$$\text{Intersection of } 4x_1 + 3x_2 \leqslant 12, \text{ and } 3x_1 + 5x_2 \leqslant 15$$
$$4x_1 + 3x_2 = 12 \text{ is also } 12x_1 + 9x_2 = 36$$
$$3x_1 + 5x_2 = 15 \text{ is also } 12x_1 + 20x_2 = 60$$
$$\overline{11x_2 = 24}$$
$$x_2 = \frac{24}{11}$$

$$x_1 = \frac{15}{11}; \text{ this vertex is located at } \frac{15}{11}, \frac{24}{11}$$

If you have completed the calculations correctly, you may read the solution to the last question in Part B and go on to Part C, Question 1. If you have not completed them correctly, go on to Part B, Question 2.

Solution to Part B, Question 2:

Using the same method as that used in the solution to Part B, Question 1b, the vertices are:

c: the vertex is located at $\frac{7}{3}, \frac{8}{9}$

d: the vertex is located at 2.71, 0

Go on to Part C, Question 1.

Solution to Part C, Question 1:

Revenue:	$151
Less production costs:	12
Less cocoa-bean cost:	76 (4 × $19)
	$ 63

If you have completed the calculation correctly, you may read the solution to Part C, Question 2, and then go on to Part D, Question 1. If you have not completed it correctly, go on to Part C, Question 2.

Solution to Part C, Question 2:

Using the same method as that used in the solution to Part C, Question 1, the contribution is: $54.
Go on to Part D, Question 1.

Solution to Part D, Question 1:

$$\text{Vertex a: } \$63x_1 + \$54x_2 = \$64(0) + \$54(3) = \$162$$

$$\text{Vertex b: } \$63(\frac{15}{11}) + \$54(\frac{24}{11}) = \$203.73$$

If you have completed the calculations correctly, you may stop figuring and read the solution to the other question in Part D. If you have not completed them correctly, go on to Part D, Question 2.

Solution to Part D, Question 2:

$$\text{Vertex c: } \$63(\frac{7}{3}) + \$54(\frac{8}{9}) = \$195.00$$

$$\text{Vertex d: } \$63(2.71) + \$54(0) = \$170.73$$

Unit **8**

Capital Budgeting

In this unit, our purpose is to develop the basic concepts of capital budgeting. We will do this in three steps.

First, you will encounter a static, risk-type inventory problem. We shall employ the decision matrix as our basis for model building in the static, risk inventory problem of a Christmas tree retailer. Because the demand for Christmas trees is not known with certainty, we call this a risk problem. The significance of "static" will become apparent shortly.

Second, we learn that some information can be obtained only at an unnecessarily high price and that it is possible to determine rationally how much value additional information can have for us.

Third, in this unit's case, the Amory Oil Corporation has a capital-budgeting problem that your diagnosis should show to be *analogous* to the (static, risk inventory) Christmas tree problem. Accordingly, you will have to trace out the threads of the analogy. You will have to make the transformation required to adapt a model developed in one context to make it suitable for another. In other words, you will be called upon to perform one of the most creative acts of management science—to make a model that has been learned in one context useful in another context that seems quite dissimilar.

STATIC, RISK INVENTORY PROBLEMS

Assume that a Christmas tree retailer is faced with the following problem. It is November 20, and he must place an order for trees to sell for the coming Christmas season. He cannot place any orders with his supplier, who is a large distributor of trees, after December 9. But he doesn't even begin to sell any trees to his customers until December 12, and most of his sales are made after December 17. Consequently, there is no opportunity to take rectifying action based upon what is learned.

The demand for trees *varies* from year to year (a *risk* situation exists). We can assume that in a number of past years, on December 26, there has been an excess of trees; these were sold for firewood, and thereby the retailer realized some salvage value. In other years, the supply of trees was exhausted too soon.

It bothers our retailer to lose sales because he has not ordered enough stock. But it also bothers him to have to dump perfectly good trees because he has overordered. Depending upon what each season brings, the retailer is more or less unhappy. In risk systems, perfection is very rare. The fact is that few retailers could tell us for sure which bothers them more—being overstocked or understocked. We propose to show why such unhappiness is unnecessary.

Let us carefully note the characteristics of this problem. It is *static* because only one order can be placed and no corrective action can be taken. The results of this single-order quantity decision can yield only one of three outcomes:

I   demand = supply: Just the right amount was ordered; or
II demand > supply: Understock penalties occur; or
III demand < supply: Overstock costs exist.

The problem is a real one, because demand must be estimated beforehand, and since demand varies, the problem is one of risk.

We shall now look at a specific problem. Say that each tree costs the Christmas tree retailer $3 and that he sells each one for $7. Furthermore, this retailer delivers without charge each tree he sells, and he pays $0.50 per tree to his delivery boys. The salvage value of a tree after December 26 averages out at $0.30. Therefore, we can develop the profit for each of the three cases (I, II, and III) in terms of x = the order quantity (supply) and z = the demand for trees.

Case I: (z = x) demand = supply	There are no trees for salvage; x trees are sold, so revenue = $7x; x trees are purchased at a cost of $3x; and x trees are delivered at a cost of $.5x. Then profit (P) is:

$$P = \$7x - \$3x - \$.5x = \$3.5x$$

Case II: (z > x) demand > supply	There are no trees for salvage; x trees are sold (only the supply can be sold), so revenue = $7x; x trees are purchased at a cost of $3x; and x trees are delivered at a cost of $.5x. Then profit (P) is:

$$P = \$7x - \$3x - \$.5x = \$3.5x$$

which is the same result as Case I.

Case III: (z < x) demand < supply	(x − z) units must be salvaged, which produces a salvage revenue of $0.30(x − z); z trees are sold (only the demand is sold; the remainder is salvage), so this revenue is $7z; x trees are purchased at a cost of $3x; z trees are delivered at a cost of $.5z. Then profit (P) is:

$$P = \$7z + \$0.30(x - z) - \$3x - \$.5z$$
$$= \$6.2z - \$2.7x$$

When z = x, P = $6.2x − $2.7x = $3.5x, which is the same result as Case I.

To keep matters simple, we shall let the demand for Christmas trees be counted in small units. (This restriction is only for convenience in presentation.) Assume that the probability of demand is estimated as follows:

z	Probability of z occurring
0	.00
1	.05
2	.10
3	.20
4	.30
5	.20
6	.10
7	.05
8	.00
	1.00

FORECASTING

This demand distribution might have been derived by the Christmas tree retailer based on his results in prior years. Should that be the case, then the retailer is relying on the fact that the demand characteristics of the market are stable and do not change. (What with the booming synthetic-tree market, this presumption may be looked upon with suspicion.) Reading the distribution above, we see that it says: There must be some demand, since the probability that z = 0 is zero; 5% of the time, the demand will be for only one tree; 10% of the time it will be for two trees; and so on. If no records of previous years' sales have been kept by the retailer, or if the retailer is entering the Christmas tree business for the first time, or if the retailer has moved to a new location, etc., other methods for estimating the probabilities must be used. It is not our purpose to go into forecasting methods at this time. That is a full term's topic in its own right. It is important, however, to indicate that useful probability estimates can sometimes be generated strictly on the basis of the retailer's hunches.

We now draw up the appropriate decision matrix, where the strategies are the different ordering policies (x), and the states of nature are the different demand levels (z). We don't need to include $z = 0$ or $z = 8$, since both have probabilities equal to zero—i.e., $p_0 = 0$ and $p_8 = 0$.

To obtain the outcome values for this matrix, we use the appropriate computing formulas (see Cases I, II, and III). For example, consider $x = 2$, $z = 3$. This falls under Case II in the upper part of our matrix, and $P = \$3.5x = \$7.0$. How about $x = 5$, $z = 4$? This is Case III, whence $P = \$6.2(4) - \$2.7(5) = \$11.3$.

PROBABILITIES	.05 $z = 1$	.10 $z = 2$	.20 $z = 3$	.30 $z = 4$	.20 $z = 5$	.10 $z = 6$	.05 $z = 7$
S_1: $x = 1$							
S_2: $x = 2$			$7.0	CASES I AND II: $P = \$3.5x$ $z \geq x$			
S_3: $x = 3$							
S_4: $x = 4$		CASE III $P = \$6.2z - \$2.7x$ $z < x$					
S_5: $x = 5$				$11.3			
S_6: $x = 6$							
S_7: $x = 7$							

As exercise A, please fill in the entire matrix. Then use your knowledge of decision-making procedures to obtain the expected values (EV) for each strategy. Indicate which ordering strategy you would choose, and tell us: What is the expected profit of this strategy? (The solution will be found at the end of this note.)

AVERAGE PROFIT—NOT AVERAGE DEMAND

Now that you have the decision matrix and its operations firmly in mind again, let us note that the model itself is straightforward—it is the cost composition of the entries in the matrix that is critical. Only when the costs are understood, properly measured, and assembled in the matrix do the outcomes of our models have any meaning.

Let us consider the following: If the salvage value had been $3, what solution would you have expected to get? Right, the answer is obvious—order 7 trees. After all, a $3 value for salvage is equivalent to operating on a consignment basis. Had the salvage value been $3, the largest expected profit would have been obtained when $x = 7$.

Many businessmen look upon a problem of this type in an incorrect way. Their reasoning goes something like this. The average demand is:

$$(.05 \times 1) + (.10 \times 2) + (.20 \times 3) + (.30 \times 4) + (.20 \times 5) + (.10 \times 6) + (.05 \times 7) = 4.00 \text{ trees}$$

This manager reasons: Since the average demand is 4 trees, I will order 4 trees. But we say, not so—the reason our maximum expected value for profit occurred with 4 trees was coincidental. The costs just happened to balance out. Often, the average demand will provide a different and incorrect answer. Our prior illustration, with salvage value of $3, should serve to emphasize this point.

> *Our objective is the maximum average profit—this does not necessarily occur when the order quantity equals the average demand.*

THE VALUE OR COST OF INFORMATION

With a moment's thought, it will be observed that the diagonal of our decision matrix represents *perfect information* for strategic selections. By this we mean that with perfect prior knowledge, we can always be prepared to order just the right amount to meet demand exactly.

That doesn't mean we can control what will happen. The Christmas tree man, after all, cannot control the states of nature—i.e., the demand levels. The ability to be always on the diagonal requires that we should always know beforehand which one of the demand levels will occur. Then we would be able to choose a strategy that would yield an outcome falling on the diagonal—i.e., let supply x = demand z. This is what we mean by *perfect information*.

How can our Christmas tree man know which state of nature will occur? He could try to survey his customers, speak to other Christmas tree merchants, correlate tree sales with relevant factors for tree sales, and so forth. We are trying to say that it isn't hopeless to be able to predict what will happen. But it is quite likely to cost more than the expense for the original forecast that yielded the probability distribution. How much extra would you be willing to pay to be able always to have outcomes that fall on the diagonal of the matrix?

Clearly, we need to know the expected value of the diagonal of the matrix. It is:

$$(.05 \times \$3.5) + (.10 \times \$7.0) + (.20 \times \$10.5) + (.30 \times \$14.0) + (.20 \times \$17.5) + (.10 \times \$21.0) + (.05 \times \$24.5) = \$14.00$$

Therefore, it makes no sense for our Christmas tree retailer to spend more than $14.00 − $10.59 = $3.41 to obtain perfect information.

> *Compulsively, because it always seems best to know things, many managers do not take into account the fact that additional information—above and beyond what they have already—may not make a sufficient contribution to warrant the additional expense.*

THE VALUE OF CONTROL

The matrix example can be looked at in still another way. How much would it be worth to the Christmas tree man to gain control over his demand level? Let's say he could do this by lowering his price, or by advertising, or perhaps by contracting with a civic club for the total demand, etc. The answer to this is quite simple, once you have given the question a few moments thought. (The solution may be found as Exercise B at the end of this note.)

We should point out that if a cost matrix is used instead of profit, the same reasoning applies throughout—but it is, of course, logical to seek the cost minimums rather than profit maximums.

PRESENT VALUE

> *In making decisions about static problems, it is often necessary to compare costs (or revenues) that occur at different times. For comparison, the time variable must be removed, as time affects the value of money. The present-value concept is an important concept for making this adjustment.*

One might ask, is revenue of $1,000 gained today the same as revenue of $1,000 gained one year hence? Hardly, for revenue gained today can be put to use immediately in accruing interest or in generating additional profits.

The revenue deferred for a year suffers the loss of the additional year of return by comparison. For example, revenue of $1,000 received today and invested at 6% interest is worth $1,060 a year hence, obviously more than the $1,000 received a year from today.

We might turn around and ask how much we would need to earn today to have it worth $1,000 in one year if we can invest our money at 6% interest; in other words, the *present value* of $1,000 received one year hence with return of 6%. This is easily computed to be $943.40 by use of the following formula:

$$\text{Present Value} = N \left(\frac{1}{1+i} \right)^n$$

where N = the size of the deferred investment
n = the number of years completed—reckoned from now—when the payment will be made
i = the interest or carrying-cost rate for money

Under this present-value concept, we see that in dollar value there is no difference in receiving $1,000 a year hence from receiving $943.40 today and being able to put it to work at a 6% return on investment.

To give another example of the present-value concept, we might look at the purchase of a $1,000 piece of equipment scheduled to be bought in two years. If we were to invest $890 today at 6% return, we would have our $1,000 at the end of two years. Thus, the present value of that expenditure is $890.

In selecting one of several possibilities for expenditure or investment, one must first transpose the alternatives to a common point in time. Present-value (or present-worth) calculations allow you to do this by bringing all future expenditures, made at different points in time, down to a common reference point, to make them comparable.

For convenience, present-value tables have been created. The present value of $1 due at the end of *n* years can be found in the table below.

PRESENT VALUE OF $1

PERIODS HENCE	1%	2%	4%	6%	8%	10%	12%	14%	15%	16%	18%	20%	22%	24%	25%	26%	28%	30%	35%	40%	45%	50%
1	0.990	0.980	0.962	0.943	0.926	0.909	0.893	0.877	0.870	0.862	0.847	0.833	0.820	0.806	0.800	0.794	0.781	0.769	0.741	0.714	0.690	0.667
2	0.980	0.961	0.925	0.890	0.857	0.826	0.797	0.769	0.756	0.743	0.718	0.694	0.672	0.650	0.640	0.630	0.610	0.592	0.549	0.510	0.476	0.444
3	0.971	0.942	0.889	0.840	0.794	0.751	0.712	0.675	0.658	0.641	0.609	0.579	0.551	0.524	0.512	0.500	0.477	0.455	0.406	0.364	0.328	0.296
4	0.961	0.924	0.855	0.792	0.735	0.683	0.636	0.592	0.572	0.552	0.516	0.482	0.451	0.423	0.410	0.397	0.373	0.350	0.301	0.260	0.226	0.198
5	0.951	0.906	0.822	0.747	0.681	0.621	0.567	0.519	0.497	0.476	0.437	0.402	0.370	0.341	0.328	0.315	0.291	0.269	0.223	0.186	0.156	0.132
6	0.942	0.888	0.790	0.705	0.630	0.564	0.507	0.456	0.432	0.410	0.370	0.335	0.303	0.275	0.262	0.250	0.227	0.207	0.165	0.133	0.108	0.088
7	0.933	0.871	0.760	0.665	0.583	0.513	0.452	0.400	0.376	0.354	0.314	0.279	0.249	0.222	0.210	0.198	0.178	0.159	0.122	0.095	0.074	0.059
8	0.923	0.853	0.731	0.627	0.540	0.467	0.404	0.351	0.327	0.305	0.266	0.233	0.204	0.179	0.168	0.157	0.139	0.123	0.091	0.068	0.051	0.039
9	0.914	0.837	0.703	0.592	0.500	0.424	0.361	0.308	0.284	0.263	0.225	0.194	0.167	0.144	0.134	0.125	0.108	0.094	0.067	0.048	0.035	0.026
10	0.905	0.820	0.676	0.558	0.463	0.386	0.322	0.270	0.247	0.227	0.191	0.162	0.137	0.116	0.107	0.099	0.085	0.073	0.050	0.035	0.024	0.017
11	0.896	0.804	0.650	0.527	0.429	0.350	0.287	0.237	0.215	0.195	0.162	0.135	0.112	0.094	0.086	0.079	0.066	0.056	0.037	0.025	0.017	0.012
12	0.887	0.788	0.625	0.497	0.397	0.319	0.257	0.208	0.187	0.168	0.137	0.112	0.092	0.076	0.069	0.062	0.052	0.043	0.027	0.018	0.012	0.008
13	0.879	0.773	0.601	0.469	0.368	0.290	0.229	0.182	0.163	0.145	0.116	0.093	0.075	0.061	0.055	0.050	0.040	0.033	0.020	0.013	0.008	0.005
14	0.870	0.758	0.577	0.442	0.340	0.263	0.205	0.160	0.141	0.125	0.099	0.078	0.062	0.049	0.044	0.039	0.032	0.025	0.015	0.009	0.006	0.003
15	0.861	0.743	0.555	0.417	0.315	0.239	0.183	0.140	0.123	0.108	0.084	0.065	0.051	0.040	0.035	0.031	0.025	0.020	0.011	0.006	0.004	0.002
16	0.853	0.728	0.534	0.394	0.292	0.218	0.163	0.123	0.107	0.093	0.071	0.054	0.042	0.032	0.028	0.025	0.019	0.015	0.008	0.005	0.003	0.002
17	0.844	0.714	0.513	0.371	0.270	0.198	0.146	0.108	0.093	0.080	0.060	0.045	0.034	0.026	0.023	0.020	0.015	0.012	0.006	0.003	0.002	0.001
18	0.836	0.700	0.494	0.350	0.250	0.180	0.130	0.095	0.081	0.069	0.051	0.038	0.028	0.021	0.018	0.016	0.012	0.009	0.005	0.002	0.001	0.001
19	0.828	0.686	0.475	0.331	0.232	0.164	0.116	0.083	0.070	0.060	0.043	0.031	0.023	0.017	0.014	0.012	0.009	0.007	0.003	0.002	0.001	
20	0.820	0.673	0.456	0.312	0.215	0.149	0.104	0.073	0.061	0.051	0.037	0.026	0.019	0.014	0.012	0.010	0.007	0.005	0.002	0.001	0.001	
21	0.811	0.660	0.439	0.294	0.199	0.135	0.093	0.064	0.053	0.044	0.031	0.022	0.015	0.011	0.009	0.008	0.006	0.004	0.002	0.001		
22	0.803	0.647	0.422	0.278	0.184	0.123	0.083	0.056	0.046	0.038	0.026	0.018	0.013	0.009	0.007	0.006	0.004	0.003	0.001	0.001		
23	0.795	0.634	0.406	0.262	0.170	0.112	0.074	0.049	0.040	0.033	0.022	0.015	0.010	0.007	0.006	0.005	0.003	0.002	0.001			
24	0.788	0.622	0.390	0.247	0.158	0.102	0.066	0.043	0.035	0.028	0.019	0.013	0.008	0.006	0.005	0.004	0.003	0.002	0.001			
25	0.780	0.610	0.375	0.233	0.146	0.092	0.059	0.038	0.030	0.024	0.016	0.010	0.007	0.005	0.004	0.003	0.002	0.001	0.001			
26	0.772	0.598	0.361	0.220	0.135	0.084	0.053	0.033	0.026	0.021	0.014	0.009	0.006	0.004	0.003	0.002	0.002	0.001				
27	0.764	0.586	0.347	0.207	0.125	0.076	0.047	0.029	0.023	0.018	0.011	0.007	0.005	0.003	0.002	0.002	0.001	0.001				
28	0.757	0.574	0.333	0.196	0.116	0.069	0.042	0.026	0.020	0.016	0.010	0.006	0.004	0.002	0.002	0.002	0.001	0.001				
29	0.749	0.563	0.321	0.185	0.107	0.063	0.037	0.022	0.017	0.014	0.008	0.005	0.003	0.002	0.002	0.001	0.001	0.001				
30	0.742	0.552	0.308	0.174	0.099	0.057	0.033	0.020	0.015	0.012	0.007	0.004	0.003	0.002	0.001	0.001	0.001					
40	0.672	0.453	0.208	0.097	0.046	0.022	0.011	0.005	0.004	0.003	0.001	0.001										
50	0.608	0.372	0.141	0.054	0.021	0.009	0.003	0.001	0.001	0.001												

EXERCISE C

What is the present value of an investment of $2,500 to be made at the end of three years? (The starting point is now.) Let the interest rate be 6% per year. The solution may be found below.

Solution to Matrix Exercise, A.

		.05	.10	.20	.30	.20	.10	.05	
		z=1	z=2	z=3	z=4	z=5	z=6	z=7	EV
	S_1: x=1	$ 3.5	$ 3.5	$ 3.5	$ 3.5	$ 3.5	$ 3.5	$ 3.5	$ 3.50
S	S_2: x=2	0.8	7.0	7.0	7.0	7.0	7.0	7.0	6.69
	S_3: x=3	−1.9	4.3	10.5	10.5	10.5	10.5	10.5	9.26
	S_4: x=4	−4.6	1.6	7.8	14.0	14.0	14.0	14.0	10.59*
	S_5: x=5	−7.3	−1.1	5.1	11.3	17.5	17.5	17.5	10.06
	S_6: x=6	−10.0	−3.8	2.4	8.6	14.8	21.0	21.0	8.29
	S_7: x=7	−12.7	−6.5	−0.3	5.9	12.1	18.3	24.5	5.90

We would tell our Christmas tree retailer to order four trees, in order to maximize his expected profit, which is $10.59.

Solution to Demand-Control Exercise, B.

The best profit in the matrix is $24.50. If the Christmas tree dealer could gain control over this system, he would make z = 7. The difference $24.50 − $10.59 = $13.91 gives us the answer we are looking for. No more than this amount should be expended to gain control over the demand level, assuming that the forecast is already on hand.

Solution to Present-Value Exercise, C.

Using the formula given:

$$\text{Present Value} = \$2,500 \left(\frac{1}{1 + .06} \right)^3$$

$$- \$2,500 \left(\frac{1}{1.06} \right)^3$$

$$= \$2,500(0.84)$$

$$= \$2,100$$

So $2,500 promised now to be paid at the end of three years has a present value of only $2,100.

Alternatively, using the table:

$$\text{Present Value} = \$2,500(0.84)$$

$$= \$2,100$$

0.84 has been found in the table as the present value of $1 at 6% three years from now. Either way of working the problem is correct.

You will have an opportunity to use the concept of present value in the Amory Corporation Case that follows.

INSTRUCTIONS FOR PREPARING THE CASE

Amory Oil Corporation

Prepare the calculations for the case through the exercises that follow. To do these calculations, you may use either the present-value formula or the present-value table; both methods are correct, but use of the table lightens the mathematical load considerably.

Please note that, although cost of information is an important concept with which you should be familiar, it is not relevant to the Amory Oil Corporation case.

In this case, assume that Dr. Dumas, your boss, has asked you for recommendations that he can pass on to the president of the Amory Oil Corporation. Dr. Dumas has pointed out to you that, because basic corporate policies are at issue here, the president has become involved.

Dr. Dumas has suggested that you use a carrying-cost rate of 10% in any calculations. He justifies this by stating that since Amory is a large company, it probably has a carrying-cost rate in excess of 10%; further, in Argentina, return rates tend to be substantially larger than those in the United States. On the other hand, inflation is rampant and serves to negate considerations of a rate above 10%. Dr. Dumas further suggests that if the imprecision of the 10% rate disturbs you, a sensitivity analysis can be employed to determine how errors in estimating the carrying-cost rate can affect the results.

In leaving you with this assignment, Dr. Dumas gives you this final bit of guidance: "The president of Amory is a bearcat on logical analysis. He will want a clear statement of your objective for analysis. He will expect your analysis to be complete, but to remain within the bounds of the objective. Finally, I have an intuitive feeling that there must be a unique solution to this inventory problem that will satisfy all parties; look for it."

DEFINE THE OBJECTIVE → SET UP CRITERIA → IDENTIFY MISSING INFORMATION → CREATE STRATEGIES → EVALUATE EACH STRATEGY (1, 2, . . . N) BY EACH CRITERION → RECOMMEND THE BEST STRATEGY

Decision Process

CASE

Amory Oil Corporation

Amory Oil Corporation is a large U.S. petroleum company with operating fields and refineries located all over the world. Amory International (a division of Amory Oil Corp.) has concluded an arrangement to organize an affiliate in Argentina. It is called Amory Petroliferos, S.p.A.

The major design stages and their components have all been completed. Planning is now moving into the more detailed stages. For example, it has been definitely decided to locate the new refinery in Rosario, which is some 200 miles north of Buenos Aires. The final configuration of the facility has been approved.

As one part of a large capital outlay, it has been decided to buy a large GWB generator from West Germany. That the unit has an expected life of 12 years is well documented by the engineering records. The equipment plans call for replacement of the unit at the end of 12 years, and it has been explicitly stated that the nature of the replacement will be determined at the beginning of the eleventh year in accord with conditions existing at that time.

The cost of spare armatures for the generator has become a major issue, for these reasons: Spares purchased at the same time as the generator cost $3,000 each; if they must be ordered at a later time, the cost rises to $26,000 for setup expenses plus $5,000 for each unit produced; it is considered unlikely that unused spares will have any value after 12 years.

A directive from the top management of Amory Oil Corporation to Amory International requires that all investments (and consequent carrying costs) be kept to an absolute minimum. On the other hand, a long-established policy—which has been reinforced by some recent experiences—proclaims that all possible steps should be taken to ensure that no unnecessary downtime occur that would increase the vulnerability of the company to adverse criticism from those interests that advocate nationalization of the oil industry.

A real difference of opinion has arisen. The controller (who reports to the finance V.P. in New York City, although he works in Argentina), after carefully studying the engineering statistics, has stated that there is so low a probability of failure that he favors ordering no spares. As a concession to the refinery manager, who wants many spares, the controller has agreed to accept the carrying cost of *one* spare. The refinery manager is adamant, however. He insists that he must have at least two spares, since the production losses of downtime (contribution) will approximate $5,000 per day; also, there are no local facilities for making other than the most minor armature repairs. Aside from the specific issue, it is evident that a conflict of policies is involved, and that whatever decision is made is quite likely to be interpreted as establishing a policy.

As a result of the importance of this particular decision, your firm, Dubarry and Dumas, has been called upon to clear the air with some expert advice. You are one of D&D's top project directors, and have been charged with the responsibility for determining how many spare armatures to purchase *with the original order.* You have been chosen for this job because the problem is considered to be central to a very sensitive personal issue. Dr. Dumas has specifically cautioned you about the fact that the controller and the refinery manager are apparently involved in a struggle for control of the facility. He believes that the long-term relationship of D&D (vis-à-vis the Amory Oil Corporation) may well be at stake.

Reliable engineering data are available on the probable number of armature failures that will occur in the 12-year period, as follows:

Number of Failures in 12 Years (N)	Probability of N Failures
0	.90
1	.05
2	.03
3	.02

Also, on the condition that one failure occurs, its expected time of failure is at the end of the sixth year. On the condition that two failures occur, it is expected that the first will have failed at the end of 4 years and the second at the end of 8 years. On the condition that 3 failures occur, the expected spacing is 3, 6, and 9 years. This information was furnished to you by the controller, who had specifically requested such data from the engineers of GWB. In order to simplify the solution, assume that if a failure does occur, only one armature can be ordered at a time (although any number can be purchased with the original order).

PROBLEM-SOLVING EXERCISES

Amory Oil Corporation

To save you time on calculations, we have prepared a programmed series of problems for this unit, which will help you to solve the case. If you solve all three sections of Question 1 correctly in Part A, you may go to Part B. If you solve Question 1 correctly in Parts B and C, you may stop figuring and just look at the computations as done by us, since you have shown that you understand the method and the problem. If you can't do Question 1 correctly in Part A, look at the solution, find your mistake, and go on to Part B. Continue this process until you have solved at least one problem in each of Parts B and C correctly. Do not look at the solutions except to check yourself.

PART A

Question 1a.   What is the algebraic expression for armature costs when the right number of spares is ordered with the generator?

Question 1b.   What is the algebraic expression for armature costs when too small a number of spares is ordered with the generator?

Question 1c.   What is the algebraic expression for armature costs when the number of failures is smaller than the number of spares ordered with the generator?

You will find the solutions to these problems on pages 155, 156.

PART B

Question 1.   If no armatures are purchased at the time of the generator purchase, what are the costs involved for each possible number of failures, as given in the case? What is the expected value of cost for this strategy? Do not consider carrying costs at this point.

You will find the solution to this problem on page 156.

Question 2.   If one armature is purchased with the generator, what are the costs involved for each possible number of failures, as given in the case? What is the expected value for this strategy? Do not consider carrying costs at this point.

You will find the solution to this problem on page 156.

Question 3.   If two armatures are purchased with the generator, what are the costs involved for each possible number of failures, as given in the case? What is the expected value for this strategy? Do not consider carrying costs at this point.

You will find the solution to this problem on page 156.

Question 4.   If three armatures are purchased with the generator, what are the costs involved for each possible number of failures, as given in the case? What is the expected value for this strategy? Do not consider carrying costs at this point.

You will find the solution to this problem on page 156.

PART C

Question 1.   What would be the present value of costs if no armatures were ordered at the time of the purchase of the generator, and one failure occurred? If one armature were ordered and two failures occurred?

You will find the solution to this problem on page 157.

Question 2.   What would be the present value of costs if no armatures were ordered at the purchase of the generator, and two failures occurred? If two armatures were ordered and three failures occurred?

You will find the solution to this problem on page 157.

Solution to Part A, Question 1a:

$$\text{Demand} = \text{Order quantity}$$

$$z = x$$

The appropriate total cost is $3,000x.

Solution to Part A, Question 1b:

$$\text{Demand} > \text{Order quantity}$$

$$z > x$$

There is a cost of $3,000x for each spare ordered with the generator. Then, in addition, $(z - x)$ spares have to be ordered afterwards. We assume that they are ordered one by one. So a cost results of $(z - x)(\$26,000 + \$5,000) = \$31,000(z - x)$

The total cost will be:

$$TC = \$3,000x + \$31,000(z - x) = \$31,000z - \$28,000x$$

Solution to Part A, Question 1c:

Demand $<$ Order quantity

$z \quad < \quad x$

There is a cost of $3,000x for each spare ordered with the generator. If there were a salvage value of S dollars per unit left over, we would decrease these costs by $S(x - z)$. Since $S = 0$ for this case, the total cost is $3,000x.

If you have completed the calculations correctly, you may go on to Part B, Question 1. If you have not completed them correctly, determine your error; then go on to Part B, Question 1.

Solution to Part B, Question 1:

$P_r(z) =$	.90	.05	.03	.02	EV
	$z = 0$	$z = 1$	$z = 2$	$z = 3$	
$x = 0$	$z = x$	$z > x$	$z > x$	$z > x$	
	$0	$31,000	$62,000	$93,000	$5,270

If you have completed the calculation correctly, you may go on to Part C, Question 1. If you have not completed it correctly, go to Part B, Question 2.

Solution to Part B, Question 2:

$P_r(z) =$	.90	.05	.03	.02	EV
	$z = 0$	$z = 1$	$z = 2$	$z = 3$	
$x = 1$	$z < x$	$z = x$	$z > x$	$z > x$	
	$3,000	$3,000	$34,000	$65,000	$5,170

If you have completed the calculation correctly, you may go on to Part C, Question 1. If you have not completed it correctly go to Part B, Question 3.

Solution to Part B, Question 3:

$P_r(z) =$	.90	.05	.03	.02	EV
	$z = 0$	$z = 1$	$z = 2$	$z = 3$	
$x = 2$	$z < x$	$z < x$	$z = x$	$z > x$	
	$6,000	$6,000	$6,000	$37,000	$6,620

If you have completed the calculations correctly, you may go on to Part C, Question 1. If you have not completed them correctly, go to Part B, Question 4.

Solution to Part B, Question 4:

$P_r(z) =$	.90	.05	.03	.02	EV
	$z = 0$	$z = 1$	$z = 2$	$z = 3$	
$x = 3$	$z < x$	$z < x$	$z < x$	$z = x$	
	$9,000	$9,000	$9,000	$9,000	$9,000

Now go on to Part C, Question 1.

Solution to Part C, Question 1:

$z = 1, x = 0$: TC = \$31,000 (0.564) = \$17,484

$z = 2, x = 1$: TC = \$3,000 + \$31,000 (0.467) = \$3,000 + \$14,477 = \$17,477

If you have completed the calculations correctly, you have reached the end of this exercise. If you have not completed it correctly, go to Part C, Question 2.

Solution to Part C, Question 2:

$z = 2, x = 0$: TC = \$31,000(0.683 + 0.467) = \$35,650

$z = 3, x = 2$: TC = \$6,000 + \$31,000(0.424) = \$6,000 + \$13,144 = \$19,144

Unit 9

Statistical Quality Control

To the extent that human judgment can assess the degree to which operations are under control, there have always been management control systems. The pyramids couldn't have been built, Napoleon could not have marched, and governments would have fallen as they rose if some forms of control had not always existed. We have much evidence that systems that survive in spite of a poor control system pay a very high penalty for this weakness.

Problems become more complex as the organizations in which they are embedded become larger, evolve more rapidly, and experience greater connectedness to the rest of the world. Judgmental control systems no longer suffice.

A new form of managerial control over operations came into existence with the discovery of statistical quality control (SQC) principles and with the invention of control charts and related methods.* During World War II, the far-ranging implications of SQC became apparent. Statistical control methods are still being developed, and new applications continually suggest themselves.

The methods of SQC add speed and sensitivity to the control of almost every type of process. These characteristics are necessary if a manager wants to maintain uniform quality of output. We shall illustrate basic SQC concepts through application to process control.

Let us start with the examination of a typical control model:

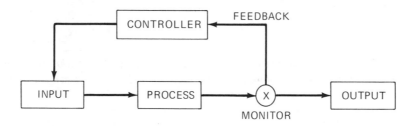

THE CONTROL FUNCTION

The segments of this model that provide control are the monitor and the controller. A *monitor* is interposed to collect information about the output. If the output is not uniform or is unacceptable, a *controller* prescribes a change in the process and/or the inputs. Through this feedback loop, adjustments in input and process are made as needed to produce output of acceptable quality.

---

*Walter A. Shewhart, working with the U.S. Department of Agriculture in the 1930s, is generally credited with being the "father of SQC." Much significant statistical methodology came from various contributors in these early years who worked with the Department of Agriculture, and Walter Shewhart was certainly one of the most important of these.

The monitor usually performs a test or inspection operation. From this station, immediate reports of significant changes (deviations) of quality are relayed to the controller. The controller then seeks to correct input and/or process to achieve acceptable or uniform quality of output.

CHANCE CAUSES

There are no processes in the universe that produce *exact* and *identical* replicas. Variability is inherent in all technological processes. Gears heat up, changes in crystalline structure occur, atomic and subatomic energy shifts are experienced, minute particles of dust are introduced into the process. These types of changes occur not just one at a time, but in such great numbers and individually on such a small scale that they are called *chance causes*. There is no point in trying to rectify or modify any one or several of these chance causes of variability; there are just too many to cope with, and they are inherent in the fundamental structure of the process.

ASSIGNABLE CAUSES

Any disturbance of a process that is not a chance-cause factor (as previously defined) is an *assignable cause* factor. As the name indicates, the source of such types of disturbance can be traced, *assigned,* and (frequently but not always) removed. Tool and gear wear are correctable; human error in setting a machine, a broken cam, or a loosened and vibrating part can be remedied. These are typical of the assignable causes that can be detected by the methods of statistical quality control (SQC).

We are interested in assignable causes affecting only those qualities of the output that concern us. A part can be inspected for many different qualities, such as length, finish, hardness, tensile strength, color, and so on. We establish a quality standard for each of the objectives that is included in our definition of output quality to be controlled.

The primary points to bear in mind are:

1.   The process (in conjunction with its specified inputs) has inherent chance-cause variability that cannot be removed—*except* by changing fundamental characteristics of the process.

2.   The blueprints, standards, etc., define a set of specifications. The process we are using may not be well suited for producing these specifications (in the economic sense) or providing "acceptable" output a "sufficiently" large percentage of the time. We shall have to spell this out in more detail at a later point in our discussion.

3.   The process may not seem to be suitable (in the economic sense mentioned above), but this conclusion is not meaningful until assignable causes of variation have been removed and the process has been stabilized. Note:

> By definition, a process that is operating without any assignable causes of variation is stable. Further, a stable process may be highly variable or it may be only slightly so. Stability does not reflect degrees of variability. It does reflect the absence of assignable causes of variation.

A stable process can become unstable when its behavior is changed by the entrance of a new factor. Monitors and methodology are designed to detect such changes so that we may remove the new assignable causes. Usually, the cost of the process increases as its inherent (chance-cause) variability decreases. We speak of this low variance as characterizing superior technology.

4.   *Sensible operations management requires that the variability characteristics of the process be fitted to the requirements of the product design*—providing neither too much nor too little inherent variability. The effects of too much are clear. The probable effects of too little are that we use better equipment than we need to, and thereby misallocate our resources.

5.   Inspection equipment also enters the picture, by contributing its own inherent variability. Whether we use gauges, micrometers, optical comparators, or hardness, saline, temperature, or pressure testers—all inspection equipment introduces some variability of its own. *Sometimes, the inspection equipment and/or the in-*

spectors are responsible for introducing assignable causes of variation. These can usually be removed once they are detected and have been traced to their sources. Inspection operations such as taste testing of foods, sniffing perfumes, or quaffing wines, are subject to the same considerations, but they can be far more difficult to handle with respect to measuring effects and diagnosing as well as removing assignable causes.

6.   A product may be specified with tolerances that are gross in comparison to the precision of the process. The inspection equipment may then be similarly unrefined. By taking gross measurements of the output, it can appear as though exact replicas are being produced—whereas a finer measurement system would reflect the variabilities that are actually occurring. For example, assume that a part must conform to the specifications 3.0 ± 0.1. A refined inspection facility would indicate that the process is actually turning out parts as follows: 3.005, 3.001, 2.995, 3.008, 2.994, . . . , etc. While there is variability, all parts are within tolerances.

TYPES OF CONTROL

One way to monitor a process is to *100 percent inspect* output. For a variety of reasons, this is seldom done. Clearly, it is more expensive than just sampling the output. It is also likely to slow down the production rate. Most important, it is seldom more accurate and usually less reliable whenever human inspection procedures are involved and the volume of throughput is substantial. Human inspectors experience fatigue; their conclusions must be verified with far greater care as the number of inspections that they are required to make per unit of time increases. In addition, we would still have to analyze the results of the 100 percent inspection in some way so that it would indicate whether or not the process remained stable. As will be seen shortly, the method devised by Walter Shewhart takes advantage of the fact that only *samples* of output are needed. Using Shewhart's method, a large portion of the 100 percent inspection data would be discarded as unnecessary for our SQC purposes. (Bear in mind that we are discussing here only the monitoring of a process. When bad parts must be sorted out, 100 percent inspection is necessary.)

Two fundamentally different measuring procedures can be used. These are:

1.   *Classification by variables,* where scaled measures along a continuum are used (e.g., 2.05 pounds, 7.03426 inches, etc.). We can measure length, weight, temperature, impact strength, dielectric strength, etc., in such a way. The fineness (or grossness) of the units of measure is related to the quality specifications for output.

2.   *Classification by attributes,* where the output is sorted into only two classes—i.e., accepted or rejected. We get this type of result from a "go—no go" inspection system. Defects (causing rejection) arc those measurements outside the range of values that are preset as acceptable. Under this classification, process quality is judged by the number or percentage of defects in a sample.

STATISTICAL QUALITY CONTROL—THE THEORY

Walter Shewhart observed that if an assignable cause entered a process, it would create a change, and that to spot this change a record of output quality would be required over time. He went on to consider that *small samples taken at proper intervals would yield just the kind of information needed to detect the presence of an assignable cause of variation.*

The process output shown below illustrates the nature of one sampling procedure. Here, the sequence of output is unit x_1 followed by x_2 followed by x_3, and so on.

Subgroup Sample I	Interval Between Samples	Subgroup Sample II	Interval Between Samples
$x_1 \, x_2 \, x_3$	$x_4 \, x_5 \, x_6 \, x_7$	$x_8 \, x_9 \, x_{10}$	$x_{11} \, x_{12} \ldots$ etc.

Let us assume that each x_i (i = output number) is measured on a continuous scale, and so we are working here with *classification by variables.* A subgroup size of three has been chosen for this hypothetical case. The interval between samples has been selected to equal four—again, purely hypothetically. We shall return at a later point to consider how to choose a subgroup size, as well as the interval between subgroups.

Following Shewhart's method, the *average value* of each subgroup ($\bar{x}_i$) is obtained, i.e.,

$$\bar{x}_I = (x_1 + x_2 + x_3)/3$$
$$\bar{x}_{II} = (x_8 + x_9 + x_{10})/3$$

.

.

.

etc.

Also, the variation *within* each subgroup is measured as a range, R. This range measure, R, is simply the largest value of x in the subgroup minus the smallest value of x in the subgroup. Thus, $R = x_{MAX} - x_{MIN}$. If $x_1 = 5$, $x_2 = 4$, and $x_3 = 2$, then $R_I = (5 - 2) = 3$.

When $x_8 = 6$, $x_9 = 3$, and $x_{10} = 8$, what is R_{II}? (Correct, $R_{II} = 5$.)

The theory of statistical quality control recognizes that the variation observed within *each subgroup* (R_I, R_{II}, . . . , *etc.*) *can be statistically related to the variation* between *the averages of the subgroups—assuming that the process is stable.* Note: $\bar{\bar{x}}$ (called the *grand mean*) is the average of the averages; that is, $\bar{\bar{x}} = (\bar{x}_I + \bar{x}_{II} + \ldots + \bar{x}_N)/N$. Then this kind of between group variability is measured by $(\bar{x}_I - \bar{\bar{x}})$, $(\bar{x}_{II} - \bar{\bar{x}})$, and so on.[*]

The two types of variability (within and between) are related when the process is stable. When it is not stable, the well-known statistical relationship (to be described shortly) will not hold. *Note that the observations taken within the subgroup are relatively close together, whereas in the interval between subgroups, sufficient time elapses to allow an assignable cause to have entered the system. The subgroup size is made small enough so that there is a good deal of homogeneity among these subgroup observations. In a stable system, this same homogeneity will be reflected in the intersubgroup behavior.*

Let's look at this theory in another way. Stability (in one of its most basic forms) means that a distribution such as the one shown below is stationary; in other words, over time it neither moves around nor changes shape. More advanced concepts of stability permit certain regular changes to occur—but we shall not deal with these more complex systems here, as our present definition covers the greatest percentage of all SQC applications.

The distribution below reflects the direct measure of individual parts for some particular characteristic (in this case, weight). It is called the distribution of the *parent population.* There are several ways to describe this distribution. We have discussed two.

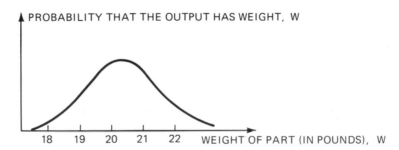

The average (or mean) locates the central tendency on a scale (such as weight). Pronounced shifts in the mean indicate a changing distribution and instability.

We have looked at range as a measure of spread, dispersion, or variability in a distribution. Pronounced changes in range indicate changes in variability, and this indicates a change in the shape of the distribution—that is, instability.

There is another measure of variability, and this is called variance.

---

[*]For the precise form of the measure that is used, see the definition of $\sigma_{\bar{x}}$ that is given later.

VARIANCE

Variance is a measure frequently used to describe the variability of a set of numbers. It is often represented by the Greek letter sigma, σ, where sigma is squared, σ^2.

Consider two groups of men whose average weight is 160 pounds. Let the groups be composed as follows:

Individual (i)	Group 1	Group 2
i = 1	140 pounds	120 pounds
i = 2	150 "	140 "
i = 3	160 "	160 "
i = 4	170 "	180 "
i = 5	180 "	200 "
Total group weight	800 pounds	800 pounds

The average weight in both groups is the same, 800/5, which equals 160 pounds. But clearly, there is something different about the two groups. The variability of the second group is greater than that of the first. We would certainly like to express this fact, and to do so effectively we can use σ^2.

To calculate variance, we subtract the average ($\overline{x}$) from all numbers x_i ($x_i - \overline{x}$); squaring each of these subtractions, $(x_i - \overline{x})^2$, to eliminate all negative numbers, since a minus number times a minus number is a plus number; multiplying each square by its associated probability, $(x_i - \overline{x})^2 p_i$; and then summing across all i numbers—for instance, $(x_1 - \overline{x})^2 p_1 + (x_2 - \overline{x})^2 p_2 + \ldots + (x_i - \overline{x})^2 p_i$.

To use the formulation above, we should recognize that the probabilities here are all equal, and therefore, 1/5. So we get:

For Group 1:

i	p_i	$(x_i - \overline{x})$	$(x_i - \overline{x})^2$	$p_i(x_i - \overline{x})^2$
1	1/5	−20	400	80
2	1/5	−10	100	20
3	1/5	0	0	0
4	1/5	+10	100	20
5	1/5	+20	400	80
			Total =	$200 = \sigma^2$

For Group 2:

i	p_i	$(x_i - \overline{x})$	$(x_i - \overline{x})^2$	$p_i(x_i - \overline{x})^2$
1	1/5	−40	1600	320
2	1/5	−20	400	80
3	1/5	0	0	0
4	1/5	+20	400	80
5	1/5	+40	1600	320
			Total =	$800 = \sigma^2$

Group 2's larger variance indicates that this group is less homogeneous than Group 1.

Note: Another measure of variability is the *standard deviation,* which is the square root of the variance (i.e., σ). In the example above, the standard deviation of Group 1 is $\sqrt{200} = 14.14$; that of Group 2 is $\sqrt{800} = 28.28$. (One can consider a range for each group within which some percentage of the total group falls. For example, a one-sigma range would be the average value plus and the average value minus one standard deviation.)

To illustrate the point above, let us consider the well-known *normal distribution,* which has 68 percent of its area falling within a plus and minus one sigma range.

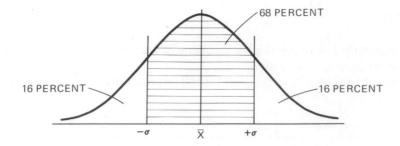

If the scale is in terms of weight, then $\bar{x}$ is the average weight; 16 percent of the units have a weight in excess of $\bar{x} + \sigma$; 16 percent of the units have weights of less than $\bar{x} - \sigma$. Note the table below, which gives some additional values for the normal distribution.

Number of Standard Deviations for the Specification ± of the Range	Probability That the Observed Measure Will Fall within the Specified Range
1.0σ	68%
1.6σ	90%
2.0σ	95%
3.0σ	99.8%

Returning to the previous data:

For Group 1:

$$160 - 14.14 = 145.86 \text{ LOWER LEVEL OF RANGE}$$
$$160 + 14.14 = 174.14 \text{ UPPER LEVEL OF RANGE}$$

This range includes three of the five individuals of Group 1, or 60 percent of the total group.

And for Group 2:

$$160 - 28.28 = 131.72 \text{ LOWER LEVEL}$$
$$160 + 28.28 = 188.28 \text{ UPPER LEVEL}$$

This range includes three of the five individuals of Group 2, or 60 percent of the total group.

To underscore the importance of variability, remember that a person who cannot swim can drown trying to cross a stream that *averages* two inches in depth, because for, say, ten feet of its width, it is over that person's head.

TEST FOR STABILITY OR CONTROL

When assignable causes enter the system, various kinds of change can occur in the parent distribution. It could shift to the right or to the left or both, and a change of shape might occur as well; that is, it could spread out or peak. Then we would not have the stationary parent population that we require for stability. To detect the existence of changes, we measure *within-group* variability and compare it to the *between-group* variability. Let us explore the reasons that make this comparison significant.

First, the within-group variability (R) of each subgroup is a *sample measure* of the variability of the parent population.

Second, the sample means, $\bar{x}_{\text{I}}$, $\bar{x}_{\text{II}}$, and so on, have a distribution of their own. The diagram below shows that *the distribution of the sample means is narrower than that of the parent population.*

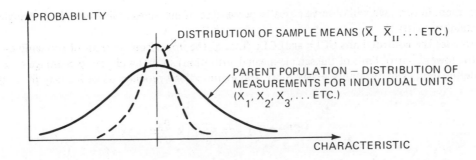

Third, the relation between the variability (spread) of a stable (stationary) parent distribution and that of the sample means is well known. It is:

$$\sigma_{\overline{x}} = \sigma_x / \sqrt{n}$$

where $\sigma_{\overline{x}}$ = the standard deviation of the distribution of the

sample means (It is measured by $\sqrt{\sum_{j}^{N}(\overline{x}_j - \overline{\overline{x}})^2 / N.}$)

σ_x = the standard deviation of the parent population

distribution (It is measured by $\sqrt{\sum_{i}^{n}(x_i - \overline{x})^2 / n.}$)

n = the number of observations included in a subgroup.

N = the number of subgroup sample means that are calculated

$\overline{x}_j$ = the mean of the subgroup

x_i = the individual reading

Clearly, if n = 1, then $\sqrt{n}$ = 1, and the two distributions would be identical—*if* the parent distribution is stable over time.

Fourth, a good test for stability results when we create *control limits* that are located some given number of standard deviations away from the average value of the distribution. We use the distribution of the sample means, but base our control limits on the variability observed *within* the subgroups.

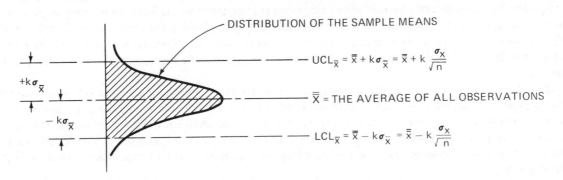

(The cross-hatched area of the sample-mean distribution shows the preselected percentage of all $\overline{x}$ values that we expect to observe within the range, as we collect actual data from the subgroup observations. If we observe less than this percentage, then, in turn, we will observe a greater percentage of measures falling outside the range—indicating that a lack of stability exists.)

We can now set the control limits $UCL_{\overline{x}}$ and $LCL_{\overline{x}}$ (that is, the upper control limit of the sample-mean distribution and the lower control limit of the sample-mean distribution) so that a chosen percentage of $\overline{x}$ observations might fall inside the limits when stability exists. Statistical methodology provides us with a way to set the control limits:

$$UCL_{\overline{x}} = \overline{\overline{x}} + k\sigma_{\overline{x}} = \overline{\overline{x}} + k\,\frac{\sigma_x}{\sqrt{n}}$$

$$LCL_{\overline{x}} = \overline{\overline{x}} - k\sigma_{\overline{x}} = \overline{\overline{x}} - k\,\frac{\sigma_x}{\sqrt{n}}$$

When a subgroup value of $\overline{x}$ is calculated and found to lie outside these control limits, the monitor then transmits to the controller a signal that is interpreted as an emergency condition.

The control limits can be moved in and out. Their distance from $\overline{x}$ is a managerial decision that recognizes the trade-off between the increased protection afforded by tighter control limits and the costs of looking for trouble (assignable causes) more frequently when none are present. Referring to a previous table, we note that if k is equal to 1, then 68 percent of all $\overline{x}$ observations should lie within the control limits. This would mean that 32 out of 100 out-of-control signals could be attributable to chance cause. When k = 1.6, 90 percent of the observations should lie within the control limits. If k = 2, 95 percent qualify, and when k = 3, we expect that 99.8 percent of all $\overline{x}$ observations will fall within the control limits. These statements apply if the *distribution of the sample means* is normal, bell-shaped, or similar in appearance to the distribution shown on page 164. Shewhart showed, however, that even if the parent population is not normal, the *means* of the subgroup samples drawn from that distribution will be close enough to normal so that our statistical considerations apply.

The common practice is to use two or three sigmas in setting control limits. Using one-sigma limits results in too many false alarms, since about 32% of the observations would be normally outside this limit, without *any assignable causes present.*

CONTROL CHARTS FOR VARIABLES

The control chart is a device for monitoring the process. It is so designed that most deviations will be accepted without sending a signal for corrective action to the controller. Only when the statistical assumption mentioned above (concerning the nature of variation within subgroups as compared to variation between subgroups from a stable system) appears to be violated does a corrective call signal emanate from the control chart. In other words, *as long as chance cause seems to be operating, the system does not respond. However, when an event occurs that has a low probability of happening in a purely chance-cause system, then the emergency (out-of-control) alarm sounds.*

Since we are working with statistical systems, it is necessary that occasionally an event will occur that falsely signals the presence of an assignable cause. There are obvious costs for going on a wild-goose chase, and we want to know how often that will happen (on the average) with any particular set of control rules. By means of k, we can adjust the sensitivity of the control system so it is properly responsive in accord with the economic realities of the comparative penalties. (The same can be said for adjusting the responsiveness of a temperature or smoke-sensitive sprinkler system.)

Using an example, let us see how this works. A shampoo manufacturer collects the following data concerning the contents in net ounces of 20 of his bottles of shampoo.

Subgroup					$\bar{x}$	$\bar{R}$
I	6.06	6.20	6.04	6.10	6.10	0.16
II	6.10	5.95	5.98	6.05	6.02	0.15
III	6.03	5.90	5.95	6.00	5.97	0.13
IV	6.03	6.05	6.10	5.94	6.03	0.16
V	6.12	6.40	6.20	6.00	6.18	0.40
					30.30	1.00

He then derives the grand mean $\bar{\bar{x}}$ and the average range $\bar{R}$.

$$\bar{\bar{x}} = \frac{30.30}{5} = 6.06 \qquad\qquad \bar{R} = \frac{1.00}{5} = 0.20$$

Since, for convenience of computation, we are using R instead of σ, we must convert our measures of R to σ. The conversion factors relating R and σ have been tabled and are widely available.[*] We call the conversion factor the A_2 factor when three sigma limits are used—that is, k = 3 and $k\sigma = 3\sigma$. The A_2 factor changes according to the number of observations that are made for a subgroup. Thus, if the subgroup size, n (the number of observations), is four, as in the example above, then A_2 = 0.73. The table given below presents some typical values for A_2 (and also for D_3 and D_4, which we shall turn to later).

Subgroup Size n	A_2	D_3	D_4
2	1.88	0	3.27
3	1.02	0	2.57
4	0.73	0	2.28
5	0.58	0	2.11
6	0.48	0	2.00
7	0.42	0.08	1.92
8	0.37	0.14	1.86
9	0.34	0.18	1.82
10	0.31	0.22	1.78
12	0.27	0.28	1.72
15	0.22	0.35	1.65
20	0.18	0.41	1.59

THE $\bar{x}$ CHART

The way in which we use A_2 is quite straightforward. We have:

$$A_2\bar{R} = k\sigma_{\bar{x}} = 3\sigma_{\bar{x}} = 3\,\frac{\sigma_x}{\sqrt{n}}$$

Therefore, for three sigma limits:

$$UCL_{\bar{x}} = \bar{\bar{x}} + A_2\bar{R}$$
$$LCL_{\bar{x}} = \bar{\bar{x}} - A_2\bar{R}$$

[**]See, for example, Martin K. Starr, *Production Management: Systems and Synthesis* (Englewood Cliffs, N.J.: Prentice-Hall, 1972), p. 509.

Accordingly, the shampoo manufacturer derives these results:

$$UCL_{\bar{x}} = 6.06 + (0.73)(0.20) = 6.206$$
$$LCL_{\bar{x}} = 6.06 - (0.73)(0.20) = 5.914$$

The $\bar{x}$ chart is constructed accordingly, and all the $\bar{x}$ values are plotted on it.

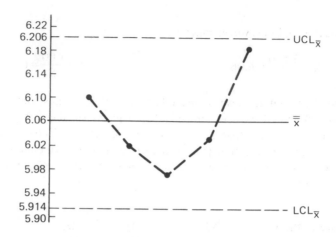

No points have fallen outside the control limits, so we can assume that the process is a stable one (at least with respect to averages). Of course, the number of samples is absurdly small. Since three sigma limits have been used, 99.8 percent of all observations should fall within the limits—assuming that the process is stable. This means that in one out of every 500 samples, we can expect to ring the emergency bell even though no emergency exists at all.

THE R CHART

Another kind of control chart for variables exists as a companion to the $\bar{x}$ chart. It is a chart that controls on variability. *Sometimes, an assignable cause creates no shift in the process average, but a change in the variability of the parent population takes place.* We turn to the R chart to help us detect this.

The control limit formulas are as follows:

$$UCL_R = D_4\bar{R}$$
$$LCL_R = D_3\bar{R}$$

The shampoo manufacturer would determine his control chart parameters:

$$\bar{R} = 0.20, D_3 \ (n = 4) = 0, D_4 \ (n = 4) = 2.28$$
$$UCL_R = (2.28)(0.20) = 0.456$$
$$LCL_R = (0.00)(0.20) = 0.000$$

The R chart is constructed, and all R values derived from the sample subgroups are plotted.

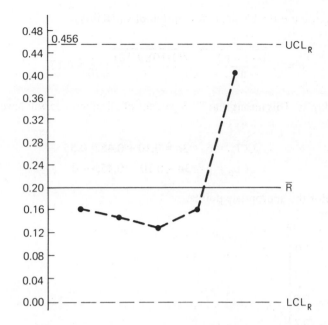

Again, no points are out of control, but we don't particularly like the configuration. There is a run of 4 points below the average and then a quite substantial jump. We shall need many more samples before we can really tell what's going on. It has not been our intention to concentrate on the example here, but rather to provide a framework for explaining the construction of the $\bar{x}$ and R charts. In certain cases, only an $\bar{x}$ chart might be used. Far more uncommon, only an R chart would be employed. Once the data for control by variables has been collected, it is not much more costly to construct the two charts, $\bar{x}$ and R, and use them both.

THE p CHART (FOR ATTRIBUTES)

Monitoring by variables is generally quite a bit more expensive than by attributes. Not all circumstances warrant the precision of exact measures along a continuum. Then a p chart[*] would suffice.

With p charts, the inspection procedure is less expensive, and the p chart is simpler to maintain. Let us return to the shampoo manufacturer to illustrate what is involved. First, presume that he uses a scale that does not weigh each bottle but merely says *accept* or *reject* according to the following rule: Accept when net ounces are *equal to or less than* 6.20 or *greater than* 5.92; that is; 5.92 < accept when net ounces are ⩽ 6.20. We now rework our previous data into these terms.

Subgroup	Number Inspected	Number Rejected	p
I	4	0	0
II	4	0	0
III	4	1	0.25
IV	4	0	0
V	4	1	0.25
TOTALS	20	2	

Whence $\bar{p} = \dfrac{2}{20} = 0.10$

[*]Where $p = \dfrac{\text{number rejected}}{\text{number inspected}}.$

For the p chart computations, we use the binomial description of variability:

$$\sigma = \sqrt{\frac{\overline{p}\,(1-\overline{p})}{n}} = \sqrt{\frac{(1/10)(9/10)}{4}} = \frac{3}{20} = 0.15$$

Let us use three sigma limits. This means that 99.8 percent of all subgroups will have a p value that falls within the control-limit bonnds.

$$UCL_p = \overline{p} + 3\sigma = 0.10 + 0.45 = 0.55$$
$$LCL_p = \overline{p} - 3\sigma = 0.10 - 0.45, \text{ or } 0$$

We construct our chart and plot the appropriate points.

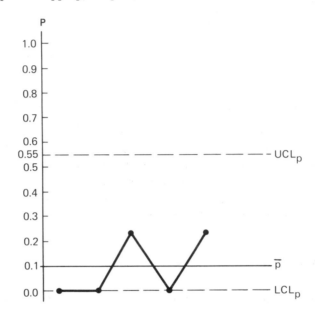

According to this p-type control chart, the shampoo manufacturer has a stable filling process. We can clearly observe that a change in the definition of rejects will affect all the parameters of the chart and may indicate an unstable process according to the new definition. It is conceivable, too, that a process may produce a high rate of rejects (dependent on tolerances and specifications) and yet be in control. This might be because the control limits are outside the design tolerances.

STARTING UP

There is a real difference between monitoring a system that is already stable and bringing a new (or modified) process under control. As a rule of thumb, we can (roughly) indicate that at least 20 subgroup readings are required for any one of these charts before the first set of parameters can be calculated and an initial chart set up. Again, as a rough guide, the majority of start-ups will indicate instability. After the process is studied and things are changed, new parameters are calculated, and this continues until the stable pattern is achieved. From there on, monitoring the stable process prevails.

Great diagnostic ability is required to read control charts and to be able to determine from the charts what has happened. Yet people with such abilities exist. Experienced practitioners of SQC have learned that certain patterns mean specific assignable causes are present.

The success of these control procedures depends in large part on the choice of appropriate subgroup sizes and the spacing between. There is no specific set of rules. The choice relates to the technology of the process. But we can say the following kinds of things:

> The strength of Shewhart's method lies in the fact that the *information of sequence* is not lost, and that *trends* can be seen.
>
> The control chart acts as an *early warning system,* much as radar provides advance warning of things to come.
>
> *The subgroup size must be* made small enough so that the output during that interval is very likely to be *homogeneous.*
>
> If the process undergoes rapid changes, then subgroup sizes of even less than 4 may well be warranted. The obvious advantage of large subgroup sizes is that the A_2 factor gets considerably smaller and so the spread of the control limits is reduced.
>
> *In all sampling procedures, large samples have greater reliability than do small ones.* Furthermore, it is usually less expensive to take a larger sample with greater spacing between samples.

The interval between subgroups should be made large enough so that a new assignable factor in the system can be detected. If these intervals are too small (relative to the nature of the process), successive samples will not be measuring potentially different things but will be much the same as a single homogeneous subgroup. If assignable effects move in slowly, making their presence known in a gradual way, then longer intervals between subgroups are desired. On the other hand, the disadvantage of long intervals resides in the fact that an assignable cause will not be spotted as quickly as it might have been if the interval had been smaller. Substantial penalties may well be the fruit of such delays.

INSTRUCTIONS FOR PREPARING THE CASE

Martronics, Inc.

Read the case. Place yourself in the role of Henry Peters. You have received the following memorandum that you must answer.

To: Henry Peters
From: W. Zander

The TX 10L 205 is still a major problem. I hope you will have recommendations for me soon. Specifically:

1.   Should we try to cancel production of this item? Our customer is important to us, as he buys many other items, but we can't afford the losses we have experienced on this product. Our costs are 20% higher than originally estimated—we must roll them back within 2 months. I hope SQC is the answer.

2.   Al Wormser wants to move the costs of his inspectors to your budget. Please give me your thoughts and the basis for your conclusions. Maybe eliminating the 100% inspection altogether will help reduce our costs, but what will this action do to the quality of outgoing product?

Note: Problem-solving exercises have been included.

Decision Process

CASE

Martronics, Inc.

Bob Martin had little technical training but a great deal of acumen, administrative ability, and knowledge of how to attract capital. By his 40th birthday, he was president of Martin Radio, Inc., with central offices located in Pittsburgh, Pennsylvania. Martin owned over 80% of his company's voting stock.

Martin Radio was a large wholesaler of radios and not a manufacturer. The consumer was not aware of this fact, since a complete line of radios was marketed under the brand name, Martronic. The line was made for Martin Radio by the Apex Corporation, based in Chicago.

In the 1940s, interest in television began to grow. For Apex, the move into television sets was a natural. And by 1945, Martin Radio had become the exclusive East Coast representative for Apex, which was fast becoming one of the largest manufacturers of television sets in the country.

At that time, it was quite apparent to everyone—including the consumer—that television sets were poorly designed. They broke down often and required far more service than Bob Martin thought desirable for the continued growth of this infant industry. Therefore, in 1950, he employed a group of electronic engineers to design a better TV that would be competitive in price.

In 1952, Martin thought he was ready to embark on the manufacture of TV sets. He formed a new company, called Martronics, Inc., and named Bill Zander, head of the original design group, to be vice-president and executive officer.

With help from a local bank and municipal cooperation, a plant was built in an industrial park on the outskirts of Pittsburgh. Martin Radio had the exclusive franchise for distributing all of Martronics' production.. The television sets that Martronics produced were well accepted by the market. By 1959, the brand was in national distribution. Even before this, Martronics had begun to move into other related lines.

The company grew swiftly under its aggressive management. It now has plants located in Pittsburgh, Dayton, Ohio, and Boca Raton, Florida. The line has been expanded to include high-fidelity amplifiers, pre-amps, AM and FM tuners, phonographs, specialized stereophonic equipment, and a growing new line of color television sets. About 30% of present sales volume is obtained from military products. These include fire-control systems, communication systems, and satellite components.

The Dayton plant was established in 1962, as a result of the award of substantial government contracts. Eventually, all government products were designed in Dayton and were then manufactured in whichever of the company's plants seemed the most suitable. The Dayton plant had annual sales last year of $5 million, over 50% of which was from government work. Boca Raton had an average of 80% military work, while less than 10% of the Pittsburgh plant's output was devoted to military work.

When Martronics lost a considerable amount of money on a just-completed, large space-program contract, Zander brought in the firm of Zift Consultants to track down why. Mr. Zift soon reported, "High scrap losses and large inspection expenses have been a sinkhole for costs. Your corporate practice of no formalized inspection during production and 100% inspection of all finished product is a practice that was obsolete years ago. You had trouble on this job because you sold a contract to specifications that your machinery couldn't produce. Our chief recommendation is that you establish SQC as soon as possible. Start with the product now giving you the greatest quality difficulty."

Zander quickly took action. He identified the high-volume transformer (TX 10L 205) as his leading trouble spot. He persuaded Henry Peters, head of quality control in a competing firm, to come to work for Martronics.

When Peters reported, Zander instructed him, "You have a blank check to install SQC. Start with transformer TX 10L 205, made in Dayton. Our costs are too high for the price we are charging. Our customer relations are bad, as we are not meeting delivery schedules, and our returns are high. We have adequate production capacity—while we have been using 4 winding machines, they are only used for 4 hours a day. You will work closely with Al Wormser, plant manager at Dayton, but you will report directly to me—you are on my staff. This contract is sizeable, so act fast. I shall be interested in your initial reaction."

After a physical observation of the transformer manufacturing process, Peters searched for all available historical data on transformer TX 10L 205. Of greatest interest to him were the data that had been recorded for the 100% inspection performed for the previous year. By using random selection, Peters chose 20 dates within the year and 10 observations for each date. He was ready to take his first cut at analysis.

Transformers' Rating
(An Impedance Index)

Subgroup	Date	Observations									
1	1/16	31	36	43	41	26	38	28	22	35	36
2	1/20	36	38	42	40	35	32	28	26	30	36
3	2/15	36	35	37	38	34	33	35	37	38	39
4	3/6	32	33	35	37	38	35	34	36	37	38
5	3/28	30	32	33	34	36	39	40	37	38	36
6	3/31	31	38	37	37	36	35	35	26	35	36
7	4/5	36	36	32	30	32	33	35	38	36	37
8	4/8	43	42	37	35	33	41	40	38	37	34
9	4/21	26	38	35	32	34	33	38	35	36	39
10	5/10	32	33	35	34	36	39	40	36	37	38
11	5/31	26	40	37	33	30	32	35	38	35	38
12	6/7	43	42	37	35	33	41	40	38	37	34
13	7/8	41	40	38	37	34	37	30	35	32	34
14	8/27	33	34	37	32	37	35	35	37	37	38
15	9/30	36	37	34	39	38	38	38	34	34	39
16	10/5	31	36	43	26	32	42	40	34	37	36
17	10/17	31	37	37	35	30	32	35	36	37	39
18	11/6	32	38	37	33	40	42	40	34	37	36
19	12/3	34	34	37	32	37	35	35	37	38	34
20	12/28	38	26	34	37	36	24	36	37	38	36

Note: The tolerance limits have been specified as $33 \leqslant TL \leqslant 39$. This information can be useful in a number of ways, not the least of which involves the construction of a p chart.

PROBLEM-SOLVING EXERCISES

Martronics, Inc.

To save you time on calculations, we have prepared a programmed series of problems for this unit, which will help you to solve the case. There are three parts to the exercises. If you solve Question 1 correctly in Parts A, B, and C, you may stop figuring and just look at the computations as done by us, since you have shown that you understand the method and the problem. If you can't do Question 1 correctly, look at the solution, try to find your mistake, and go on to Question 2. Continue this process until you have solved at least one problem in all parts correctly. Do not look at the solutions except to check yourself.

PART A

Question 1. For each of the subgroups 1-5, calculate the sample mean, $\overline{x}$.

You will find the solution to this problem on page 181.

Question 2. For each of the subgroups 6-10, calculate the sample mean, $\bar{x}$.

You will find the solution to this problem on page 181.

Question 3. For each of the subgroups 11-15, calculate the sample mean, $\bar{x}$.

You will find the solution to this problem on page 181.

Question 4. For each of the subgroups 16-20, calculate the sample mean, $\overline{x}$.

You will find the solution to this problem on pages 181, 182.

PART B

Question 1. For each of the subgroups 1-5, calculate the sample range, R.

You will find the solution to this problem on page 182.

Question 2. For each of the subgroups 6-10, calculate the sample range, R.

You will find the solution to this problem on page 182.

Question 3. For each of the subgroups 11-15, calculate the sample range, R.

You will find the solution to this problem on page 182.

Question 4.   For each of the subgroups 16-20, calculate the sample range, R.

You will find the solution to this problem on pages 182, 183.

PART C

Question 1.   For each of the subgroups 1-5, calculate the percent defective, p.

You will find the solution to this problem on page 183.

Question 2.   For each of the subgroups 6-10, calculate the percent defective, p.

You will find the solution to this problem on page 183.

Question 3.   For each of the subgroups 11-15, calculate the percent defective, p.

You will find the solution to this problem on page 183.

Question 4.   For each of the subgroups 16-20, calculate the percent defective, p.

You will find the solution to this problem on page 183.

Solution to Part A, Question 1:

According to the formula: $\overline{x}_I = (x_1 + x_2 + x_3 + \ldots + x_{10})/10$

Subgroup	Total Observations	Sample Mean $\overline{x}$
1	336	336/10 = 33.6
2	343	343/10 = 34.3
3	362	362/10 = 36.2
4	355	355/10 = 35.5
5	355	355/10 = 35.5

If you have completed the calculations correctly, you may read the solutions to the other questions in Part A and go on to Part B, Question 1. If you have not completed them correctly, go on to Part A, Question 2.

Solution to Part A, Question 2:

Subgroup	Total Observations	Sample Mean $\overline{x}$
6	346	346/10 = 34.6
7	345	34.5
8	380	38
9	346	34.6
10	360	36

If you have completed the calculations correctly, go on to Part B, Question 1. If you have not completed them correctly, go on to Part A, Question 3.

Solution to Part A, Question 3:

Subgroup	Total Observations	Sample Mean $\overline{x}$
11	344	344/10 = 34.4
12	380	38
13	358	35.8
14	355	35.5
15	367	36.7

If you have completed the calculations correctly, go on to Part B, Question 1. If you have not completed them correctly, go on to Part A, Question 4.

Solution to Part A, Question 4:

Subgroup	Total Observations	Sample Mean $\overline{x}$
16	357	357/10 = 35.7
17	349	34.9
18	369	36.9
19	353	35.3
20	342	34.2

Now go on to Part B, Question 1.

Solution to Part B, Question 1:

According to the equation: $R = x_{MAX} - x_{MIN}$

Subgroup	Sample Range R
1	43 − 22 = 21
2	42 − 26 = 16
3	39 − 33 = 6
4	38 − 32 = 6
5	40 − 30 = 10

If you have completed the calculations correctly, you may read solutions to the other questions in Part B and go on to Part C, Question 1. If you have not completed them correctly, go on to Part B, Question 2.

Solution to Part B, Question 2:

Subgroup	Sample Range R
6	12
7	8
8	10
9	13
10	8

If you have completed the calculations correctly, you may go on to Part C, Question 1. If you have not completed them correctly, go on to Part B, Question 3.

Solution to Part B, Question 3:

Subgroup	Sample Range R
11	14
12	10
13	11
14	6
15	5

If you have completed the calculations correctly, you may go on to Part C, Question 1. If you have not completed them correctly, go on to Part B, Question 4.

Solution to Part B, Question 4:

Subgroup	Sample Range R
16	17
17	9
18	10
19	6
20	14

Now go on to Part C, Question 1.

Solution to Part C, Question 1:

Subgroup	# Inspected	# Defective	p
1	10	6	.60
2	10	6	.60
3	10	0	0
4	10	1	.10
5	10	3	.30

If you have completed the calculations correctly, you may read the solution to the other problems in Part C. This is the end of the exercises for you. If you have not completed the calculations correctly, go on to Part C, Question 2.

Solution to Part C, Question 2:

Subgroup	p
6	.20
7	.30
8	.40
9	.20
10	.20

If you have completed the calculations correctly, you have reached the end of the exercises. If you have not completed them correctly, go on to Part C, Question 3.

Solution to Part C, Question 3:

Subgroup	p
11	.40
12	.40
13	.40
14	.10
15	0

If you have completed the calculations correctly, you have reached the end of the exercises. If you have not completed them correctly, go on to Part C, Question 4.

Solution to Part C, Question 4:

Subgroup	p
16	.60
17	.30
18	.40
19	.10
20	.20

Unit 10

Systems and Subsystems

> The *systems approach* to a problem requires that *all related* elements be studied together. The system must be optimized as an *integrated whole,* or at least with a full awareness of the totality.

A system is frequently broken down into parts; then *each part* is studied and optimized in isolation from the other parts. While this approach yields a set of optimal *subsystem* solutions, it is most important to note that *often a very poor total system's performance results when the optimal subsystems are recombined.*

If a total systems approach is to be effective, you must understand and properly use the concepts of analysis and synthesis. Analysis is the taking apart; synthesis is the putting back together.

Analysis requires division, segmentation, and fractionation. The inspection of each segment is followed by whatever steps are deemed necessary for improvement.

Synthesis is integration and combination. It requires the judicious development of appropriate conditions for togetherness.

Improvement should be sought for the system and may be pursued on an individual or on a "team" basis. (If you think of teams and what it takes to play the game, you are closing in on the essence of the systems concept.)

Let us look at an abstract model of these considerations.

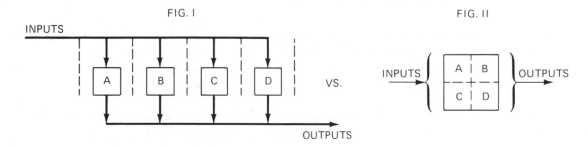

Assume that in Figure I, the cost performance of each subsystem (A, B, C, and D) is minimized. Do you think that this means that the total cost performance of the system (ABCD) illustrated by Figure II will be a minimum? Many managers do—but they are not necessarily right. One thing we can be sure of: As a problem moves up the organizational ladder toward the overall perspective of top management, the probability that the subsystem view is wrong increases rapidly. (The same type of reasoning applies to profits or benefits of any other kind as well.)

Why is this so? It is because interdependencies can exist between the parts that relate their individual performances to that of the whole in a *non-additive* fashion, such as 2 + 2 = 5. Impossible? Not at all! Consider the word *synergy*. According to the dictionary, *synergy* means "cooperative action of discrete agencies such that the total effect is greater than the sum of the two effects taken independently, as in the action of the mixtures of certain drugs."

Synergistic effects are generally a large *total system's* property. They may occur when the subsystems are individually optimal, but this is not required; it is not even usually the case.* If the components of a rocket were designed separately to achieve the best possible guidance system, best possible reentry system, best possible propulsion system, optimal carrier dynamics and in-space configuration, and so on, the result would be a "bird" that could not fly. The learning of that lesson has been very costly in well-known instances.

Until the total system's lesson has been learned, it is not unusual for the manager to think that the *best* possible performance for all individual components will produce a reasonable approximation to the best overall systems performance. But, under these circumstances, most highly interrelated and complex systems perform badly or fail.

We wish to underscore two major points that are often lost sight of: *First: Real, ongoing systems are seldom totally free and unconstrained with respect to all resource allocations and systems capabilities.* For example:

> Sufficient production capacity may not exist to make as much of each product as the distribution system can handle in a profitable fashion.
>
> There may not be enough telephone, airport, or electrical capacity to fully absorb peak loads. We could design the system for peak loads, but then what about the economics of the idle capacity that would exist the rest of the time?
>
> When multiple-item inventories must be carried, we may not have sufficient cash to invest in the optimal inventory quantities for each and every item.

Second: Optimal solutions can be obtained only when all the information necessary for optimality is available. Frequently, only partial information exists. Then, we cannot talk about a single optimal solution. We can't possibly know what it is. Rather, we have *many possible* optimals. The "true" one would be apparent *if* we had all the necessary information. Since we do not, we can only trace out the range of all possible optimals. Shortly, this concept will be amply illustrated. For the moment, let us call all members of the *set of potential optimals* the set of *rational* solutions.

> *We shall now show that the optimal inventory policies for each of a number of individual items may not be equivalent to the item inventory policies that are dictated by an overall optimal systems design. This is the most important lesson to be learned in this unit.*

DERIVATION OF THE OPTIMAL AVERAGE INVENTORY

Now we can turn to a specific situation that is designed to illustrate both the points that we mentioned above. Assume that inventory decisions must be made for three different items—I, II, and III. The purchase cost of each of these we shall denote by c_I, c_{II}, and c_{III}. The amounts ordered from the vendor for each item will be represented as x_I, x_{II}, and x_{III}. Then the average amount of cash that will be tied up in inventory for any item, i, will be $a_i = c_i x_i / 2$, i = I, II, or III.

For the three items, we obtain the total average dollar inventory as follows: $a_I + a_{II} + a_{III} = (c_I x_I / 2 + c_{II} x_{II} / 2 + c_{III} x_{III} / 2)$. In more general terms, this can be written:

$$A = \sum_{i=I}^{M} a_i = \sum_{i=I}^{M} c_i x_i / 2$$

---

*The sum over time of the parts of a Beethoven symphony is another good example of synergism.

where A = the *total average* dollar inventory invested in all (M) different items. (Σ is the Greek capital sigma, which stands for *sum*. The i = I below and M above the Σ tell us to add the average dollar inventories across all the items.)

The value of A will depend on the rules that are being used to determine the x's. Let's assume that *for each item's order quantity*, x_i is selected as the *optimal* number of units. This is, as we have previously seen:

$$x(OPT)_i = \sqrt{\frac{2z_i C_r}{c_i C_c}}$$

where z_i is the (annual) demand for the ith item, C_r is the cost of an order, and C_c is the carrying-cost rate expressed as a percent (per year).

Let's assume that the Beta Corporation has three items, as shown below, where C_r = \$4.00, and C_c = 9%, or .09 per year.

Item	c_i	z_i (per year)	$x(OPT)_i$	$c_i(X_i)$	a_i
1	\$ 2.00	800	188.6	377.2	188.6
2	\$ 8.00	450	70.7	565.6	282.8
3	\$100.00	49	6.6	660.0	330.0
				1602.8	801.4 A

Note: The fact that $x(OPT)_i$ values are fractional is no cause for concern. The fractional numbers should be used for all calculations in all cases. However, when the items can only be counted as integers, then orders should be placed for the rounded integer amount.

Then, *for each item,* the optimal average dollar inventory will be represented as $a(OPT)_i$. We wish to define A (the total average dollar inventory) in terms of the optimal item order quantities, $x(OPT)_i$, and the optimal item dollar average inventories, $a(OPT)_i$. We shall call this particular value of A, the optimal total average dollar inventory, A(OPT).

First, let us obtain the optimal value for each item.

Equation 1

$$a(OPT)_i = (c_i)(x(OPT)_i/2) = \frac{c_i}{2}\sqrt{\frac{2z_i C_r}{c_i C_c}} = \frac{1}{2}\sqrt{\frac{2z_i C_r c_i^2}{C_c c_i}} = \left(\sqrt{c_i z_i}\right)\left(\sqrt{\frac{C_r}{2C_c}}\right)$$

(You should study these calculations until you are certain that you understand them. The result they yield is most important.) We can then go on:

Equation 2

$$A(OPT) = \sum_i^M (c_i)(x(OPT)_i/2) = \sum_i^M \left(\sqrt{c_i z_i}\right)\left(\sqrt{\frac{C_r}{2C_c}}\right) = \sqrt{\frac{C_r}{2C_c}} \sum_i^M \sqrt{c_i z_i}$$

We note that $\sqrt{\frac{C_r}{2C_c}}$ is a constant and is not meant to be affected by the particular item, i, that we are considering.

For the Beta Corporation, we have $\sqrt{\frac{C_r}{2C_c}} = \sqrt{\frac{\$4}{.18}} = \$4.715$.

Item	$\sqrt{c_i z_i}$	$a(OPT)_i$	(Equation 1)
1	\$ 40	\$188.60	
2	60	282.90	
3	70	330.05	
	\$170	\$801.55	

Also, $A(OPT) = \$170(4.715) = \$801.55$ (Equation 2).

THE CRITICAL RATIO FOR ALLOCATING INVENTORY DOLLARS

The ratio $a(OPT)_i / A(OPT)$ *is highly useful.** *It describes the ratio of average dollars that should be invested in a particular item as compared to that of the* total *average dollar inventory investment.* This ratio (for any ith item) is:

Equation 3

$$\frac{a(OPT)_i}{A(OPT)} = \frac{\left(\sqrt{c_i z_i}\right)\left(\sqrt{\frac{C_r}{2C_c}}\right)}{\sqrt{\frac{C_r}{2C_c}} \; \overset{M}{\underset{i}{\Sigma}}\sqrt{c_i z_i}} = \frac{\sqrt{c_i z_i}}{\overset{M}{\underset{i}{\Sigma}}\sqrt{c_i z_i}}$$

We can appreciate the incisiveness of mathematics when we observe how many terms have been cancelled out and how pleasingly simple this final mathematical description has become.

Note in this equation that (1) $c_i z_i$ is the annual dollar volume for the ith item; (2) the ratio involves the square root of each item's (annual) dollar volume—i.e., $\sqrt{c_i z_i}$; (3) the denominator of the ratio is the sum of the square roots of annual dollar volume across all the items, *not* the square root of the sum of dollar volumes for all items; (4) neither the ordering cost, C_r, nor the carrying-cost rate, C_c, have to be known in order to establish this ratio in Equation 3; (5) generally, the information about c_i and z_i is well known or obtainable for all i items—z_i can be calculated from the stockcards, and c_i is available from the purchasing department records; (6) therefore, this ratio can usually be determined in practice.

For the Beta Corporation, the following calculations pertain at this point:

Item	$\sqrt{c_i z_i}$	Ratio
1	\$ 40	40/170 = .235
2	60	60/170 = .353
3	70	70/170 = .412
	\$170	

Assume, now, that we don't have A(OPT) dollars available to be invested (on the average) in inventory. (That would be \$801.55 for the Beta Corporation.) Instead, we must limit our total average dollar inventory to A dollars, where $A < A(OPT)$.** (Say that only \$600 is available to Beta, for example.) The obvious question is, How many dollars should be apportioned to *each* item's average inventory from the total of A dollars? There are alternative ways of arriving at an answer to this question:

Strategy A—not rational: Carry the optimal amounts, $a(OPT)_i$, for all i items that we consider important. Then cut back severely on the average dollar inventories of the remaining items. To do this, we would have to work back and forth with the numbers, adjusting the a_i's so that always $\overset{M}{\underset{i}{\Sigma}} a_i = A$. Then at the same time, the proportions allocated to each a_i must satisfy us.

*Equation 1 ÷ Equation 2.

**We are all familiar with cases where the controller announces that the dollars invested in inventory are too high. Consequently, the condition that we have just described is very real.

For the Beta Corporation, this strategy might yield these results:

Item	a_i	$a_i(\text{OPT})$
1	$188.60	$188.60
2	282.90	282.90
3	128.50	330.05
	$600.00	$801.55

Do you know why this is not the best that we can do?

Strategy B—rational: Let the constrained dollar ratios (based on A) follow the same pattern as the optimal ones (based on A(OPT)); that is:

Equation 4

$$\frac{a_i}{A} = \frac{a(\text{OPT})_i}{A(\text{OPT})} = \frac{\sqrt{c_i z_i}}{\overset{M}{\underset{i}{\Sigma}}\sqrt{c_i z_i}}$$

For the Beta Corporation, results of this approach are shown below under the "Rational" heading:

			Rational	Irrational	Optimal
Item	(Ratio × A)	=	a_i	a_i	a_i
1	.235 × 600	=	$141.00	$188.60	$188.60
2	.353 × 600	=	211.80	282.90	282.90
3	.412 × 600	=	247.20	128.50	330.05
			$600.00	$600.00	$801.55

Mathematical proof[*] exists that this rational procedure is the only one to follow under the circumstances where A, as specified by management, is less than A(OPT). If it turns out that A = A(OPT), then of course, a_i will be the optimal average dollar inventory for each item. As we proceed, we shall offer logical proof that the ratio rule above is rational and that no other rule can be rational.

To begin with, let us compare the total costs of the rational, irrational, and optimal policies as shown in the table above. We have:

$$TC_i = a_i C_c + \frac{z_i}{x_i} C_r \ (\text{where } x_i = \frac{2a_i}{c_i})$$

Rational (based on A = $600 and following the ratio rule):

$$TC_1 = (141)\ (.09) + (800/141)\ (4) = \$\ 35.39$$
$$TC_2 = (211.8)(.09) + (450/52.95)(4) = \$\ 53.06$$
$$TC_3 = (247.2)(.09) + (49/4.944)\ (4) = \$\ 61.89$$
$$\text{Total} = \overline{\$150.34}$$

Irrational (based on A = $600, but not following the ratio rule):

$$TC_1 = (188.6)\ (.09) + (800/188.6)\ (4) = \$\ 33.94$$
$$TC_2 = (282.9)\ (.09) + (450/70.725)(4) = \$\ 50.91$$
$$TC_3 = (128.5)\ (.09) + (49/2.57)\quad\ (4) = \$\ 87.83$$
$$\text{Total} = \overline{\$172.68}$$

[*]See M. Starr and D. Miller, *Inventory Control: Theory and Practice* (Englewood Cliffs, N.J.: Prentice-Hall, 1962), pp. 93-104.

Optimal (based on A = $801.55):

$$TC_1 = (188.6) \; (.09) + (800/188.6) \; (4) = \$ \; 33.94$$
$$TC_2 = (282.9) \; (.09) + (450/70.725)(4) = \$ \; 50.91$$
$$TC_3 = (330.05)(.09) + (49/6.60) \quad (4) = \$ \; 59.40$$
$$\text{Total} = \overline{\$144.25}$$

As we expected, the total cost of the optimal policy is lowest. Next in line is the rational policy, and then the irrational one.

INTERPRETATION OF THE RATIO

Remember that A(OPT) is based on all a(OPT)$_i$'s, and these in turn are formed from x(OPT)$_i$'s. The determination of x(OPT)$_i$'s requires *certain* knowledge of the costs, C_r and C_c; that is:

Equation 5

$$x(OPT)_i = \sqrt{\frac{2z_i C_r}{c_i C_c}} = \left(\sqrt{\frac{2z_i}{c_i}} \right) \left(\sqrt{\frac{C_r}{C_c}} \right) = \left(\sqrt{\frac{2z_i}{c_i}} \right) (k)$$

$$\text{where } k = \sqrt{C_r/C_c}$$

If C_r and/or C_c are *unknown* and cannot be obtained,[*] then we cannot derive a(OPT)$_i$ and we shall never know the appropriate value for A(OPT). Then, what we can do is the following:

1. Let the value of $k = \sqrt{C_r/C_c}$ vary. Choose, for example, r different estimates of k. Start with some small number for k and gradually increase it until the estimate is a large number.
2. For each hypothetical value of $k = \sqrt{C_r/C_c}$, obtain a *set* of x$_i$'s (one for each of the i items), where

$$x_i = \left(\sqrt{\frac{2z_i}{c_i}} \right) (k).$$

3. Using each of these x$_i$'s, calculate the equivalent a$_i$'s. You will have a *set* of a$_i$'s for each hypothetical value of $k = \sqrt{C_r/C_c}$.
4. Sum the a$_i$'s to yield A. There will be one value of A for each hypothetical setting of $k = \sqrt{C_r/C_c}$.

For each different estimate of k	We derive a set of x's	And then, a set of a's	The sum of the a's for each estimate of k produces a value of A

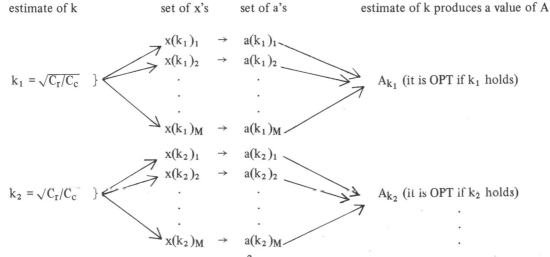

*This was not the case for the Beta Corporation, where $k = 6\frac{2}{3}$.

$$k_r = \sqrt{C_r/C_c} \quad \Big\}$$

$$
\begin{array}{ccc}
x(k_r)_1 & \rightarrow & a(k_r)_1 \\
x(k_r)_2 & \rightarrow & a(k_r)_2 \\
\cdot & & \cdot \\
\cdot & & \cdot \\
\cdot & & \cdot \\
x(k_r)_M & \rightarrow & a(k_r)_M
\end{array}
\qquad A_{k_r} \text{ (it is OPT if } k_r \text{ holds)}
$$

As an illustrative exercise, let us pretend that the Beta Corporation value of k equals 10 rather than 6 2/3 as was previously the case. Then:

$$x_1 = \left(\sqrt{\frac{2(800)}{2}} \right)(10) = 282.84 \rightarrow a_1 = 282.84$$

$$k = 10 \qquad x_2 = \left(\sqrt{\frac{2(450)}{8}} \right)(10) = 106.07 \rightarrow a_2 = 424.28 \qquad 1{,}202.12$$

$$x_3 = \left(\sqrt{\frac{2(49)}{100}} \right)(10) = 9.90 \rightarrow a_3 = 495.00$$

So, if k = 10, then A(OPT) = $1,202.12. And if k = 5, then A(OPT) = $601.08, which is very close to the constrained value of $600 that was previously assumed for our calculations. We may note that with k = 5, the indicated order quantities would be $x_1 = 141.42$, $x_2 = 53.04$, and $x_3 = 4.95$, which are very close to the results that were previously derived by means of the ratio. Clearly, *the management constraint on A that limits it to about $600 imputes a cost ratio for k that is approximately 5.*

If we knew the actual value of $k = \sqrt{C_r/C_c}$, we would choose the appropriate k and obtain the corresponding A(OPT). But if we assume that we don't know it, then what we have been doing is to derive the *set of all possible optimals. The "true" optimal must be one of them.* Taken together, all of them are the set of potential optimals. Any value of A that is chosen by management might be *the one.*

> *When the manager specifies a value for A, in effect he or she chooses (imputes) a value for the ratio of the costs that apply to the situation. The square root of the cost ratio is k. It is based on intuition and judgment concerning the total average dollar inventory that would be appropriate for the situation.*

THE CRITICAL RATIO FOR ALLOCATING THE NUMBER OF ORDERS

In a previous unit, we showed that as the number of orders increases in a given period of time, the average inventory decreases; and that the reverse is also true. We also showed that the mathematical model for the optimal order quantity was derived from an equation that included both carrying costs and ordering costs:

Total costs (per yr.) = Carrying costs (per yr.) + Ordering costs (per yr.)

or

$$TC = \frac{cx}{2}(C_c) + \frac{z}{x}(C_r)$$

which can be stated:

$$TC = aC_c + nC_r$$

For the ith item, this would be:

$$TC_i = a_i C_c + n_i C_r$$

where n_i = the number of orders (z_i/x_i) made in the given period of time.

Let us determine the optimal number of orders to be placed, $n(OPT)_i$, in the same way we have previously derived the optimal average dollar inventories, $a(OPT)_i$.

Equation 6

$$n(OPT)_i = \frac{z_i}{x(OPT)_i} = \frac{z_i}{\sqrt{\dfrac{2z_iC_r}{c_iC_c}}} = z_i\sqrt{\frac{c_iC_c}{2z_iC_r}} = \sqrt{\frac{c_iC_cz_i^2}{2z_iC_r}} = \left(\sqrt{\frac{C_c}{2C_r}}\right)\left(\sqrt{c_iz_i}\right)$$

The similarity to the result for $a(OPT)_i$ is striking. We can also obtain the expression for the total number of orders by summing across all items. This total number of orders in a given period of time will be called N.

$$N = \sum_i^M n_i = \sum_i^M (z_i/x_i)$$

And in turn,

$$N(OPT) = \sum_i^M n(OPT)_i = \sqrt{\frac{C_c}{2C_r}} \sum_i^M \sqrt{c_iz_i}$$

To return for a moment to the Beta Corporation, we would find:

Item	$\sqrt{c_iz_i}$	$n(OPT)_i$	(see Equation 6)
1	40	4.24	
2	60	6.36	
3	70	7.42	
	N(OPT) =	18.02	

where

$$\sqrt{\frac{C_c}{2C_r}} = \sqrt{\frac{.09}{\$8}} = .106$$

The ratio $n(OPT)_i/N(OPT)$ describes the allocation of the optimal total number of orders to each of the i = M items. Thus:

Equation 7

$$\frac{n(OPT)_i}{N(OPT)} = \frac{\left(\sqrt{\dfrac{C_c}{2C_r}}\right)\left(\sqrt{c_iz_i}\right)}{\left(\sqrt{\dfrac{C_c}{2Cr}}\right)\left(\sum_i^M \sqrt{c_iz_i}\right)} = \frac{\sqrt{c_iz_i}}{\sum_i^M \sqrt{c_iz_i}}$$

Let us use this formulation with our previously derived values for $n(OPT)_i$.

Item	$n(OPT)_i/N(OPT)$	=	$\sqrt{c_iz_i}/\sum_i^M \sqrt{c_iz_i}$	
1	4.24/18.02	=	40/170	ok
2	6.36/18.02	=	60/170	ok
3	7.42/18.02	=	70/170	ok

All the relations check out.

Now, as before, let us assume that we don't know the actual costs, C_r and C_c. Therefore, we can't determine N(OPT). Say we choose some total number of orders, N per year. How should these N orders be allocated to each item? The logical reply is to make use of the rational pattern based on the optimal ratio, as follows.

Equation 8

$$\frac{n_i}{N} = \frac{n(OPT)_i}{N(OPT)} = \frac{\sqrt{c_i z_i}}{\sum\limits_i^M \sqrt{c_i z_i}}$$

The same mathematical proofs are available[*] to show that this is the only correct relationship to use. If it turns out that the manager's estimate for N is equal to N(OPT), then each n_i will be the optimal number of orders. If not, the n_i's will at least be allocated in the proper, rational proportions.

We shall not repeat for N the full interpretation of the ratio (Equation 8), since it was given previously for A and the story remains the same. However, we do wish to point out that in addition to a rational set of A's, now there is also a rational set of N's.

EXERCISE

Assume that the costs are unknown and that the manager of the Beta Corporation has specified that the total number of orders for Items 1, 2, and 3 must not exceed 10 per year. How would you allocate the individual item orders? (The solution will be found at the end of the note.)

$$\frac{40}{170} = .2353 \qquad\qquad .2353(N) = .2353(10) = 2.353$$

$$\frac{60}{170} = .3529 \qquad\qquad .3529(N) = .3529(10) = 3.529$$

$$\frac{70}{170} = .4118 \qquad\qquad .4118(N) = .4118(10) = \underline{4.118}$$

$$10.000 = N \text{ orders/yr}$$

THE RATIONAL SET OF OPTIMAL (A $\times$ N)'s

Can we choose any A and any N and then allocate the a_i's and the n_i's in accord with the following?

$$a_i = \frac{A\sqrt{c_i z_i}}{\sum\limits_i^M \sqrt{c_i z_i}} \qquad \text{and} \qquad n_i = \frac{N\sqrt{c_i z_i}}{\sum\limits_i^M \sqrt{c_i z_i}}$$

[*]Starr and Miller, *Inventory Control: Theory and Practice.*

Definitely not! The manager can *choose* a particular value for A. By doing so, he will have determined the rational value for N. If he chooses the value for N, then this choice will automatically set the value of A. In other words, either A or N can be constrained—*but not both.*

To show that this is so, we need only observe what happens when we multiply:

$$[A(OPT)] \; [N(OPT)] = \left[\left(\sum_i^M \sqrt{c_i z_i} \right) \; \left(\sqrt{\frac{C_r}{2C_c}} \right) \right] \left[\left(\sum_i^M \sqrt{c_i z_i} \right) \; \left(\sqrt{\frac{C_c}{2C_r}} \right) \right]$$

By this operation we have obtained the set of *all possible optimal* combinations (for different values of C_c and C_r) of the total inventory, A, and the total number of orders placed, N, in a given time period. This equation reduces to:

Equation 9

$$AN = \frac{1}{2} \left(\sum_i^M \sqrt{c_i z_i} \right)^2 = W$$

(W is a constant, because the item costs and their demands are available from the records and are not affected by our system decisions.) The diagram below shows a curve, called a hyperbola, which maps Equation 9.

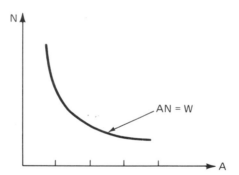

It is *critical* to note that the costs, C_r and C_c, cancelled out of Equation 9. Therefore, the hyperbola includes all possible values of these costs. AN = W *is the rational cost curve.* Given any specific costs C_r and C_c, a particular point on the curve will be found.

A given rational value for N automatically fixes the rational value for A. A given rational value for A automatically fixes the rational value for N.

We repeat, *any* point on this curve might be the actual optimal. If the costs were known, that point could be found by using Equation 10.

Equation 10

$$\frac{A(OPT)}{N(OPT)} = \frac{\sum_i^M \sqrt{c_i z_i} \; \left(\sqrt{\frac{C_r}{2C_c}} \right)}{\sum_i^M \sqrt{c_i z_i} \; \left(\sqrt{\frac{C_c}{2C_r}} \right)} = \frac{C_r}{C_c}$$

If C_r and C_c are known, or if the ratio is known, then the optimal point for A and N can be immediately determined.[*] If the ratio C_r/C_c is not known, then either A or N (but not both) can be specified by judgment. But they must both lie on the rational cost curve.

[*]*Note:* AN = W, so A = W/N and A/N = C_r/C_c = W/N^2. Hence, N^2 = W(C_c/C_r). The same reasoning applies when solving for A.

For the Beta Corporation:

$$AN = \frac{1}{2}\left(\sum_i^M \sqrt{c_i z_i}\right)^2 = \frac{1}{2}(170)^2 = 14,450$$

The optimal point, when $C_r = \$4$ and $C_c = .09$, would be:

$$A/N = \frac{\$801.55}{18.02} = 44.4$$

Also, it is:

$$\frac{C_r}{C_c} = \frac{\$4}{.09} = 44.4$$

Consider the results when N is fixed: N = 10 per year. A then must equal 1,445 and A/N = 144.5
Remember that we fixed A = $600; then N must equal 24.08 and A/N = 24.92.

These points are all shown on the curve below. Any point not falling on the curve represents an irrational policy.

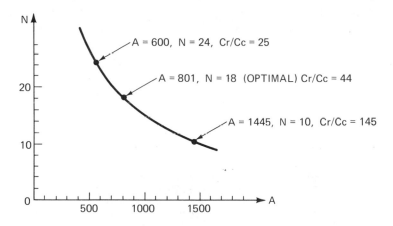

IMPUTATION

Thinking in reverse, based on what a company is *actually doing,* we can impute the costs that their actions imply. So if a company is following a particular policy, we should be able to calculate from its records the value of W as well as those of A and N. Then, following Equation 10, A/N imputes a specific cost ratio, C_r/C_c—on the *assumption* that the company is performing in an optimal (or close to optimal) fashion. Of course, this assumption may not be valid, but the imputed cost ratio will help us to know if it is valid. For example, if A/N is 50,000 and it is reasonable to assume that C_c is about 10 percent per year, then $C_r = \$5,000$ per order, which might be so far out of line that it signals that something is wrong.

Further, assume that A = $500,000 and N = 10 per year, whence A × N = 5,000,000. If W is found to be 1,000,000, it can be deduced that irrational policies are being used. Assume that A is $500,000; then to be on the curve, N should be set equal to 2 per year. Suppose N is considered reasonable at 10; A must then be $100,000 to remain on the curve. Clearly, although we don't know what is optimal here, we do know what constitutes irrational behavior.

SYSTEM AND SUBSYSTEM OPTIMALS

Let us examine the implications of the concepts we have developed. If there are no constraints on the system and all the costs are known, then optimal policies would be derived for each item. These would be a set of $x(OPT)_i$ (for all i = M items), which could be directly translated into $a(OPT)_i$'s and $n(OPT)_i$'s.

Assume that in a company, individual optimal policies gave us an A = $100,000 and an N = 10 per year. Also assume that the cost ratio C_r/C_c is equal to 10,000. Now, invoke a system's constraint; for instance, the manager states that because of competing investment alternatives, he feels that the total dollar average inventory should be held at $75,000. In effect, he is stating that because of certain conditions that the model did not take into consideration, the imputed cost ratio is as follows:

1. $N = W/A = 1,000,000/\$75,000 = 13\ 1/3$*
   $C_r/C_c = A/N = \$75,000/13\ 1/3 = \$5,625$

Then, we can determine new a_i and n_i using $\sqrt{c_i z_i}\,/\,\overset{M}{\underset{i}{\Sigma}}\,\sqrt{c_i z_i}$ such that

2. $\overset{M}{\underset{i}{\Sigma}}\,a_i = \$75,000,$ and $\overset{M}{\underset{i}{\Sigma}}\,n_i = 13\ 1/3$

Our model has instructed us how to modify the subsystems (that is, the inventory for each item) so that the performance of the total system (all the items taken together) is the best that is possible under the total system's constraints.

We see that an overriding logic pertains when systems are constrained and that the best possible policies for all items individually produce an inferior policy for the total system. Without exception, the system's solution must be found.

Solution to Systems-Ordering Exercise

We have:

Item	$\sqrt{c_i z_i}$	$n_i = N\ (\sqrt{c_i z_i}\,/\,\overset{M}{\underset{i}{\Sigma}}\,\sqrt{c_i z_i})$
1	40	$10(40/170) = $ 2.353 orders per year
2	60	$10(60/170) = $ 3.529 orders per year
3	70	$10(70/170) = $ 4.118 orders per year
	170	10.000 = N per year

*The fraction does not really pose a problem. We may either consider that orders are planned over a 3-year period, when 40 orders will have been placed, or round off to 13 orders per year.

INSTRUCTIONS FOR PREPARING THE CASE

Cormflakes Corporation

Read the case carefully. Perform the programmed exercises. Doing so will help consolidate your knowledge of certain equations and relationships given in the reading and may later reduce your computational load. As a caution, we point out that you may want many more numbers than are asked for in these exercises, as you carry out your analysis.

Place yourself in the role of "ace analyst," working for the firm of McWhood and Wilkerson. You have been asked for recommendations by Mr. McWhood. Please respond with a full analysis, starting with a statement of your decision objective.

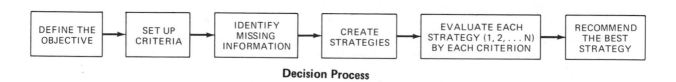

Decision Process

Cormflakes Corporation

T.D. Leghorn invented and patented a process for mixing various grains together to produce breakfast cereals that are highly resistant to the sogginess that normally results after milk is added. Some attractive offers were made to Mr. Leghorn for the exclusive rights to his process. He turned these down in spite of the fact that the negotiating companies were large enough to be able to offer him attractive positions at handsome salaries.

It was Leghorn's notion that since these companies so evidently wanted his process, it must have plenty of profit potential for him. Accordingly, he rejected the use of market research of any kind. This attitude ran counter to the advice of many of his business friends, who warned him about the problems of dealing in the grain market and of achieving supermarket shelf space that was so tightly contested by the giants of the field.

Up to the present, it appears that Leghorn is entirely correct in his contention. In fact, the product's resistance to sogginess has proved to have such a great competitive advantage that Leghorn's company, Cormflakes Corporation, has grown at a far more rapid rate than has the rest of the industry.

Cormflakes Corporation has been following a policy of reinvesting all nonworking cash, Mr. Leghorn being the staunchest advocate of this policy. All opportunities for investment have been reviewed and, if there was reasonable chance for at least a 16% rate of return, assuming that money was available, the investment was made. Thus far, such opportunities have been many, as the marketplace has been receptive to the Cormflakes products. The types of investment that have been sought are primarily those that broaden distribution, add to the product line, and reduce costs.

Leghorn knew that it would only be a matter of time before the large companies that had tried to buy him out entered the market with competing products. To prepare for this eventuality, he charged his management group with using all resources to get a firm foothold in the markets open to them and to bring operations to a level of maximum efficiency.

The management group at Cormflakes was skillful and imaginative, and the requests for capital funds exceeded what was available. This prompted Leghorn to meet with Frank Harvey, his comptroller. The results of the meeting were summed up in Leghorn's final remarks:

"Frank, we agree, then, that we should look at our inventory policy. We may be too fat here or we may be just right. In any event, we may be able to squeeze some money out that we can use to advantage elsewhere. If nothing else, we may be able to improve our costs. I wish you accountants could come up with a way to get the carrying and ordering costs of inventory into our internal reports, so we would routinely know how we are doing.

"Please get after the consultants, McWhood and Wilkerson, to make a study just as soon as possible. Have them look at our inventory of grains to start off. Prepare some basic information for them so that we don't waste time."

Harold McWhood appeared at the company the following week. After Frank Harvey outlined to him Leghorn's goals for study, he asked to see the inventory records.

A study of the records gave evidence that Cormflakes acted inconsistently in this area of its operations—sometimes there was indication that the company had little use for capital; at other times it appeared to conserve capital. This contradiction prompted Harold to sound out the comptroller on past inventory policy. The general idea of Frank's reply was contained in the following:

"While we never knew for sure, we always felt we were doing a good job on inventories. Cormflakes got away from speculation in the commodity markets at an early stage. To me, our stocks of grain seemed about right. We have never run out of stock."

Harold McWhood listened carefully, but he felt that the remark about not running out of stock might be symptomatic of an overprotective (overstocking) policy. He had experienced unbalanced policies in "young" companies many times and knew that it was characteristic in these situations to overstock in order to avoid any threat of production slowdowns or shutdowns.

At the end of the day, McWhood returned to his office. The next morning, he called in his ace analyst. After explaining the situation at Cormflakes, he passed on the following assignment:

"Take a look at their four major grains. See if you agree with me that they have too much money tied up in some and not enough in others. Don't lose sight of their present product mix and whether it is the right one. Then, if you agree with me that something is wrong here, make up a tentative recommendation for revised procedures. Perhaps you will be able to come up with a good fix on the carrying cost of inventory—but if not, that's all right, as long as you rationalize the overall inventory question.

"Work on Cormflakes's two major products—Funbits and Crundels. I have brought back the basic information that you will need, and it's here in Tables I and II.

"Let me have your recommendations as soon as possible. Bear in mind that this is more than a problem of numbers. Mr. Leghorn has operational objectives that should guide your thinking."

TABLE I

	Funbits	Crundels
Wheat	2 oz./box	1 oz./box
Corn	2 oz./box	3 oz./box
Oats	1 oz./box	2 oz./box
Rye	2 oz./box	1 oz./box
Batter and Toast Dept.	0.12 min./box	0.08 min./box
Package and Ship Dept.	0.05 min./box	0.10 min./box
Profit per box	3¢	4¢
Present prodution pattern (boxes per year)	625,000	500,000

Notes: 1. There are 250 eight-hour working days in a Cormflakes year. The company's present ordering practice is shown in Table II, with some other relevant information.

2. There are no grain shortages. Therefore, all necessary supplies can be on hand if they are previously specified.

3. The cost of an order has been reasonably well established at $100, and each type of grain must be ordered separately.

4. According to the controller, the line operations appear to be fairly well balanced, and costs of changing over from Funbits to Crundels or vice versa can be neglected.

TABLE II

Stock Item	Approximate Number of Pounds per Bushel	Expected Cost per Bushel	Order Quantity (in bushels)
Wheat	60	$1.80	911.46
Corn	55	$1.40	1,041.67
Oats	33	$0.70	1,026.55
Rye	56	$1.25	1,953.13

PROBLEM-SOLVING EXERCISES

Cormflakes Corporation

To save you time on calculations, we have prepared a programmed series of problems for this unit, which will help you to solve the case. If you solve Question 1 correctly in Parts A, B, and C, you may stop figuring and just look at the computations as done by us, since you have shown that you understand the method and the problem. If you can't do Question 1 correctly, look at the solution, try to find your mistake, and go on to Question 2. Continue this process until you have solved at least one problem in each of the three parts correctly. Do not look at the solutions except to check yourself.

PART A

Question 1a.   What is the optimal product mix for Cormflakes Corporation?

Work out your solution in the space below; then compare your answer with ours, shown on page 204.

Question 1b.   What are the annual grain requirements, z_i (bushels/yr.), for wheat and corn at the optimal product-mix level (in bushels)?

You will find the solution to this problem on page 204.

Question 2.   What are the annual grain requirements, z_i (bushels/yr.), for oats and rye at the optimal product-mix level?

You will find the solution to this problem on page 204.

PART B

Question 1.   Under the optimal product mix, what is the optimal annual order quantity for wheat? optimal number of orders? optimal average dollar inventory? Assume $C_c = 0.16$ per year.

Work out your solution in the space below; then compare your answer with ours, shown on page 205.

Question 2.   Under the optimal product mix, what is the optimal annual order quantity for corn? optimal number of orders? optimal average dollar inventory? Assume $C_c = 0.16$.

Work out your solution in the space below; then compare your answer with ours, shown on page 205.

Question 3.   Under the optimal product mix, what is the optimal annual order quantity for oats? optimal number of orders? optimal average dollar inventory? Answer the same questions for rye. Assume $C_c = 0.16$.

Solution on page 205.

PART C

Question 1.   Compute $[A(OPT)]$ $[N(OPT)]$ for the optimal product mix.

Solution on page 205

Solution to Part A, Question 1a:

Optimal product mix =

	X_F	X_C	Total Resources Available
Restriction 1: Batter and Toast Dept.	0.12	0.08	480 min.
Restriction 2: Package and Ship Dept.	0.05	0.10	480 min.
Profit per box	3¢	4¢	

Wherefore: $0.12\,X_F + 0.08\,X_C \leqslant 480$
$0.05\,X_F + 0.10\,X_C \leqslant 480$
MAXIMIZE $(0.03\,X_F + 0.04\,X_C)$

The vertices would be:

	X_F	X_C	Total Profit
	0	4,800	$192.00
	4,000	0	$120.00
This is optimal:	1,200	4,200	$204.00
Present policy is:	2,500	2,000	$155.00

If you have not answered correctly, go back through the solution and find your mistakes.

Solution to Part A, Question 1b:

Wheat:

Funbits— 1,200 boxes/day × 250 days × 2 oz./box =   600,000 oz./yr.
Crundels—4,200 boxes/day × 250 days × 1 oz./box = 1,050,000 oz./yr.
Total = 1,650,000 oz./yr.

1,650,000 oz. = 103,125 lbs.
103,125 lbs. ÷ 60 lbs./bushel = 1,718.75 bushels/yr.

Corn: Using similar calculations, z_i = 4,261.36 bushels/yr.

If you have answered correctly, look at the answer to Part A, Question 2, and go to Part B, Question 1. If not, go on to Part A, Question 2 and perform the calculations.

Solution to Part A, Question 2:

Oats:

Funbits— 1,200 boxes/day × 250 days × 1 oz./box =   300,000 oz./yr.
Crundels—4,200 boxes/day × 250 days × 2 oz./box = 2,100,000 oz./yr.
Total = 2,400,000 oz./yr.

2,400,000 oz. = 150,000 lbs.
150,000 lbs. ÷ 33 lbs./bushel = 4,545.45 bushels/yr.

Rye: Using similar calculations, z_i = 1,841.52 bushels/yr.

Go to Part B, Question 1.

Solution to Part B, Question 1:

Wheat:

$$x(OPT) = \sqrt{\frac{2z_i C_r}{c_i C_c}} = \sqrt{\frac{2 \times 1,718.75 \times \$100}{\$1.80 \times 0.16}} = 1,092.51 \text{ bushels/order}$$

$$n(OPT) = \frac{z_i}{x(OPT)} = \frac{1,718.75}{1,092.51} = 1.57 \text{ orders per year}$$

$$a(OPT) = (c_i) [x(OPT)/2] = \frac{\$1.80 \times 1,092.51}{2} = \$983.26$$

If you have answered correctly, look at the answers to Part B, Questions 2 and 3, and go to Part C, Question 1. If not, go on to Part B, Question 2, and perform the calculations.

Solution to Part B, Question 2:

Corn:

$$x(OPT) = \sqrt{\frac{2z_i C_r}{c_i C_c}} = \sqrt{\frac{2 \times 4,261.36 \times \$100}{\$1.40 \times 0.16}} = 1,950.59 \text{ bushels/order}$$

$$n(OPT) = \frac{z_i}{x(OPT)} = \frac{4,261.36}{1,950.59} = 2.18 \text{ orders per year}$$

$$a(OPT) = (c_i) [x(OPT)/2] = \frac{\$1.40 \times 1,950.59}{2} = \$1,365.41$$

If you have answered correctly, look at the answer to Part B, Question 3, and go to Part C, Question 1. If not, go on to Part B, Question 3, and perform the calculations.

Solution to Part B, Question 3:

Using the same formulas as for Questions 1 and 2, the answers are as follows:

Oats: $x(OPT) = 2,849.01$; $n(OPT) = 1.60$; $a(OPT) = \$997.15$
Rye: $x(OPT) = 1,357.03$; $n(OPT) = 1.36$; $a(OPT) = \$848.14$

Go on to Part C, Question 1.

Solution to Part C, Question 1.

	$\sqrt{c_i z_i}$	$\sqrt{c_i z_i}/\Sigma\sqrt{c_i z_i}$
Wheat	55.62	.23
Corn	77.24	.33
Oats	56.41	.24
Rye	47.98	.20
	237.25	

$$AN = 1/2 \left(\overset{M}{\Sigma} \sqrt{c_i z_i}\right)^2 = W = 28,143$$

Unit **11**

Simulation and Queueing Theory

Input/output models (resources "in" and products "out") form the basis of the production and operations field. These I/Os describe the basis of production systems. In turn, I/Os can be studied whenever a physical transformation of any kind occurs.

Specifically, inputs arrive at a service station for processing. After the transformation is completed (service rendered), they leave as outputs of the system.

Inputs (arrivals) → Service Station → Outputs (serviced)

THE SERVICE FUNCTION

The service station has some given capacity—it may be able to process, say, 5, 50, or 1,000 units per hour. If the station treats 5 units per hour on a regular basis, taking precisely 12 minutes per unit, then it is a *deterministic processor*. Precise, repetitive machine operations can be viewed in this fashion.

However, it may take 12 minutes *on the average* to do the job, which can require 9, 10, 11, 12, 13, 14, 15 minutes, and so on, with different probabilities. Workers' performance is generally found to behave in this way. When the service time varies and is probabilistically distributed, then we have a *nondeterministic* (or random, or stochastic) processor.

THE DEMAND FOR SERVICE

Arrivals to the service station may follow a deterministic pattern. The doctor who gives appointments to his patients (say, every half hour) is at least trying to regulate his arrival rate. Frequently, arrivals are nondeterministic, and a statistical distribution is required to describe the character of the inputs. This description applies to people arriving at the bank teller's window, for example. As with distributed service times, an *average* interval between arrivals may be obtained when these intervals vary in a regular and stable pattern.

DESIGN OF THE SYSTEM

When both the arrival intervals and the service times are deterministic, the service station's capacity can be designed to match precisely the arrival load that is placed on it. Thus, if exact-12-minute intervals are fixed between arrivals, then an equivalent service time will assure constant throughputs, with neither (1) delay of units requesting service, nor (2) idle time on the part of the service station.

When either the arrival intervals or the service time (or both) are nondeterministic, then a deeper problem exists in *matching the service capacity with the demand* that is placed on it. Under such circumstances, two things can happen: (1) Waiting lines, or *queues,* can form in front of the service station. That is:

Queue
Inputs———→ | ... □ □ □ □ | (□) Service Station ———→Outputs

—or (2) the system can be empty at times, and thereby the service station will be idle.

Imagine that a run of short arrival intervals occurs by chance, and at the same time, a number of longer-than-average service times are experienced. A waiting line forms. It is easy enough to picture the reverse conditions to explain how idle time can occur for the facility.

Many different queueing models exist to describe realistic situations. For example, there are *single-channel systems,* such as the one shown above, or *multiple-channel systems,* as illustrated below.

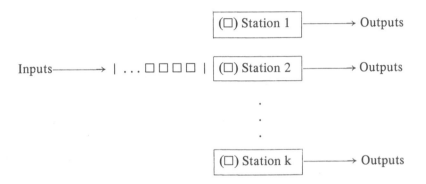

In a *deterministic* case, the multichannel system would be perfectly balanced if arrival intervals were 12 minutes and each of 3 stations requires 36 minutes to provide service. With these times, 5 units per hour require service (60/12 = 5), and each station can service 1 2/3 units per hour (60/36 = 1 2/3). Since there are 3 stations, the throughput is balanced, and neither waiting lines nor idle stations will occur. When the system is nondeterministic, this concept of balance must be altered to fit the circumstances of randomness.

Some queueing models limit the length of the waiting line that can be permitted to develop. Thus, when a garage is filled, the next arrival is turned away. Planes enter a waiting line when they are stacked over an airport; when the stack capacity is exceeded, the next plane must be shunted to other stacks or, in some cases, to other airport facilities. The waiting line between two machines may be severely restricted when the parts being processed sequentially are large castings; then what happens is that the first facility is shut down until the second catches up with it, and there is room for the first facility's output.

Line priorities, such as first-in, first-out (FIFO) or last-in, first-out (LIFO), batch processing, line switching, and line defection (leaving a line because of discouragement), are just a few of the many variants that can be coped with effectively by using queueing methods.

THE ELEMENTS OF QUEUEING THEORY

The models of queues (or waiting lines) belong to one of the most fundamental classes of processes that the operations manager ever encounters.

Queueing theory is a highly mathematical subject when treated in analytic (traditional mathematical) form. It claims some of the most advanced mathematics that will be found in the operations research field. Simulation (a particular kind of model, often developed in computer language) permits an alternative approach that is frequently useful. We shall concentrate on the methods of simulation in this unit.

Simulation as an Approach

In the study of process flows, simulation can be helpful in the simple, determinate situation as well as in systems involving complex, interdependent variables.

When relevant factors are statistically distributed, the gamut of potential systems behaviors can be generated by simulation methods. The total range of performance can then be studied to determine whether everything that could happen is acceptable. In some cases, irregular distributions may apply; for the most part, no analytic methods exist for treating such irregular systems, but simulation can do the job.

Simulation is also useful to compress time—years of systems performance can be simulated in minutes. Also, far more detail (more variables and their relations) can be included in a simulation than is generally feasible with analytic models.

Furthermore, totally different technical abilities are required to handle simulations from those needed for analytic models. The mathematical training requirements are less, but the need for systems abilities, programming knowledge, and computer time are significantly greater. We do not intend to get involved in this unit with any specialized computer aspects of simulations. The applicability of large-scale computers will become evident, however, as we proceed.

There are many types of queueing models. As a minimum, an entire course devoted to queueing would be necessary to treat the major classes of variants that have been developed. In the remainder of this unit, we shall develop one model that is highly useful when the probabilities of all possible arrival and servicing interval times have been established.

Monte Carlo Simulation

Let us examine a *nondeterministic, single-channel* case where arrivals and service times are distributed in accordance with interval probabilities as shown:

Arrival Intervals:

λ is the arrival-rate average

$\lambda = 20$ units per hour; average interval $= 60(1/\lambda)$ min.

Interval (minutes)	Interval Probability
2	0.20
3	0.60
4	0.20
	1.00

Service Times:

μ is the service-rate average

$\mu = 24$ units per hour; average service time $= 60(1/\mu)$ min.

Service Time (minutes)	Service-Time Probability
1	0.10
2	0.40
3	0.40
4	0.10
	1.00

These distributions can be simulated through assignment of Monte Carlo numbers.

Monte Carlo Assignments

Consider that 100 chips, marked 00 to 99, have been put into a bowl marked "Arrival Distribution." The arrival interval of 2 minutes has a .20 probability of occurring (see arrival chart above). You would take .20 of 100 chips, or the 20 chips marked 00-19, to represent the event that the arrival interval was 2 minutes. The chart indicates that there is a .60 probability of the arrival interval being 3 minutes, so you let the 60 chips 20-79 represent a 3-minute interval. Similarly, 20 chips marked 80-99 represent the .20 probability of a 4-minute interval.

Consider that another bowl marked "Service Times" also contains 100 chips marked 00 to 99. Referring to the service-times chart, we see that there is a .10 chance of a 1-minute service time. Thus, the 10 chips 00-09 represent this interval. A 2-minute service time is represented by the 40 chips 10-49, because of the .40 probability of this event's occurring. Similarly, 40 chips represent a 3-minute service time, and 10 chips represent a 4-minute service time.

The arrival-interval and service-time charts have been expanded to include the Monte Carlo assignments.

Arrival Intervals:

$$\lambda = 20 \text{ per hour; average interval} = 60(1/\lambda) \text{ min.}$$

Interval (minutes)	Interval Probability	Monte Carlo Assignments
2	0.20	00-19
2	0.60	20-79
4	0.20	80-99
	1.00	

Service Times:

$$\mu = 24 \text{ per hour; average service time} = 60(1/\mu) \text{ min.}$$

Service Time (minutes)	Service-Time Probability	Monte Carlo Assignments
1	0.10	00-09
2	0.40	10-49
3	0.40	50-89
4	0.10	90-99
	1.00	

The *specific* numbers given to the chips in either bowl is of no consequence. What counts is that the *proper proportion* of the 100 chips is *keyed* to each type of event. Thus, as long as the right amount of uniquely numbered chips has been assigned to each event class, the structure of the distribution has been properly depicted.

Random Numbers

In carrying out our analysis of this simulation for the nondeterministic case, we need to use random numbers. However, before illustrating how the random numbers are put to use, let us pause for a brief explanation of what random numbers are.

Any random number is by definition as likely to be chosen as any other number. So if we draw a single-digit random number, it could be any digit—0, 1, 2, 3, 4, 5, 6, 7, 8, or 9—with equal likelihood. Furthermore, the next single-digit random number selected is necessarily independent of the previous one—and the same rules concerning the equal likelihood of all digits 0-9 continue to apply.

To get random numbers, you may either turn to a table of random numbers* or else generate them. The computer can be programmed to be a most efficient random generator—but we won't get into that. You could generate random numbers using a perfectly balanced roulette wheel or other mechanical devices, including coins, cards, and dice. The critical thing is to make absolutely certain that no biases creep in that favor the appearance of any one number over another. To expedite matters, we present herewith a very limited table of 100 two-digit random numbers for your immediate use. (The first three rows have, in fact, been rigged a bit so that the example that follows could demonstrate quickly some of the points we wish to make.)

58	09	02	32	41	68	06	79	74	42
72	18	43	71	36	94	15	87	21	99
18	86	23	82	42	35	11	29	60	33
15	31	77	90	31	07	20	55	54	12
86	57	44	23	36	77	62	96	44	16
83	66	19	36	69	92	70	38	36	28
14	05	21	57	57	89	15	69	15	80
06	79	87	17	48	02	87	47	24	10
16	94	66	79	18	82	23	62	74	28
76	91	80	95	20	61	54	85	02	05

You may enter the table at any point; then it is best to read consistently, by either rows, columns, or diagonals, or any regular pattern. The reason for this is to avoid any bias that you may have with respect to number affinities that cause you to select certain kinds of numbers at a greater frequency than the others.

Application of Random Numbers to Simulation

We use random numbers in simulation to ensure that a good sample is drawn—one that cannot be anticipated. Only in this way can the situation observed in the simulation be known to be unstaged, unpremeditated, and representative.

Let us return to our example. We shall enter the table of random numbers at the upper left and read across each row in turn. Our first number is 58. This we apply to the *arrival* distribution. The Monte Carlo assignment 20-79 includes 58, and so we have just sampled an arrival interval of 3 minutes. Let us say that this arrival occurs at Time 03. The next random number is 09, and we refer it to the *service-time* distribution in order to find out when the arrival will have completed its servicing. The service-time Monte Carlo assignment 00-09 identified our random number 09 with a service time of one minute. Random number 02, which is drawn next, is included in the arrival Monte Carlo assignment 00-19, so this arrival time is 2 minutes. This means that 2 minutes after the first arrival, the second arrival occurs. The table below continues in the same fashion. We strongly recommend that you follow through the steps to make sure that the procedure is entirely clear to you.

			Random Numbers			
Start	Time 00	Time in Queue	Arr.	Svce.	Idle System	Finishes Service
1st arrival	03	—	58	09	00-03	04
2nd arrival	05	—	02	32	04-05	07
3rd arrival	08	—	41	68	07-08	11
4th arrival	10	10-11	06	79	—	14
5th arrival	13	13-14	74	42	—	16
6th arrival	16	—	72	18	—	18
7th arrival	19	—	43	71	18-19	22
8th arrival	22	—	36	94	—	26
9th arrival	24	24-26	15	87	—	29
10th arrival	27	27-29	21	99	—	33
11th arrival	29	29-33	18	86	—	36
12th arrival	32	32-36	23	82	—	39
13th arrival	35	35-39	42	35	—	41
14th arrival	37	37-41	11	29	—	43
15th arrival	40	40-43	60	33	—	45

*For such a table, see Martin K. Starr, *Production Management: Systems and Synthesis,* 2nd ed. (Englewood Cliffs, N.J.: Prentice-Hall, 1972), p. 514.

We observe that in the first 40 minutes,* the service facility was idle 6 (3 + 1 + 1 + 1 = 6) minutes. This is 6/40 = 0.15, or 15 percent of the time. Of course, the first 3 minutes was really startup time. If we leave it out of our calculations, then the facility was idle 7.5 percent of the time.

The waiting-line computations are a bit more tricky, so let us look at what occurred in a tabular form.

Time	Who Is in Queue	Time	Who Is in Queue
00-01	—	20-21	—
01-02	—	21-22	—
02-03	—	22-23	—
03-04	—	23-24	—
04-05	—	24-25	#9
05-06	—	25-26	#9
06-07	—	26-27	—
07-08	—	27-28	#10
08-09	—	28-29	#10
09-10	—	29-30	#11
10-11	#4	30-31	#11
11-12	—	31-32	#11
12-13	—	32-33	#11, #12
13-14	#5	33-34	#12
14-15	—	34-35	#12
15-16	—	35-36	#12,/#13
16-17	—	36-37	#13
17-18	—	37-38	#13, #14
18-19	—	38-39	#13, #14
19-20	—	39-40	#14
		40-41	#14, #15
		41-42	#15

Let's make a frequency distribution of the number in queue during the first 40 minutes.

Number in Queue	Frequency	Probability
0	23	23/40
1	13	13/40
2	4	4/40
	40	1.00

We find that the queue was never longer than 2 units.** If we had taken a sufficiently larger sample than 15 arrivals and 40 minutes, we would have experienced longer queues. All our measures take on more meaning with an increasing sample size. Here, the average number in queue is calculated to be (0 × 23/40) + (1 × 13/40) + (2 × 4/40) = 21/40, or slightly more than half a unit.

Simulation Architecture

Each simulation situation is different. There are obvious ground rules for building a satisfactory simulation, but not for constructing a great one. In many respects, simulation-model procedure is management's equivalent of architecture. The manager must intuit what is important and how to represent it as a flow of happenings over time. He must have in mind what to measure as a reflection of the system's performance. Once he develops confidence in his abilities to construct (or more likely to oversee the construction of) a simulation representation of his sytem, he can turn to computer programmers who are able to translate the model into computer language. Then all the tedious pencil and paper work is removed. Furthermore, satisfactory sample sizes can be easily achieved.

---

*We could have used 45 minutes, since the idle-system record is available up to that time. As the simulation record grows longer, such tail effects become negligible.

**Again, for convenience, we have taken the first 40 minutes as the length of our sample in this illustration.

Obviously, not all problems lend themselves to simulation. Learning which problems do is another part of the job. At best, we can say the following: *Where complex scheduling, line-balancing, and systems-flow problems involve various types of risk and interdependent decisions, simulation will usually turn out to be an appropriate method of attack.*

Vital Stone Corporation

After you have studied the text and case, prepare the calculations that you will need for your decision making. We suggest that you go through only 15 machine breakdowns for each repair crew size; while this is far too few to provide a valid base for consideration of the different numbers of repairmen, it should be sufficient to familiarize you with the concept. (The real Bob Castle would go much further and would be likely to use his company's computer facilities.)

To save yourself time, you can use the five simulations given in the case as your starting point. These are laid out in schematic form in the simulation exercises following the case. (Read the case before looking at the schematics).

Put yourself in the role of Bob Castle and prepare recommendations for Mr. Stone. Take a broad managerial viewpoint, with due regard for management issues and implications.

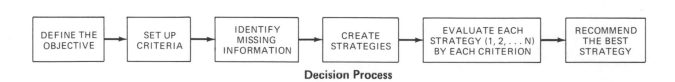

Decision Process

CASE

Vital Stone Corporation

Vital Stone Corporation is a small growth company. It was established a few years ago to manufacture and distribute a technologically-new line of products in the expanding marketplace of the construction industries. R.V. Stone is the inventor of the new product process. He holds all the basic patents; he has not assigned them to the corporation. As he founded the company and is majority stockholder, it is hardly surprising that he is also president and chairman of the board. In other words, all corporate power is vested in Mr. Stone, and he has not seen fit to dissipate it.

The core product is an entirely new type of laser gun. It is most effectively used to produce rapid, high-strength joints and seams. A variety of ingenious peripheral attachments and adapters have also been patented by Stone, who spends much of his time in his Boston laboratory, extending the range and scope of his initial ideas.

Clearly, Stone is a brilliant inventor. Perhaps he would be an equally outstanding businessman if he wished to be, but he has stated that he has "neither the inclination in that direction nor the time to devote in that manner." His base patent has many years to run, and with that protection, Stone has felt little pressure to study his operations with care. Nevertheless, he exhibits continuing interest in the way the business is run.

For example, on one of his irregular but not infrequent visits to his plant, he observed to Mr. Dryer, the plant manager, that about three out of four times he has visited, there has been an idle repairman standing around, talking with the other workers, and occasionally even dozing right on the main plant floor. Once he saw a three-man card game being played. Dryer explained the situation to Mr. Stone as follows:

"We have five XF-28 production machines now, Mr. Stone. They are identical and of your own design. You know very well that together they comprise our most crucial equipment. They are also so delicate that they represent our greatest vulnerability in meeting customer deliveries.

"All the other machines in the shop are standard, general-purpose equipment that can be easily repaired. Our investment in the five XF-28s is hundreds of times greater than that of all our other facilities combined. So we have four repairmen available to put the XF-28s back into action the minute any one of them goes down. Now, you know how tricky these XFs are. Lately, each machine has been breaking down, on the average, every 20 hours of service. Our latest reports indicate that it takes 8 hours (on the average) to service the unit and return it to operating condition. True, sometimes we can get the unit back in service in an hour or so. But at other times, the precise adjustments required when we burn a tube will cause more than two days to elapse before we're back and running. It seems like we've always got a couple of them down. As you know, we're trying to do something about that. Anyway, I'm certainly not sure that four repairmen is the right number. However, I'd rather have repairmen sitting around than machines."

Mr. Stone's reply was brief. He said, "I don't disagree, but I detest indolence. Find something for the repairmen to do while they're waiting around for an XF-28 breakdown. Their idleness is disruptive to the rest of the work force."

"Can't do that," Mr. Dryer replied. "The union rules have us tied up on all sides. First, XF-28 repairmen are prohibited from doing anything but class A repair work. Even the repair or maintenance of standard machines is out, because it involves a different skill class. In any case, our general-purpose equipment is serviced by the equipment operators themselves. They have that job description included in their pay class. Of course, it allows them to repair and service only the standard equipment. The workers insist that no one else be allowed to do general-purpose repairs because it's a part of their rated times. They're not going to give that cushion up without a real struggle, and I'd like to avoid that. We've got good morale here. I don't want to upset the applecart. So, that's it. I can't find anything else for the XF-28 repairmen to do even though they are expert technicians."

Stone went back to his lab, but he couldn't forget the repairman problem. Eventually, after some reading, he concluded that the situation might at least be clarified by a queueing-theory study. Consequently, he called Dryer and asked him to assign to Bob Castle, the quality-control engineer, the task of formulating the problem in queueing-theory terms.

Shortly thereafter, Stone called Castle into his office. "Bob, I believe Mr. Dryer has told you of the investigation I want done on the XF-28. I don't think this problem can be handled in analytic terms, but I do feel that a Monte Carlo simulation will give us our answers. I know you have done some work with this approach—which is why I asked to have you assigned to this problem.

"It's my hypothesis that the exponential distribution will hold for both the arrival and service intervals. This distribution is frequently used to describe a purely random process, and these are the circumstances we have here. There is no reason to expect any sequential pattern or run of long and short intervals. In other words, the intervals between arrivals or servicing periods are independent of the length of all previous intervals."

Stone reached for a book on his desk, which was opened to a page showing an exponential-type distribution:

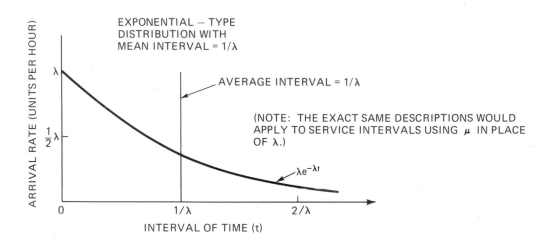

"You will note that at $1/\lambda$ we have a line showing the mean value of the distribution.

"You shouldn't have any trouble with your analysis. I am particularly interested in the total costs of repair time and delay time (time on queues) with 1, 2, 3, and 4 repairmen. Mr. Dryer can give you input information, but let me have the results of your study."

Castle went back to his office to tackle his assignment. He envisioned the situation as a multiple-channel case, where arrivals were machines breaking down, the service stations were the repairmen, and the service times were repair times. From a conversation with Dryer, he determined an arrival rate, $\lambda = 1/20$ per hour, and a service rate, $\mu = 1/8$ per hour for each machine. He also learned that the equivalent weekly amortization per machine was about $600 and that a repairman's weekly salary was $200.

From literature suggested to him by Mr. Stone, Castle learned that one of the simplest ways to make Monte Carlo assignments using the exponential distribution was to draw a curve of the cumulative exponential distribution. He noted carefully the explanation in the text:

Draw a series of random numbers from a table of random numbers. Let's say we get 22, 59, 55, 83, 05, 06, 59, 10, 05, 30, 41, 68, ... Monte Carlo assignments can be obtained by multiplying the random numbers by 0.01. This product is then used to enter the chart along the y-axis.

Since the table given in the text consists of 2-digit numbers, the value 100 will never appear. For accuracy, we point this out; in the interest of practicality, we suggest that you gloss over this discontinuity. Other randomization methods would provide a remedy.

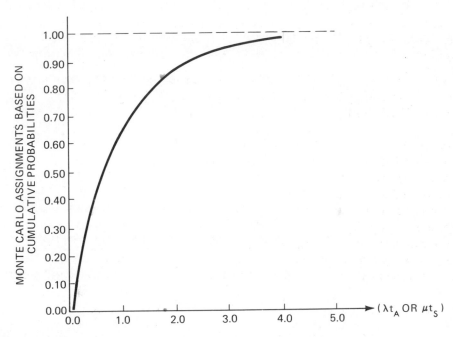

For each random number drawn from a table of such numbers, we find its equivalent Monte Carlo number on the vertical axis, then read off the equivalent horizontal-axis value. Place the first of each pair of random numbers under λt_A and the second of the pair under μt_S. (t_A is the arrival interval; t_S is the service period.)

Random Number	λt_A	μt_S
22	0.25	
59		0.90
55	0.80	
83		1.80
05	0.05	
06		0.06
59	0.90	
10		0.10
05	0.05	
30		0.35

Castle used the given values of $\lambda = 1/20$ and $\mu = 1/8$ for the XF-28 situation to determine the arrival intervals t_A and the service periods t_S:

$$\lambda t_A = 1/20 t_A = 0.25 \qquad t_A = 5.00 \text{ hours}$$
$$= 0.80 \qquad t_A = 16.00 \text{ hours}$$
$$= 0.05 \qquad t_A = 1.00 \text{ hour}$$
$$= 0.90 \qquad t_A = 18.00 \text{ hours}$$
$$= 0.05 \qquad t_A = 1.00 \text{ hour}$$

$$\text{and } \mu t_S = 1/8 t_S = 0.90 \qquad t_S = 7.20 \text{ hours}$$
$$= 1.80 \qquad t_S = 14.40 \text{ hours}$$
$$= 0.06 \qquad t_S = 0.48 \text{ hours}$$
$$= 0.10 \qquad t_S = 0.80 \text{ hours}$$
$$= 0.35 \qquad t_S = 2.80 \text{ hours}$$

He noted that he could run the simulation for as long as he liked so as to generate as many breakdowns for each machine as he wished. In his calculations, he determined all idle time and the number of machines waiting for service. With respect to the latter, he was careful to see that there was a repairman available before service was started.

SIMULATION EXERCISES

Vital Stone Corporation

The five simulations given in the case are provided as your starting point. We suggest you go through only 15 machine breakdowns for each repair-crew size. Some practice with simulation is desirable even when the principles are fully understood.

Clock	1	2	3	4	5	No. of Idle Repairmen	Time on Queue (number of hours of delay)
			Machines				
0.00						4	
1.00						2	
2.00			⊥		⊥	3	
3.00							
4.00						4	
5.00							
6.00							
7.00							
8.00						3	
9.00							
10.00							
11.00							
12.00							
13.00						4	
14.00							
15.00							
16.00						3	
17.00							
18.00				⊥		2	
19.00						3	
20.00							
21.00							
22.00							
23.00							
etc.							
		30.40					

It should be observed in the above simulation, that the number of hours of delay (based upon five simulations) is zero. Also, to facilitate matters, let us practice reading the chart. We note that machine 1 broke down after five hours

219

and returned to use at 5 + 7.20 = 12.20 hours. Machine 2 broke down 16 hours after the simulation began and returned to working condition at 16 + 14.40 = 30.40 hours. Machine 3 broke down 1 hour after the simulation began and returned to service at 1 + 0.48 hours. Similar statements can be made for the other machines.

Continuing with the Monte Carlo method, random numbers are drawn to determine how long each machine works after it has been returned to service. Thus, for example, if machine 1 breaks down for the second time after 1 hour, then that will occur at 12.20 + 1 = 13.20 hours.

FEEDBACK CASES

What Are They and Why Are They Used?

The means by which a person learns best are not obvious. However, the subject of learning has been studied. It is known that lectures accompanied by homework problems that are never graded are one of the poorest approaches to learning. There is no feedback to the student, and feedback is the basis for learning. Graded homework provides some information, but if the information fed back is only that the answer is right or wrong, that kind of response provides no teaching assistance to correct what is wrong. Without such corrective feedback, the student remains passive and unmotivated.

The type and rate of feedback used are critical factors affecting the success of the feedback process for learning. Often, the case method provides an overabundance of fuzzy feedback via case discussions. Typically, the communication begins with too much irrelevant financial information, plus random—although often lengthy—descriptions of situations and of persons and their personalities. Both of these are undesirable, because they create an illusion of knowledge and of transferable experience. Such cases foster feedback in a fuzzy medium and at the wrong rate.

Feedback cases, on the other hand, are well structured and concise. Much of their materials are related to the presence of clearly identifiable right and wrong methods for solving problem components of the case. The methodology and concepts underlying how numerical answers are arrived at should be well stated. We want the student to know that he or she has learned how to use a technique correctly. Thus, repeated opportunity is given for the student to practice a method, and a positive signal is given when the method is mastered. This is effective feedback (with concept and approach understood), whereas letter grades on homework, without full description of the methods required, represents ineffective feedback.

Cases without any answers provide no feedback. Without feedback there is no learning; and consequently, such cases are wasteful of the students' time and make their use dependent on obtaining good in-class instruction.

The cases that comprise this text utilize feedback pedagogy, which distinguishes them from cases as they are normally conceived. The feedback cases are short. They attempt to exclude irrelevant information. In addition, they are presented with instructions for preparing the case and programmed exercises after the case. Programmed answers are shown wherever it is necessary to develop a model for obtaining specific types of (usually numerical) answers to supply insights about the problem. Also, these cases are accompanied by lectures that are written with specific focus on the methods that can successfully resolve the cases. The focused lectures help to define the nature of the problems, and they offer relevant methodology providing analogies that are readily transferable to the substance of the case. As we go by analogy from the lectures to the case (via Instructions for Preparing the Case), so, from the case, the student can make applications by analogy to reality situations. Computational burdens are alleviated by means of programmed answers, enabling concentration on conceptual issues. Because the cases are specific and problem-oriented, extraneous information (if it does appear) can be identified and then discarded. Since the programmable answers are not *sufficient* for dealing with these cases, conceptual reasoning is required. So with this text we obtain the appropriate ingredients for effective learning: There is motivation to learn through real-life contexts, feedback concerning the appropriate analytic approach, and relief from tedious computations by the programmed-method approach.

Good cases are based on the broad, systems view of reality. The dimensions of such cases should encompass production, finance, marketing, accounting, industrial relations, and many other categories of functions that exist in the real system of the problem. Management thinking should include planning, organizing, staffing, directing, and controlling. As the cases show, the management science methodology is entirely applicable to processes other than manufacturing. These cases are models that can be tuned to the management of service organizations, marketing and market research departments, money and financial systems, retailing, mining, transportation, and communication.

Methods, properly formulated, become transferable. The decision problem of Verity Mining can easily be extended by analogy to merger and acquisition problems. The decision trees of the Vulcan Rubber Company can be applied to pilot plants, test markets, commodity buying, and so on. Analogy transfer is as available as real situational learning and imagination allow. The same kind of breakeven analysis used by Marquis Detection Company is being used by thousands of companies all over the world, but it should be used by many thousands more. Teaneck's project problem is hardly restricted to sewers. It could be applied as well to bids for contracts for hospitals or schools, and to construction projects of buildings, ships, and tunnels. The same kind of statements concerning transferability by analogy can be made for Lafayette, with its multiple decision-criteria problems, Lucky Bell and its very general inventory situation, Chocoban's use of linear programming to best allocate scarce resources, Amory Oil's approach to a repeating type of capital-budgeting decision, Martronics's employment of statistical quality control, Cormflakes Corporation's need to address its systems problems, and Vital Stone's simulation, which epitomizes the transferability of methodology by analogy.

Given application, we must still address implementation. Throughout these cases, as it is in real-life systems, the key to implementation is an agreement between the managers and the model builders, from the very beginning, concerning objectives and the problem-solving methodology to be employed. It is one thing to tell the manager what will be the outcome of using a certain strategy, and another to tell the manager what strategy to use. Some managers opt for the former and some for the latter. The specific situation may help to determine what is appropriate, but the manager's style is crucial. Some managers prefer to have continuous implementation support during and after the decision is made and converted to action. Other managers want a final study report and then freedom to implement without further contact from the study group.

The student, having completed all or several of the feedback cases in this text, should now realize that:

· Techniques have been learned from each case.
· The application of techniques has been developed so that transfer to other situations by analogy is facilitated.
· Multiple dimensions that apply in all interesting real situations should be sought out to eliminate trivial problem solving. Especially avoid defining a problem so that a technique can be used. Techniques follow problems, not vice versa.
· Implementation requires agreement concerning managerial objectives.

These feedback cases have been used by many students, and they have been honed and adapted to be most effective in improving the learning experience.

Glossary

A   *Total* average dollar inventory.

a_i   The average dollar inventory for the ith item.

Analog model   See *Model.*

Analysis   Breaking down a system into its parts so that they can be studied with intensity as segmented components.

Analytic models   By "analytic models," we refer to classical mathematical equations that represent the relevant variables and their relationships in such a way that the model can either be solved for an optimal configuration, ordering, or setting of the values of the variables, or provide a description of outputs that will occur (not necessarily optimal) with given inputs. Analytic queueing models are not able to provide optimization, but they do provide description of waiting times, idle time, etc. Simulation approximates these measures.

A(OPT)   The optimal total average dollar inventory.

Arrival intervals   The periods between the arrivals of units that come to the station for servicing. (They can vary or be constant.)

Assignable causes   Nonchance causes of variation, which can be traced to their source and generally removed.

Attributes, classification   All output is sorted into only two classes—e.g., accept and reject. (See *Variables, classification.*)

Average dollar inventory   The average investment in stock over some period of time.

Balanced I/Os   The system is so designed that its capacity to serve is economically matched with the load placed upon it. Deterministic balance requires a simple matching of the I and O rates, whereas nondeterministic balance employs complex matching of expected values and variances in terms of economic measures of queueing properties and idle facilities.

Batch processing   More than one unit is served at the same time—e.g., consider an elevator as the service station.

Batch-type production   The items are grouped in a batch and processed in these batches through various stages. All items are completed at approximately the same time.

Branches   Separable activities of a PERT network; or separable sequences of decisions and/or chance events of a decision tree.

Brand shares   The percentage of sales (or of customers) that a company commands in the marketplace. Brand share does not give any indication of profit or of the total volume of revenue (or the total number of customers) generated or existing in that marketplace.

Breakeven chart   A diagrammatic means of depicting the relations among fixed costs, variable costs, and revenues, where the point at which neither profit nor loss is made is called the breakeven point. It is also possible to find a breakeven point, or point of indifference, between two alternatives by comparing their total costs and finding the point at which they are equal.

Carrying-cost rate   A percentage applicable to the cost of an item per unit of time. It is composed of the interest (% per time) lost on money that is tied up in inventory. But it must also include other temporal expenses, such as those of storage, insurance, and taxes.

Chance cause   A random effect in the system that cannot be controlled or removed. The outcome, heads or tails, in an unbiased coin toss is attributable only to chance cause. (See also *Chance event*). Also, nonassignable causes of variation. These are causes of variation that are inherent in the process (to contrast, see *Assignable causes*).

Chance event   A probabilistic outcome associated with prior choices of actions in a decision tree. (See also *Chance cause*).

Chance-event circle   Represents the occurrence of a chance event in the decision tree.

Christmas tree problem   See *Static inventory problem.*

Constraints   Subobjectives that limit the range of activities that are available to the decision maker. For example, the major objective could be to maximize sales revenue subject to the constraint of a one-million-dollar advertising budget.

Control   The exercise of direction, guidance, and restraining power over that which is to be controlled. It involves specification of goals, regulation of controllable factors, and verification of goal attainment.

Correlate   To relate, generally by statistical methods, but also by intuitive inferences, the relations between two types of events; e.g., when "housing starts" increase, the sales of kitchen appliances rise.

Costs, fixed   Investments in which cost is in no way tied to the volume of production, such as rentals based on time, not use.

Costs, total   The sum of variable and fixed costs for a given production level or percentage of capacity utilization.

Costs, variable   Operating costs that are directly related to the number of units produced—for example, the charge on an automobile rental for miles that are driven.

CPM   Critical-path method.

Critical path   The longest path of activities in the project system.

Decision matrix   (see *Matrix*) In the decision matrix, the rows are generally strategies. One strategy must be chosen. The matrix columns are events of nature, one of which must occur.

Decision point   A choice is required between different action alternatives.

Decision-point box   Represents the decision point in the tree.

Decision tree   (see *Sequential decision process*) The decision tree depicts in extensive form the sequence of decision choices and possible chance events.

Degrees of freedom   For our purposes, the degree to which constraints allow flexibility in defining what will constitute acceptable solutions. Thus, if only a single point is allowed, there are no degrees of freedom.

Depreciation   The decline in value of an asset owing to wear and tear (variable cost) and obsolescence (fixed cost). Various accounting procedures exist for charging depreciation costs to the company and the product. Straight-line depreciation for n years is simplest, in that for each of the n years, the same amount of expense is charged, and at the end of that time the book value of the asset is zero.

Derivative   A measure of the rate of change of a (curve) function; i.e., the slope at any point on that (curve) function—or in a simplified sense, the way that y changes with incremental changes of x.

Deterministic properties   There is no variance and therefore no distribution of the event in question. Thus, if arrivals are said to be deterministic at 100 per hour, then they are always exactly that number.

Deviations   Measures that diverge from the expected or standard value.

Dimensional analysis   Dimension is the name of the scale and of the units of measurement. Dimensional analysis requires the examination of the nature of a result in order to determine whether it is consistent with our objectives (i.e., if we want to study "apples" there should be no "artichokes" mixed in). Also, a consistency check of the model to make certain that only proper operations are used; e.g., only similar units can be added to each other.

Dimensionless number   See *Pure number.*

Discount model   A model that takes into account the percentage rebate given for purchasing more than a given quantity of an item in determining the optimum order size.

Domination   If a constraint is superfluous because another constraint overrides it (is more restrictive) at every point, then we say the superfluous constraint is dominated.

Dynamic inventory problem   The items under consideration are demanded over a reasonably long period of time, so that more than one order is required.

Economic lot-size model (ELS)   This is an inventory model used to plan optimal run sizes for a serial-type, line production system.

Economic order quantity model (EOQ)   This is the inventory model used for making outside purchases from a vendor or for scheduling batch production.

ELS   See *Economic lot-size model.*

EOQ   See *Economic order quantity model.*

Expected value   The average or mean value of a set of numbers.

Exponentially distributed   The probabilities with which different values of x occur are described by ae^{-ax}, where $x \geqslant 0$. When x = 0, the probability is a, and when x approaches infinity, the probability approaches zero. The area under this distribution is equal to 1.

Feedback   Information about the output of a process, which is then fed back to the process to control its output performance.

FIFO   First-in, first-out establishes the ordering with which units entering the system are to be treated. The term is familiarly used in establishing a systematic way of costing inventory.

Forecasting   Developing a specific risk distribution for a particular situation.

Gantt charts   The precursor project-planning method to PERT.

Goodwill costs   The penalty associated with the loss of rapport that occurs when the customer becomes unhappy with the service he is receiving. This is a particularly difficult cost to determine, since it involves human and economic relations.

Grand mean   The average of a set of averages.

Hedging   This involves the buying and selling of commodity futures. A company fearing that a commodity price rise will occur can buy now a given amount of the commodity for delivery in a future month. To hedge, an organized commodities exchange is required.*

Imputed cost   One that is not actually specified but is implied by company policies.

Index   A relative measure of the value of an outcome. A set of indices provides a basis for comparing members of the set.

Inequalities   A more general statement than an equality, since it specifies only direction. Instead of "equal to," we can describe unequal relations, such as "A is less than B" (or "B is greater than A"). See Unit 7.

Inequations   When the "equals sign" is replaced in an equation with one of the signs of inequality, the equation is transformed into an inequation. It is useful to note that most operations (such as x and ÷) that apply to equations apply as well to inequations. However, if we multiply both sides by -1, the sign of the inequality changes. For example:

$$\begin{array}{ll} \text{Multiplying by } (-1){:} & 3x_1 + 2x_2 \leqslant 30 \\ \text{Whence:} & -3x_1 - 2x_2 \geqslant -30 \\ & 30 \geqslant 3x_1 + 2x_2 \end{array}$$

Inputs   These are different forms of resources, materials, and energy that are purchased and then introduced into the system for the purpose of transformation into desired end results.

Inventory   A resource that is stocked to meet a demand.

Lead time (LT)   The elapsed interval between the placing of an order and its delivery (but it must also include other sources of delay).

LIFO   Last-in, first-out establishes the ordering (see *FIFO*).

Linear   A straight-line function, $y = mx + b$.

Linear function   When y varies with x so that a constant amount of change in x produces a constant amount of change in y, a straight-line representation in graphic form would apply. This is called a linear function; a nonlinear function would be shown by a curved line of changing slope.

Linear programming   See *Programming models*.

Log transformation of utility   Because of the way in which the logarithmic curve slopes over (increasing at a decreasing rate), we obtain a measure that reflects diminishing returns. This characterizes the utility that one commonly has for increasing quantities of money.

LP   Linear programming.

Matrix   A structure of cells designed to contain data. Generally, the cells are arrayed in rows and columns. (See *Decision matrix.*)

Model   A representation of reality that attempts to explain the behavior of some aspect of that reality.

> *Analog model*   Generally, this is more abstract than a physical (or prototype) model. The analog model is related to the conception of an analogy—i.e., a relation of likeness between two things.
>
> *Prototype model*   This is a physical image of the reality. It is frequently a scale model, such as an airplane that can be flown in a wind tunnel.
>
> *Qualitative model*   These are representations of reality that do not involve numbers and/or equations. They are likely to comprise logical statements as expressed by language models as well as by physical prototypes.

*See Martin K. Starr, *Production Management: Systems and Synthesis,* 2nd ed. (Englewood Cliffs, N.J.: Prentice-hall, 1972), pp. 267-70.

Quantitative model A model that is likely to involve mathematical formulations and equations. But it is also true that any set of *numbers* can be considered a quantitative model. In this respect, a profit-and-loss statement and a balance sheet are good examples. A more abstract quantitative model is on in which equations constructed of abstract symbol apply, rather than an specific set of numbers.

Monitor An observer (man or machine) installed to take either continuous or sample information about a system.

Monte Carlo Reminiscent of the roulette wheels of the gambling casino, the Monte Carlo procedure is a systematic means for simulating a range of event occurrences according to a specific probability distribution.

Multiple-channel systems More than one service station has been provided to treat the load on the system.

Multiple-item order A single purchase requisition on which a variety of different items are included.

Multistage decision problems See *Sequential decision process*.

N Total number of orders placed in a given period.

Network A series of activity branches and nodes; they resemble an electrical network, but here the circuits are assigned their special meanings by analogy with a real-world system.

Network, extensive A network in which no branch may be traveled more than once; i.e., no feedback or looping back is permitted in the network.

n_i The number of orders placed for the ith item in a given period of time.

Nodes Points in the network at which more than one activity converge or diverge; i.e., either a new job cannot begin until some set of preceding ones is completed, or several new activities cannot begin until one particular one has been completed. For decision trees, the node can be either a decision point in a sequence of decisions or a chance event that must go one way or another.

Non-single-scale cases These are situations where various scales that cannot be added (such as status and money) together contribute to the overall measure of the goodness of the system.

Off-line The system is not producing our item but is doing other work.

On-line The system is engaged in producing our item.

Operations Actions taken to produce a desired (transformation) effect. They are work functions, intended for accomplishing, making, and doing. Such actions usually involve technological factors as well as information transformations.

Optimal The (absolute) best solution that can be obtained, given specific objectives and conditions of the system.

Optimal value The best possible outcome value.

Order cost The variable component of the total order cost. These costs can properly be charged per purchase requisition.

Outcome The result of a particular strategy and a specific state of nature. It is the independent factor in the system and is directly related to the goals for which that system is being studied. Phrased another way, it is the result that can be observed and is derived to explain the behavior of the system. It must be consistent with the objectives, but may have to be transformed to be representative of the utilities of the decision maker.

Out-of-stock cost The penalty that must be paid for not being able to deliver a particular item upon demand.

Outputs These are the end results of working on the inputs. The resources at the input have to be transformed into the desired set of outputs.

Parameters These are the "constants" that explain the behavior of a system. We note that changing the value of these constants is permitted and, in some cases, represents our control over the system's configuration.

Parent population The distribution of measurements of individuals, also called the universe, as contrasted with distributions of sample means.

Path   A sequence of contiguous branches in the network. There are many combinations of branches, each of which constitutes a path; several paths may share common branches.

Payoffs   The outcome of a decision problem transformed to represent its true utility to the decision maker.

Perfect information   The prior knowledge of exactly which state of nature will occur so that the best possible strategy can be chosen.

PERT   Program Evaluation and Review Technique, developed by the U.S. Navy Special Projects Office in conjunction with Booz, Allen and Hamilton for the Polaris project.

PERT/COST   A modified PERT system that includes cost considerations in addition to time, deadlines, and schedule.

Polygon   A geometric construction in two, three, or more dimensions, which *for our purposes* encloses three or more angles such that a line connecting *any* two points of the polygon must lie entirely within that polygon. (We call this a convex polygon.)

Prediction   (See *Perfect information*.) Prediction is the attempt to specify exactly which state of nature will occur.

Present worth   The value today of payments and investments that are promised in the future.

Product mix   The combination of products that are output from the production line, ranging from a single item to a highly varied mix. We mean both type and quantity.

Productivity coefficients   Each resource constraint is of the form: $ax_1 + bx_2 + \ldots + nx_n \leqslant R$. The productivity coefficients a, b, ... n represent the amount of resource, R, that must be used up to produce one unit of their respective outputs, $x_1, x_2, \ldots x_n$.

Programming models   Those models in which a single objective is to be either maximized or minimized, subject to a fully delineated set of constraints, and in which a systematic procedure is employed. In this regard, linear programming is a form of mathematical programming wherein the objective and the constraints assume linear equational form.

Project   A set of activities that is essentially nonrepetitive; i.e., the interval from the beginning to the end is sufficiently long that the "cycles" can be considered to be independent entities.

Prototype   See *Model*.

Pure number   A number that has no dimension. It represents a ratio relationship between similarly dimensioned quantities. For example, the ratio of 144 square inches to 12 square inches is equal to the pure number 12. This is also called a dimensionless number.

Quadrant   A plane is divided into four sectors or quadrants by the placement of x and y axes. The first quadrant contains all positive values of x and of y. It is, therefore, by convention the upper right-hand sector.

Qualitative model   See *Model*.

Quantitative model   See *Model*.

Queueing theory   The description of what will take place when arrivals (which may be randomly distributed) come to a service station (whose service times may be randomly distributed). The queue is a waiting line that can form when units must wait for service because the station is busy.

Random numbers   These are numbers that have been generated in such a way that any one number is as likely to appear and be chosen as any other number.

Rational solutions   A range of solutions that contains all possible optimal solutions (as the values of the parameters are changed) and excludes all non-optimal solutions.

Reorder point That level of inventory at which it is necessary to initiate reordering procedures. The order must be placed with the vendor so that it can be delivered at that moment in time when it is needed.

Risk When it cannot be said with certainty what is going to occur, but the various possibilities can be named and their relative likelihoods described in a believable way, risk exists. If the relative likelihoods cannot be described or lack believability, uncertainty exists. If the various possibilities cannot be named, ambiguity exists.

Run sizes The number of units manufactured at one time in a given lot.

Salvage value In a static inventory problem, after the selling interval, the goods have lost value. If they have not gone to zero value, what remains is the salvage value.

Sensitivity analysis An investigation of the stability of a solution to purposeful changes that are introduced into the model solely with the intent of testing the stability of the solution. Also, a measure of the responsiveness of a system based on the nature and amount of change produced in the system by a given change in conditions. Usually, coefficients are changed, first employing a maximum estimate and then a minimum estimate for the value of the coefficient to see if within this range the solution is affected.

Sequential decision process A sequence of decisions must be made leading to a variety of chance events, and we wish to evaluate the effect of reaching different decisions (e.g., ABCD vs. A'BCD vs. ABC'D, etc.) in terms of the entire sequence.

Serial-type production Line production by which units come off the line in sequence, one after the other. At any moment in time, a unit may be entering the system while another one may be completed and leaving it.

Service periods The various lengths of time that it takes to service units that appear at the service station.

Setup cost The expense required to set up the production line with tools, fixtures, and procedures so that it can process a particular type of item. Usually, this entails changeover from another configuration suited to a different product.

Simple transformation When a single scale is magnified or reduced in some regular fashion (such as by changing inches to feet, pints to quarts, or ounces to pounds), then a simple transformation exists.

Simulation model A descriptive model that mirrors the interconnection of events in a system without perfect precision. It can be used to generate a sequence of related effects much as a physical scale model can be tested. Generally, however, the simulation model exists in the form of a set of logical (albeit mathematical) statements that can be programmed for computer manipulation. The precision of simulated measures improves as the sample size increases.

Single-channel systems There is only one service station.

Single-scale systems Only one dimension applies, such as "dollars" or "units of preference." We can transform the nonsingle scales of "oranges" and "apples" to a single scale called "fruit."

Slack Noncritical paths are those that are not as long as the critical ones in the program system. The difference in assigned work time between a noncritical path and the critical one is called slack.

Slippage Any noncritical path has a certain amount of slack by which activities can be delayed without in any way affecting the completion date of the project; this is slippage. But slippage along the critical path will cause lateness in meeting the project target date.

SOH Stock on hand.

Solution space Those points that represent possible combinations of $x_1, x_2, \ldots, x_n$. That is, they do not violate any constraints.

Stability No assignable causes of variation exist in the process (see *Assignable causes.*)

States of the environment The same as states of nature.

States of nature   That part of a decision environment that is not under the decision maker's control. For example, we can consider different kinds of weather. Usually we exclude competitors' strategies.

Static   Only one decision is permitted, so that no corrective actions can be taken after the fact.

Static inventory problem   The items are purchased for a specific selling season. At the end of that time, the market changes, and the items lose value either totally or in part.

Stochastic   Describing nondeterministic (random) behavior—i.e., an event that can take on at least two values, with probabilities used to describe the relative likelihood of each event occurring.

Strategy   The part of the decision problem that is under the decision maker's control. It is composed of activities that form a plan of action.

Subgroup size   The size of the sample of observations that is taken at intervals.

Suboptimal   Describing the occurrence of something less desirable than the optimal result.

Subsystems   Smaller parts of the large system. They are isolated from the major system in order to permit analysis of the component behaviors of the larger system. They are systems in their own right, but the use of the term *subsystem* indicates that several such subsystems will be put together in order to form and study the larger one.

Synthesis   The methods applicable to combining elements of a system. Also, reconstructing and recombining the parts of a system to form the whole.

System   A system is a chosen set of elements whose interactions, dependencies, conditions, and effects are to be studied as a group. The system is like a box—its contents (plus the box) define that system.

Systemic costs   The cost of processing, analyzing, and evaluating data.

Systems modules   Subsystems that are non-overlapping, in the sense that a set of modules can be added together to form the larger system. For example, an apple can be sliced into four quarters. These can be reassembled into a total apple. Subsystems do not always have this modular characteristic; sometimes they overlap. For example, consider an apple sliced vertically as one systems view, diagonally as another, and horizontally as a third. These different ways of slicing the same apple give different views of the core, etc., but they cannot be added together to give the full apple. They are, therefore, not modules. However, they are very useful as different subsystem views of the apple.

Tolerances   Engineering and design ranges that are specified (e.g., blueprints) to indicate product measurements that conform to the standards of acceptance.

Trade-off   Slack paths have an excess of resources; if some resources can be reassigned from slack paths to the critical one, this trade-off will shorten the time to completion of the project. (The time along the slack paths will increase, while that required by the critical path will decrease.) Trade-off, more generally, means giving up some payoff of one kind to get more payoff of another kind.

Transformation   Change of state from some original condition to a different end condition.

Utility   The real value or payoff value of the outcome to the decision maker.

Value analysis   The familiar production-improvement approach that concentrates on whether the right materials are being used in the best possible way. Effort is concentrated on decreasing costs while maintaining quality of output. See Starr, *Production Management*, pp. 292-93.

Variables   Factors that can take on different values. For example, the speed of a car is an important variable if one wishes to know how long it will take to drive from one place to another. This variable usually runs between zero and 100 miles per hour. *Relevant variables* are those factors that are associated with the characteristics of the system in which we are interested.

Variables, classification   The variables are measured along a continuum—e.g. 2.54 centimeters (see *Attributes, classification*).

Vendor   The supplier of goods and services.

Vertex   Each point of a polygon formed by the intersections of the sides of the polygon (see *Polygon*).